Dangerous Goods Emergency Action Code List
2017

London: TSO

part of Williams Lea Tag

Published by TSO (The Stationery Office), part of Williams Lea Tag, and available from:

Online
www.tsoshop.co.uk

Mail, Telephone, Fax & E-mail
TSO
PO Box 29, Norwich, NR3 1GN
Telephone orders/General enquiries: 0333 202 5070
Fax orders: 0333 2020 5080
E-mail: customer.services@tso.co.uk
Textphone 0333 202 5077

TSO@Blackwell and other Accredited Agents

The publication is produced by NCEC (National Chemical Emergency Centre). NCEC is part of Ricardo-AEA Ltd. Registered Office Shoreham Technical Centre, old Shoreham Road, Shoreham-by-Sea, West Sussex, BN43 5FG. Registered in England and Wales No.8229264.

This publication is produced with the co-operation of the Home Office and builds on the previous publication, in the same name, produced by them and published by the Stationery Office Limited.

© Ricardo-AEA Ltd 2017

All rights reserved.

ISBN 978 0 11 754160 3

Printed in Great Britain on material containing 75% post-consumer waste and 25% ECF pulp.

Printed in the United Kingdom by TSO

J003292724   C12   04/17

Foreword

(i) This document supersedes the Dangerous Goods Emergency Action Code List 2015.

(ii) Duty holders are required to use this document for the application of the appropriate Emergency Action Codes (EACs) under Schedule 1 of the Carriage of Dangerous Goods and Use of Transportable Pressure Equipment Regulations 2009 (CDG 2009), as amended; and of the Carriage of Dangerous Goods and Use of Transportable Pressure Equipment Regulations (Northern Ireland) 2010 (CDG 2010), as amended. These regulations implement the Regulations Concerning the International Carriage of Dangerous Goods by Rail (RID[1]), and the European Agreement Concerning the International Carriage of Dangerous Goods by Road (ADR[2]).

(iii) The assignment of emergency action codes and additional personal protection codes at Section 4 of this document is based upon the physical and chemical properties of the particular dangerous goods.

(iv) This document is effective immediately in connection with the use of ADR/RID 2017 Edition and is mandatory from 1 July 2017 and the Emergency Action Code List 2015 should no longer be used from that date.

(v) Sections 4 and 5 of this Document will continue to be revised in line with any changes made to the RID and ADR Agreements (normally every two years), as provided for in domestic regulations.

---

1 Règlements Internationales Relatif au Transport des Marchandises Dangereuses par Chemin de Fer
2 Accord Européen Relatif au Transport International des Marchandises Dangereuses par Route

Contents

Section 1: Introduction to the Emergency Action Codes — 7
Introduction — 7
Danger Labels — 9

Section 2: Displaying Emergency Action Codes — 13
Assigning Emergency Action Codes — 13
Assigning Emergency Action Codes to multi-loads — 14

Section 3: Application of Emergency Action Codes for the Emergency Services — 17
Interpretation of Codes — 17
    Extinguishing Media — 18
    Personal Protection — 18
    Violent Reaction — 19
    Contain/Dilute — 19
    E "Public Safety Hazard" — 21

Section 4: Numerical List of Dangerous Goods — 23
Explanation of headings in Numerical List — 23
    Column 1: United Nations (UN) Number — 23
    Column 2: Substance — 24
    Column 3: Emergency Action Code (EAC) — 24
    Column 4: Advice on Additional Personal Protection (APP) — 24
    Column 5: Hazards — 25
    Column 6: Hazard Identification Number (HIN) — 26
List of Dangerous Goods — 31

Section 5: Alphabetical List of Dangerous Goods — 141

Acknowledgements — 199

Section 1

Introduction to the Emergency Action Codes

1.1 Introduction

1.1.1 Emergency Action codes (EACs), also known as Hazchem codes, are for the use of the emergency services in conjunction with Emergency Action Code Cards. EACs indicate to the emergency services actions that may be necessary, during the first few minutes of an incident involving dangerous goods, should the officer in charge of the incident deem it necessary to take immediate actions.

1.1.2 This document shall not be used for the purposes of markings on the orange coloured plate without reference to the Carriage of Dangerous Goods and Use of Transportable Pressure Equipment Regulations 2009 (CDG 2009), as amended; or of the Carriage of Dangerous Goods and Use of Transportable Pressure Equipment Regulations (Northern Ireland) 2010 (CDG 2010), as amended; and ADR/RID. The fact that a United Nations (UN) number and emergency action code (EAC) for a given substance are shown in this document does not necessarily mean they should be used for the marking of road tankers, rail tank wagons or tank containers used for the carriage of that substance. An annotation (1) in the EAC column of Section 4 indicates that it is not applicable to the carriage of dangerous goods under RID or ADR.

1.1.3 This document contains all items listed by the United Nations in their publication "Recommendations on the Transport of Dangerous Goods Model Regulations (nineteenth revised edition)" with the exception of substances in UN Class 1, i.e. explosives. EACs are not allocated to radioactive materials and these are annotated (2) in the EAC column of Section 4 of this document.

1.1.4 For internal transport operations in Great Britain there are two forms of placarding/plate marking permitted for tank transport and carriage in bulk under CDG 2009 (as amended); or CDG (Northern Ireland) 2010 (as amended). Both of these include the hazard warning diamond and the UN number. Road and Rail vehicles must also display one of two additional identification numbers.

- GB registered road and rail vehicles on domestic journeys must display the Emergency Action (Hazchem) Code
- All other vehicles must display the Hazard Identification Number (HIN) (see paragraphs 4.1.13–4.1.18).

1.1.5 Examples of these two systems are shown below. The requirements are contained in CDG 2009 (as amended); or CDG (Northern Ireland) 2010 (as amended).

Hazard Warning Panel

RID/ADR (Hazard Identification Number) orange coloured plate and placard

1.2 Danger Labels

1.2.1 The following are danger labels that will be shown during the transport of dangerous goods:

CLASS 1 – Explosive substances or articles

Division 1.1, 1.2 and 1.3   Division 1.4   Division 1.5   Division 1.6

CLASS 2 – Gases

Flammable gases   Non-flammable, non-toxic gases

Toxic gases

CLASS 3 – Flammable liquids

INTRODUCTION TO THE EMERGENCY ACTION CODES | 9

CLASS 4.1 – Flammable solids, self-reactive substances and desensitized explosives

CLASS 4.2 – Substances liable to spontaneous combustion

CLASS 4.3 – Substances which, in contact with water, emit flammable gases

CLASS 5.1 – Oxidising substances

CLASS 5.2 – Organic peroxides

CLASS 6.1 – Toxic substances

CLASS 6.2 – Infectious substances

CLASS 7 – Radioactive material

CLASS 8 – Corrosive substance

CLASS 9 – Miscellaneous dangerous substances and articles

1.2.2 Under the requirements of the 2017 editions of ADR and RID <u>all</u> goods classified as dangerous in carriage, whether or not assigned to another Class, may need to have the EHS mark displayed on their packaging <u>if</u> they meet the EHS criteria contained in 2.2.9.1.10 of ADR and RID.

Environmentally hazardous substance mark

1.2.3 The following are marks that may appear on vehicles during the transport of dangerous goods and would appear in addition to the danger labels at 1.2.1.

Mark for elevated temperature substances   Dangerous goods packed in limited quantities

Risk of Asphyxiation warning sign   Fumigation warning sign

Section 2

Displaying Emergency Action Codes

2.1 Assigning Emergency Action Codes

2.1.1 The codes allocated and shown in the list apply to tank transport and carriage in bulk of the single substance by road or rail except where it is also annotated (1). These codes will not necessarily apply for non-transport incidents although they may be used to provide some indication of the action that may be necessary.

2.1.2 Radioactive materials have not been allocated emergency action codes and are annotated (2).

ADR 5.3.2.1.4 and RID 5.3.2.1.1 and 5.3.2.1.2 stipulate that transport units, containers or wagons carrying packaged radioactive material with a single UN number, required to be carried under exclusive use and with no other dangerous goods, display orange-coloured plates bearing the appropriate hazard identification number (HIN) and UN number.

2.1.3 The prefix '●' will sometimes appear before the EAC in the third column, e.g. UN 1193 Ethyl Methyl Ketone appears as ●2YE. The '●' here indicates to the emergency services that alcohol resistant foam is the preferred firefighting medium but this prefix **shall not** be displayed on plates, i.e. EACs displayed on road or rail vehicles will either be two characters without an 'E' or three characters including an 'E'. In a similar way an APP code will sometimes appear in the 4th column of the List at Section 4 indicating additional information for the emergency services but again this **shall not** be displayed on plates.

2.1.4　In some cases, where there is more than one EAC for a single UN number, it will be necessary to determine the EAC by reference to the packing group, e.g. for UN 1224 – the EAC will be 3YE for ketones of packing group II whereas the EAC will be 3Y for ketones of packing group III. In these cases the relevant packing groups will be identified in the 'Substance' column.

2.2　Assigning Emergency Action Codes to multi-loads

2.2.1　The following procedure shall be used to assign EACs when each of the dangerous goods comprising the multi-load is listed for carriage in a tank under RID or ADR.

1st character of the code

2.2.2　The number forming the first character of the code for a multi-load is the highest of the numbers occurring in the EACs for the individual dangerous goods.

2nd Character of the code

2.2.3　The letter forming the second character of the code shall be determined from the first letter of the EAC for each of the dangerous goods from the chart below.

Code chart for the determination of emergency action codes for multi-loads

	P	R	S	T	W	X	Y	Z
P	P	P	P	P	W	W	W	W
R	P	R	P	R	W	X	W	X
S	P	P	S	S	W	W	Y	Y
T	P	R	S	T	W	X	Y	Z
W	W	W	W	W	W	W	W	W
X	W	X	W	X	W	X	W	X
Y	W	W	Y	Y	W	W	Y	Y
Z	W	X	Y	Z	W	X	Y	Z

2.2.4 If the letter forming the second character of the code for each of the dangerous goods is the same, then that letter will automatically form the second character of the EAC for the multi-load.

2.2.5 If, however, the letter forming the second character of the code for each of the dangerous goods is different, then one of those letters shall be selected along the top of the horizontal line) and then a second letter shall be selected down the far left-hand column, i.e. the two bold sections. The letter in the square where the appropriate column and row meet is the 'resultant letter' for those two substances. If there are only two dangerous goods to be carried in the multi-load, then that resultant letter is the letter forming the second character of the EAC for that multi-load.

2.2.6 If there are more than two dangerous goods to be carried in the multi-load, then use the 'resultant letter' obtained in paragraph 2.2.5 along the top horizontal line as above and select another letter down the far left-hand column as above. The letter in the square where the appropriate column and row meet is the new 'resultant letter'. If there are no more dangerous goods to be carried in the multi-load, then that 'resultant letter' is the letter forming the second character of the code. If there are any further dangerous goods to be carried then this procedure must be repeated until all the other letters have been used.

Letter 'E'

2.2.7 The letter 'E' shall be included as the third character in the multi-load emergency action code if it occurs in the EAC of any of the dangerous goods to be carried. If the letter 'E' does not occur in any of the EACs of the dangerous goods to be carried, the EAC shall be just a two character code determined from paragraphs 2.2.2 to 2.2.6 above.

Example:

2.2.8 The following is an example of how to calculate the emergency action code for a multi-load.

There are three substances to be carried as a multi-load, having emergency action codes of 3Y, 2S and 4WE.

1st Character (number)

The first character of the EAC for each of the three substances is 3, 2 and 4. The highest number must be taken as the first character of the code for the multi-load and therefore the first character shall be **4**.

2nd Character (letter)

The second character for the EAC for each of the three substances is Y, S and W. Taking the Y along the top row of the chart and the S along the left hand column, the intersection is at Y and therefore the character for the first two substances would be Y. This resultant character (Y) is then taken along the top row and the character for the third substance (W) is taken along the left hand column. The intersection point is now W. The second character of the code for the three substances shall therefore be **W**.

Letter 'E'

The third substance has an 'E' as a third character and therefore the multi-load shall also have an '**E**'.

The resultant emergency action code for the three substances carried as a multi-load shall therefore be **4WE**.

Section 3

Application of Emergency Action Codes for the Emergency Services

3.1 Interpretation of Codes

3.1.1 The interpretation of an emergency action code is determined using Emergency Action Code pocket cards, the latest version of which is shown below.

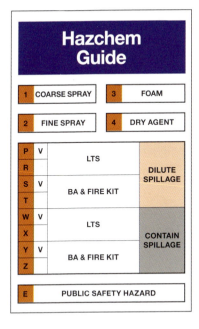
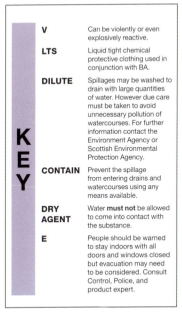

Note: Laminated Emergency Action Code Cards – "Hazchem Scale Cards" – are available from NCEC. Similar cards are also available from TSO (ISBN 978 0 11 341295 2)

Extinguishing Media

3.1.2 The firefighting extinguishing medium is determined by reference to the first character of the EAC as follows:

1 denotes **coarse water spray**

2 denotes **fine water spray**

3 denotes **normal foam** i.e. protein based foam that is not alcohol resistant

4 denotes dry **agent** – water **MUST NOT** be allowed to come into contact with substance

3.1.3 ●2 and ●3, which sometimes appear in the List, are not displayed on the vehicle plates or on the Emergency Action Code Cards and will only be shown as 2 and 3 respectively. This information can therefore only be obtained by reference to this document or another appropriate source, e.g. fire control. ●2 denotes **alcohol resistant foam** but, if not available, fine water spray can be used. ●3 denotes **alcohol resistant foam** but, if not available, normal foam can be used.

Note: Any higher number than the one shown can be used but a lower number must not be used.

Personal Protection

3.1.4 Where the second character of the EAC is S, T, Y or Z normal firefighting clothing is appropriate, i.e. self-contained open circuit positive pressure compressed air breathing apparatus conforming to BS EN 137 worn in combination with fire kit conforming to BS EN 469, firefighters' gloves conforming to BS EN 659 and firefighters' boots conforming to Home Office Specification A29 (rubber boots) or A30 (leather boots).

Note: Boots conforming to Home Office Specification A30 (leather boots) may not provide adequate chemical resistance and therefore caution should be exercised in the use of these boots.

3.1.5 Where the second character of the EAC is P, R, W or X chemical protective clothing with liquid tight connections for whole body (Type 3) conforming to the relevant standards such as BS 8428 or EN 14605, in combination with breathing apparatus specified in paragraph 3.1.4, shall be used.

Violent Reaction

3.1.6 Where the second character of the EAC is a P, S, W or Y there is a danger that the substance can be violently or explosively reactive. This danger may be present due to one of the following:

- Violent or explosive decomposition of the material involved, including ignition or friction.
- The ignition of a flammable gas or vapour cloud (this danger exists for all flammable gases and flammable liquids with a flash point below 60°C).
- The rapid acceleration of combustion due to the involvement of an oxidiser.
- A reaction with water which is itself violent, and may also evolve flammable gases.

3.1.7 The actual danger present can be determined from the vehicle placards or by reference to the United Nations Class in this document or another appropriate source, e.g. fire control.

Contain/Dilute

3.1.8 Where the second character of an EAC is W, X, Y or Z spillages, contaminated fire and decontamination run-off should be prevented from entering drains and surface and groundwaters. Where the second character of the code is P, R, S or T and there is an immediate threat to people, spillages and decontamination run-off may be washed to drains with large quantities of water. In such cases due care must be exercised to avoid unnecessary pollution of surface and groundwaters and wherever possible control measures such as the sealing of drains should be employed. More detailed advice on pollution control techniques and equipment can be found on the 'Environmental Protection' pages of the Published National Operational Guidance Programme (http://www.ukfrs.com/guidance/published-guidance).

Note 1: It should be noted that pollution offences within environmental legislation do apply to the Fire & Rescue Service. There maybe a defence available to FRS if pollution results from a discharge they made in an emergency, but this defence will only apply if all the criteria set out in the relevant legislation have been met.

Note 2: In recognition of the practical difficulties at incidents, the liaison between the environment agencies and the Fire and Rescue Service has been formalised. These are in the form of a Protocol in England and Wales and in Scotland and Northern Ireland that set out the roles and responsibilities of both parties together with the arrangements that should be followed when dealing with incidents where pollution may occur. These arrangements are detailed on the 'Environmental Protection' pages of the Published National Operational Guidance Programme (http://www.ukfrs.com/guidance/published-guidance).

Note 3: Ideally most spillages/run off and decontamination run-off should be contained. However, environment agencies accept that life saving will take precedence over environmental protection activities. Nevertheless, all steps that are reasonably practicable should be taken to contain contaminants and the Fire & Rescue Service should always inform the environment Agencies as soon as possible so that appropriate advice can be given. Specific information on the legal position of the Fire & Rescue Services at incidents can be found on the 'Environmental Protection' pages of the Published National Operational Guidance Programme (http://www.ukfrs.com/guidance/published-guidance).

Note 4: Potentially polluting substances include even apparently harmless substances such as food and beverages, which can cause serious problems if discharged into a water body: e.g. a spillage of a soft drink or beer above domestic quantities can constitute a pollutant as it can lead to deoxygenation of the water. Firefighting foams are also a potential source of pollution and their entry into a drainage system and or ground and surface waters should be prevented whenever possible.

Note 5: Other helpful guidance on environmental issues is available on the 'Environmental Protection' pages of the Published National Operational Guidance Programme (http://www.ukfrs.com/guidance/published-guidance).

E "Public Safety Hazard"

3.1.9 An 'E' following the first two characters of an EAC indicates that there may be a public safety hazard outside the immediate area of the incident, and that the following actions should be considered:

3.1.10 People should be warned to stay indoors with all doors and windows closed, preferably in rooms upstairs and facing away from the incident. Ignition sources should be eliminated and any ventilation stopped.

3.1.11 Effects may spread beyond the immediate vicinity. All non-essential personnel should be instructed to move at least 250 metres away from the incident.

3.1.12 Police and Fire and Rescue Service incident commanders should consult each other and with a product expert, or with a source of product expertise.

3.1.13 The possible need for subsequent evacuation should be considered, **but it should be remembered that in most cases it will be safer to remain in a building than to evacuate**.

Situations where evacuation may be necessary include the following:

EXAMPLES	ASSESSMENT
1.i. Smoke from product fire which is allowed to burn out. (Often safest and least environmentally damaging option.) 1.ii. Small/low concentration long lasting toxic emission.	1. Nuisance effects will last several hours. Smoke or gas concentrations in open air are unpleasant but short-term exposure is not likely to be dangerous.
2. A larger long lasting toxic gas emission which will be carried towards an inhabited area after a predicted wind change not due for at least two hours.	2. Area considered for evacuation will not be exposed to significant danger for at least an hour, preferably longer.
3. Evacuation of people from an isolated house in the country may be feasible, possibly using additional BA sets.	3. Downwind area is very sparsely populated and resources are available to protect people during their evacuation.
4.i. Righting a loaded road tanker or rail tank wagon, especially one carrying a liquefied gas. 4.ii. Recovering or clearing petrol from drains.	4. Area considered for evacuation could be exposed to danger as a result of actions necessary to restore normality at a time determined by the recovery team.

Section 4

Numerical List of Dangerous Goods

4.1 Explanation of headings in Numerical List

4.1.1 The headings provided in each column of this Section are defined below:

Column 1: United Nations (UN) Number

4.1.2 The identification number shown in the first column of the list is that allocated by the United Nations and contained in the "Recommendations on the Transport of Dangerous Goods Model Regulations (nineteenth revised edition)". These entries can also be found in the Regulations Concerning the International Carriage of Dangerous Goods by Rail [RID](2017) and in the European Agreement Concerning the International Carriage Dangerous Goods by Road [ADR] (2017).

4.1.3 Certain United Nations numbers carry more than one entry, each having a differing EAC, e.g. UN. 1866 and UN 1986. In these cases the substances are carried in differing forms whose properties pose different hazards and require separate EACs.

4.1.4 Many United Nations numbers carry the abbreviation 'N.O.S'. This abbreviation denotes 'Not Otherwise Specified'. These numbers are used for substances or articles which do not have a discrete entry in the list of UN numbers and represent the hazard or hazards the substance or article possesses, e.g. UN 2929 'Toxic Liquid, Flammable, Organic, N.O.S'.

4.1.5 The List in this Section is displayed in UN number order. If only the substance name is known, the UN number can be found by reference to the alphabetical list of substances in Section 5.

Column 2: Substance

4.1.6 The names of substances in the second column of the list are by 'Proper Shipping Names'. Where more than one EAC is allocated to a single UN number, the allocation of EAC is identified by the packing group following the 'Proper Shipping Name'.

4.1.7 The alphabetical list of substances in Section 5 indicate the appropriate UN number for that substance. Substances shown in **BOLD CAPITAL TYPE** in this list indicate the 'Proper Shipping Name'. Normal type indicates an alternative name with the appropriate UN number under which the substance will appear in this Section.

Column 3: Emergency Action Code (EAC)

4.1.8 Emergency Action Codes (commonly known as Hazchem codes) are designed to be used by the emergency services in conjunction with Emergency Action Code Cards, which are intended to be carried by emergency service personnel. The cards indicate the action that may be necessary (except additional personal protection (APP) and the use of alcohol resistant foam) during the first few minutes of an incident.

Column 4: Advice on Additional Personal Protection (APP)

4.1.9 These codes appear as A or B in the List.

Note: These codes do not appear on vehicle placards or on the Emergency Action Code Cards. Whenever an APP code is assigned to a substance, further information shall be sought from the appropriate authority who have access to this information, e.g. fire and rescue service control.

4.1.10 **Code letter A:** Indicates that fire kit as specified in paragraph 3.1.4 with gas-tight chemical protective clothing as specified in paragraph 4.1.11 should be worn. The fire kit is intended to protect against one or more of the following additional hazards which are indicated in the List by the appropriate character(s) in brackets, following the 'A', as shown below:

- **(c)** Liquefied gas with a boiling point below -20°C
- **(fg)** Flammable gas
- **(fl)** Flammable liquid
- **(cf)** Liquefied flammable gas with a boiling point below -20°C
- **(h)** The substance may be carried above 100°C
- **(co)** Oxidising gas with a boiling point below -20°C
- **(!)** The substance may have a particularly deleterious effect on chemical protective clothing

Where a thermal hazard is present [A(c), A(cf), A(co), and A(h)] suitable thermal resistant gloves should be worn, such as those conforming to BS EN511:2006 or BS EN407:2004.

4.1.11 **Code letter B:** The chemical protective clothing should be gas-tight conforming to BS EN 943 part 2 in combination with the breathing apparatus specified in paragraph 3.1.4.

Column 5: Hazards

4.1.12 This is sub-divided to show the primary hazard of the substance, which determines the Class into which the substance is assigned, and, where appropriate, the subsidiary risks. The classifications identified are those adopted by the United Nations Committee of Experts on the Transport of Dangerous Goods and on the Globally Harmonised System of Classification and Labelling of Chemicals, and are as follows:

Class 1 – Explosives (Note: not included in this document)
Class 2.1 – Flammable gases
Class 2.2 – Non-flammable, non-toxic gases
Class 2.3 – Toxic gases
Class 3 – Flammable liquids and desensitised liquid explosives
Class 4.1 – Flammable solids, self-reactive substances and solid desensitised explosives
Class 4.2 – Substances liable to spontaneous combustion
Class 4.3 – Substances which in contact with water emit flammable gases
Class 5.1 – Oxidising substances

Class 5.2 – Organic peroxides

Class 6.1 – Toxic substances

Class 6.2 – Infectious substances

Class 7 – Radioactive material

Class 8 – Corrosive substances

Class 9 – Miscellaneous dangerous substances and articles

Note: In this column the number following a decimal point always indicates a sub-division of a class.

Column 6: Hazard Identification Number (HIN)

4.1.3 The HIN consists of two or three figures. In general, the figures indicate the following hazards:

- 2 Emissions of gas due to pressure or to chemical reaction
- 3 Flammability of liquids (vapours) and gases or self-heating liquids
- 4 Flammability of solids or self-heating solids
- 5 Oxidizing (fire-intensifying) effect
- 6 Toxicity (or risk of infection)
- 7 Radioactivity
- 8 Corrosivity
- 9 Risk of spontaneous, violent reaction

Note: Spontaneous violent reaction within the meaning of figure 9 includes the possibility of the risk of explosion, disintegration and polymerization reaction with the release of considerable heat or flammable and/or toxic gases.

4.1.14 Doubling of a figure indicates an intensification of that particular hazard.

4.1.15 Where the hazard associated with a substance can be adequately indicated by a single figure, this is followed by zero.

4.1.16 The following combinations of figures, however, have a special meaning: 22, 323, 333, 362, 382, 423, 44, 446, 462, 482, 539, 606, 623, 642, 823, 842 90 and 99. See below.

4.1.17 If the letter 'X' prefixes a hazard identification number, this indicates that the substance will react dangerously with water. For these substances, water may only be used with the approval of experts.

4.1.18 The hazard identification numbers have the following meanings:

20	Asphyxiant gas or gas with no subsidiary risk
22	Refrigerated liquefied gas, Asphyxiant
223	Refrigerated liquefied gas, flammable
225	Refrigerated liquefied gas, oxidising (fire intensifying)
23	Flammable gas
239	Flammable gas, which can spontaneously lead to violent reaction
25	Oxidising (fire-intensifying) gas
26	Toxic gas
263	Toxic gas, flammable
265	Toxic gas, oxidising (fire-intensifying)
268	Toxic gas, corrosive
30	Flammable liquid (flash-point between 23°C and 60°C inclusive) or flammable liquid or solid in the molten state with a flash point above 60°C, heated to a temperature equal to or above its flash point, or self-heating liquid
323	Flammable liquid which reacts with water, emitting flammable gases
X323	Flammable liquid which reacts dangerously with water, emitting flammable gases*
33	Highly flammable liquid (flash-point below 23°C)
333	Pyrophoric liquid
X333	Pyrophoric liquid, which reacts dangerously with water*
336	Highly flammable liquid, toxic
338	Highly flammable liquid, corrosive
X338	Highly flammable liquid, corrosive, which reacts dangerously with water*
339	Highly flammable liquid which can spontaneously lead to violent reaction

* Water not to be used except by approval of experts

Code	Description
36	Flammable liquid (flash-point between 23°C and 60°C inclusive), slightly toxic or self-heating liquid toxic
362	Flammable liquid, toxic, which reacts with water, emitting flammable gases
X362	Flammable liquid, toxic, which reacts dangerously with water, emitting flammable gases*
368	Flammable liquid, toxic, corrosive
38	Flammable liquid (flash-point between 23°C and 60°C inclusive), slightly corrosive or self-heating liquid, corrosive
382	Flammable liquid, corrosive, which reacts with water, emitting flammable gases
X382	Flammable liquid, corrosive, which reacts dangerously with water, emitting flammable gases*
39	Flammable liquid, which can spontaneously lead to violent reaction
40	Flammable solid, or self-reactive substance, or self-heating substance, or polymerising substance
423	Solid which reacts with water, emitting flammable gas, or flammable solid which reacts with water, emitting flammable gases or self-heating solid which reacts with water, emitting flammable gases*
X423	Solid which reacts dangerously with water, emitting flammable gases, or flammable solid which reacts dangerously with water, emitting flammable gases, or self-heating solid which reacts dangerously with water, emitting flammable gases*
43	Spontaneously flammable (Pyrophoric) solid
X432	Spontaneously flammable (pyrophoric) solid which reacts dangerously with water, emitting flammable gases*
44	Flammable solid, in the molten state at an elevated temperature
446	Flammable solid, toxic in the molten state, at an elevated temperature
46	Flammable or self-heating solid, toxic
462	Toxic solid which reacts with water, emitting flammable gases
X462	Solid which reacts dangerously with water, emitting toxic gases*
48	Flammable or self-heating solid, corrosive
482	Corrosive solid which reacts with water, emitting corrosive gases
X482	Solid which reacts dangerously with water, emitting corrosive gases*
50	Oxidising (fire-intensifying) substance
539	Flammable organic peroxide
55	Strongly oxidising (fire-intensifying) substance

*Water not to be used except by approval of experts

556	Strongly oxidising (fire-intensifying) substance, toxic
558	Strongly oxidising (fire-intensifying) substance, corrosive
559	Strongly oxidising (fire-intensifying) substance, which can spontaneously lead to violent reaction
56	Oxidising substance (fire-intensifying), toxic
568	Oxidising substance (fire-intensifying), toxic, corrosive
58	Oxidising substance (fire-intensifying), corrosive
59	Oxidising substance (fire-intensifying) which can spontaneously lead to violent reaction
60	Toxic or slightly toxic substance
606	Infectious substance
623	Toxic liquid, which reacts with water, emitting flammable gases
63	Toxic substance, flammable (flash-point between 23°C and 60°C inclusive)
638	Toxic substance, flammable (flash-point between 23°C and 60°C inclusive), corrosive
639	Toxic substance, flammable (flash-point not above 60°C inclusive), which can spontaneously lead to violent reaction
64	Toxic solid, flammable or self-heating
642	Toxic solid, which reacts with water, emitting flammable gases
65	Toxic substance, oxidising (fire-intensifying)
66	Highly toxic substance
663	Highly toxic substance, flammable (flash-point not above 60°C inclusive)
664	Highly Toxic substance, flammable or self-heating
665	Highly toxic substance, oxidising (fire-intensifying)
668	Highly toxic substance, corrosive
X668	Highly toxic substance, corrosive, which reacts dangerously with water
669	Highly toxic substance which can spontaneously lead to a violent reaction
68	Toxic substance, corrosive
69	Toxic or slightly toxic substance, which can spontaneously lead to violent reaction
70	Radioactive material
768	Radioactive material, toxic, corrosive

* Water not to be used except by approval of experts

78	Radioactive material, corrosive
80	Corrosive or slightly corrosive substance
X80	Corrosive or slightly corrosive substance, which reacts dangerously with water*
823	Corrosive liquid which reacts with water, emitting flammable gases
83	Corrosive or slightly corrosive substance, flammable (flash-point between 23°C and 60°C inclusive)
X83	Corrosive or slightly corrosive substance, flammable (flash-point between 23°C and 60°C inclusive), which reacts dangerously with water*
839	Corrosive or slightly corrosive substance, flammable (flash-point between 23°C and 60°C inclusive), which can spontaneously lead to violent reaction
X839	Corrosive or slightly corrosive substance, flammable (flash-point between 23°C and 60°C inclusive), which can spontaneously lead to violent reaction and which reacts dangerously with water*
84	Corrosive solid, flammable or self-heating
842	Corrosive solid which reacts with water, emitting flammable gases
85	Corrosive or slightly corrosive substance, oxidising (fire-intensifying)
856	Corrosive or slightly corrosive substance, oxidising (fire-intensifying) and toxic
86	Corrosive or slightly corrosive substance, toxic
88	Highly corrosive substance
X88	Highly corrosive substance, which reacts dangerously with water*
883	Highly corrosive substance, flammable (flash-point between 23°C and 60°C inclusive)
884	Highly corrosive solid, flammable or self-heating
885	Highly corrosive substance, oxidising (fire-intensifying)
886	Highly corrosive substance, toxic
X886	Highly corrosive substance, toxic which reacts dangerously with water*
89	Corrosive or slightly corrosive substance, which can spontaneously lead to violent reaction
90	Environmentally hazardous substance; miscellaneous dangerous substances
99	Miscellaneous dangerous substance carried at an elevated temperature

* Water not to be used except by approval of experts

List of Dangerous Goods

UN No	Substance	EAC	APP	Hazards Class	Sub Risks	HIN
1001	ACETYLENE, DISSOLVED	2SE		2.1		239
1002	AIR, COMPRESSED	2T		2.2		20
1003	AIR, REFRIGERATED LIQUID	2P	A(co)	2.2	5.1	225
1004	UN No. no longer in use					
1005	AMMONIA, ANHYDROUS	2XE	A(c)	2.3	8	268
1006	ARGON, COMPRESSED	2T		2.2		20
1007	UN No. no longer in use					
1008	BORON TRIFLUORIDE	2RE	B	2.3	8	268
1009	BROMOTRIFLUOROMETHANE (REFRIGERANT GAS R 13B1)	2TE		2.2		20
1010	BUTADIENES, STABILIZED or BUTADIENES AND HYDROCARBON MIXTURE, STABILIZED	2YE		2.1		239
1011	BUTANE	2YE		2.1		23
1012	BUTYLENES MIXTURE or 1-BUTYLENE or cis-2-BUTYLENE or trans-2-BUTYLENE	2YE		2.1		23
1013	CARBON DIOXIDE	2T		2.2		20
1014	UN No. no longer in use					
1015	UN No. no longer in use					
1016	CARBON MONOXIDE, COMPRESSED	2SE		2.3	2.1	263
1017	CHLORINE	2XE	A(c)	2.3	8, 5.1	265
1018	CHLORODIFLUOROMETHANE (REFRIGERANT GAS R 22)	2TE		2.2		20
1019	UN No. no longer in use					
1020	CHLOROPENTAFLUOROETHANE (REFRIGERANT GAS R 115)	2TE		2.2		20
1021	1-CHLORO-1,2,2,2-TETRAFLUOROETHANE (REFRIGERANT GAS R 124)	2TE		2.2		20

UN No	Substance	EAC	APP	Hazards Class	Sub Risks	HIN
1022	CHLOROTRIFLUOROMETHANE (REFRIGERANT GAS R 13)	2TE		2.2		20
1023	COAL GAS, COMPRESSED	2SE		2.3	2.1	263
1024	UN No. no longer in use					
1025	UN No. no longer in use					
1026	CYANOGEN	2PE	A(cf)	2.3	2.1	263
1027	CYCLOPROPANE	2YE		2.1		23
1028	DICHLORODIFLUOROMETHANE (REFRIGERANT GAS R 12)	2TE		2.2		20
1029	DICHLOROFLUOROMETHANE (REFRIGERANT GAS R 21)	2TE		2.2		20
1030	1,1-DIFLUOROETHANE (REFRIGERANT GAS R 152a)	2YE		2.1		23
1031	UN No. no longer in use					
1032	DIMETHYLAMINE, ANHYDROUS	2PE	A(fg)	2.1		23
1033	DIMETHYL ETHER	2YE		2.1		23
1034	UN No. no longer in use					
1035	ETHANE	2YE		2.1		23
1036	ETHYLAMINE	2PE	A(fg)	2.1		23
1037	ETHYL CHLORIDE	2YE		2.1		23
1038	ETHYLENE, REFRIGERATED LIQUID	2YE		2.1		223
1039	ETHYL METHYL ETHER	2SE		2.1		23
1040	ETHYLENE OXIDE or ETHYLENE OXIDE WITH NITROGEN up to a total pressure of 1MPa (10bar) at 50°C	2PE	A(fg)	2.3	2.1	263
1041	ETHYLENE OXIDE AND CARBON DIOXIDE MIXTURE with more than 9% but not more than 87% ethylene oxide	2SE		2.1		239
1042	UN No. no longer in use					
1043	FERTILIZER AMMONIATING SOLUTION with free ammonia	2RE[1]	B	2.2		
1044	FIRE EXTINGUISHERS with compressed or liquefied gas	[1]		2.2		
1045	FLUORINE, COMPRESSED	2PE[1]	B	2.3	5.1, 8	

(1) Not applicable to the carriage of dangerous goods under RID or ADR

UN No	Substance	EAC	APP	Hazards Class	Hazards Sub Risks	HIN
1046	HELIUM, COMPRESSED	2T		2.2		20
1047	UN No. no longer in use					
1048	HYDROGEN BROMIDE, ANHYDROUS	2RE	A(c)	2.3	8	268
1049	HYDROGEN, COMPRESSED	2SE		2.1		23
1050	HYDROGEN CHLORIDE, ANHYDROUS	2RE	A(c)	2.3	8	268
1051	HYDROGEN CYANIDE, STABILIZED containing less than 3% water	2WE[(1)]	A(fl)	6.1	3	
1052	HYDROGEN FLUORIDE, ANHYDROUS	2XE	B	8	6.1	886
1053	HYDROGEN SULPHIDE	2WE	A(cf)	2.3	2.1	263
1054	UN No. no longer in use					
1055	ISOBUTYLENE	2YE		2.1		23
1056	KRYPTON, COMPRESSED	2TE		2.2		20
1057	LIGHTERS or LIGHTER REFILLS containing flammable gas	[(1)]		2.1		
1058	LIQUEFIED GASES, non-flammable, charged with nitrogen, carbon dioxide or air	2TE		2.2		20
1059	UN No. no longer in use					
1060	METHYLACETYLENE AND PROPADIENE MIXTURE, STABILIZED	2YE		2.1		239
1061	METHYLAMINE, ANHYDROUS	2PE	A(fg)	2.1		23
1062	METHYL BROMIDE with not more than 2% chloropicrin	2XE	B	2.3		26
1063	METHYL CHLORIDE (REFRIGERANT GAS R 40)	2YE		2.1		23
1064	METHYL MERCAPTAN	2WE	A(fg)	2.3	2.1	263
1065	NEON, COMPRESSED	2T		2.2		20
1066	NITROGEN, COMPRESSED	2T		2.2		20
1067	DINITROGEN TETROXIDE (NITROGEN DIOXIDE)	2PE	B	2.3	5.1, 8	265
1068	UN No. no longer in use					
1069	NITROSYL CHLORIDE	2RE[(1)]	B	2.3	8	

(1) Not applicable to the carriage of dangerous goods under RID or ADR

UN No	Substance	EAC	APP	Hazards Class	Sub Risks	HIN
1070	NITROUS OXIDE	2P	A(co)	2.2	5.1	25
1071	OIL GAS, COMPRESSED	2SE		2.3	2.1	263
1072	OXYGEN, COMPRESSED	2S		2.2	5.1	25
1073	OXYGEN, REFRIGERATED LIQUID	2P	A(co)	2.2	5.1	225
1074	UN No. no longer in use					
1075	PETROLEUM GASES, LIQUEFIED	2YE		2.1		23
1076	PHOSGENE	2XE	B	2.3	8	268
1077	PROPYLENE	2YE		2.1		23
1078	REFRIGERANT GAS, N.O.S.	2TE		2.2		20
1079	SULPHUR DIOXIDE	2RE	B	2.3	8	268
1080	SULPHUR HEXAFLUORIDE	2TE		2.2		20
1081	TETRAFLUOROETHYLENE, STABILIZED	2SE		2.1		239
1082	TRIFLUOROCHLOROETHYLENE, STABILIZED (REFRIGERANT GAS R 1113)	2WE	A(cf)	2.3	2.1	263
1083	TRIMETHYLAMINE, ANHYDROUS	2PE	A(fg)	2.1		23
1084	UN No. no longer in use					
1085	VINYL BROMIDE, STABILIZED	2YE		2.1		239
1086	VINYL CHLORIDE, STABILIZED	2YE		2.1		239
1087	VINYL METHYL ETHER, STABILIZED	2YE		2.1		239
1088	ACETAL	●3YE		3		33
1089	ACETALDEHYDE	●2YE		3		33
1090	ACETONE	●2YE		3		33
1091	ACETONE OILS	●2YE		3		33
1092	ACROLEIN, STABILIZED	●2WE	B	6.1	3	663
1093	ACRYLONITRILE, STABILIZED	●3WE	A(fl)	3	6.1	336
1094 to 1097	UN Nos. no longer in use					
1098	ALLYL ALCOHOL	●2WE	A(fl)	6.1	3	663
1099	ALLYL BROMIDE	2WE	A(fl)	3	6.1	336

UN No	Substance	EAC	APP	Hazards Class	Hazards Sub Risks	HIN
1100	ALLYL CHLORIDE	3YE		3	6.1	336
1101 to 1103	UN Nos. no longer in use					
1104	AMYL ACETATES	•3Y		3		30
1105	PENTANOLS, packing group II	•3YE		3		33
1105	PENTANOLS, packing group III	•3Y		3		30
1106	AMYLAMINE, packing group II	•2WE	A(fl)	3	8	338
1106	AMYLAMINE, packing group III	•2W	A(fl)	3	8	38
1107	AMYL CHLORIDE	3YE		3		33
1108	1-PENTENE (n-AMYLENE)	3YE		3		33
1109	AMYL FORMATES	3Y		3		30
1110	n-AMYL METHYL KETONE	3Y		3		30
1111	AMYL MERCAPTAN	3WE	A(fl)	3		33
1112	AMYL NITRATE	3Y		3		30
1113	AMYL NITRITE	3YE		3		33
1114	BENZENE	3WE	A(fl)	3		33
1115 to 1119	UN Nos. no longer in use					
1120	BUTANOLS, packing group II	•2YE		3		33
1120	BUTANOLS, packing group III	•2Y		3		30
1121	UN No. no longer in use					
1122	UN No. no longer in use					
1123	BUTYL ACETATES, packing group II	3YE		3		33
1123	BUTYL ACETATES, packing group III	3Y		3		30
1124	UN No. no longer in use					
1125	n-BUTYLAMINE	•2WE	A(fl)	3	8	338
1126	1-BROMOBUTANE	2YE		3		33
1127	CHLOROBUTANES	3YE		3		33
1128	n-BUTYL FORMATE	•3YE		3		33
1129	BUTYRALDEHYDE	•3YE		3		33

UN No	Substance	EAC	APP	Hazards Class	Hazards Sub Risks	HIN
1130	**CAMPHOR OIL**	3Y		3		30
1131	**CARBON DISULPHIDE**	2WE	A(fl)	3	6.1	336
1132	UN No. no longer in use					
1133	**ADHESIVES** containing flammable liquid, packing groups I & II	●3YE		3		33
1133	**ADHESIVES** containing flammable liquid, packing group III	●3Y		3		30
1133	**ADHESIVES** containing flammable liquid (having a flash point below 23°C and viscous according to ADR 2.2.3.1.4), packing group III	●3YE(1)		3		
1134	**CHLOROBENZENE**	2Y		3		30
1135	**ETHYLENE CHLOROHYDRIN**	●2W	A(fl)	6.1	3	663
1136	**COAL TAR DISTILLATES, FLAMMABLE,** packing group II	3WE	A(fl)	3		33
1136	**COAL TAR DISTILLATES, FLAMMABLE,** packing group III	3W	A(fl)	3		30
1137	UN No. no longer in use					
1138	UN No. no longer in use					
1139	**COATING SOLUTION,** packing groups I & II	●3YE		3		33
1139	**COATING SOLUTION,** packing group III	●3Y		3		30
1139	**COATING SOLUTION** (having a flash point below 23°C and viscous according to ADR 2.2.3.1.4), packing group III	●3YE(1)		3		
1140 to 1142	UN Nos. no longer in use					
1143	**CROTONALDEHYDE** or **CROTONALDEHYDE, STABILIZED**	●2WE	A(fl)	6.1	3	663
1144	**CROTONYLENE**	3YE		3		339
1145	**CYCLOHEXANE**	3YE		3		33
1146	**CYCLOPENTANE**	3YE		3		33
1147	**DECAHYDRONAPHTHALENE**	3Y		3		30

(1) Not applicable to the carriage of dangerous goods under RID or ADR

UN No	Substance	EAC	APP	Hazards Class	Sub Risks	HIN
1148	**DIACETONE ALCOHOL,** packing group II	•2YE		3		33
1148	**DIACETONE ALCOHOL,** packing group III	•2Y		3		30
1149	**DIBUTYL ETHERS**	3Y		3		30
1150	**1,2-DICHLOROETHYLENE**	2YE		3		33
1151	UN No. no longer in use					
1152	**DICHLOROPENTANES**	3Y		3		30
1153	**ETHYLENE GLYCOL DIETHYL ETHER,** packing group II	•3YE		3		33
1153	**ETHYLENE GLYCOL DIETHYL ETHER,** packing group III	•3Y		3		30
1154	**DIETHYLAMINE**	•2WE	A(fl)	3	8	338
1155	**DIETHYL ETHER (ETHYL ETHER)**	•3YE		3		33
1156	**DIETHYL KETONE**	•3YE		3		33
1157	**DIISOBUTYL KETONE**	3Y		3		30
1158	**DIISOPROPYLAMINE**	•3WE	A(fl)	3	8	338
1159	**DIISOPROPYL ETHER**	3YE		3		33
1160	**DIMETHYLAMINE AQUEOUS SOLUTION**	•2WE	A(fl)	3	8	338
1161	**DIMETHYL CARBONATE**	3YE		3		33
1162	**DIMETHYLDICHLOROSILANE**	4WE	A(fl)	3	8	X338
1163	**DIMETHYLHYDRAZINE, UNSYMMETRICAL**	•2WE	A(fl)	6.1	3, 8	663
1164	**DIMETHYL SULPHIDE**	3YE		3		33
1165	**DIOXANE**	•2YE		3		33
1166	**DIOXOLANE**	•2YE		3		33
1167	**DIVINYL ETHER, STABILIZED**	3YE		3		339
1168	UN No. no longer in use					
1169	**EXTRACTS, AROMATIC, LIQUID,** packing group II	3YE		3		33
1169	**EXTRACTS, AROMATIC, LIQUID,** packing group III	3Y		3		30

UN No	Substance	EAC	APP	Hazards Class	Sub Risks	HIN
1169	**EXTRACTS, AROMATIC, LIQUID,** (having a flash point below 23°C and viscous according to ADR 2.2.3.1.4), packing group III	•3YE[(1)]		3		
1170	**ETHANOL (ETHYL ALCOHOL)** or **ETHANOL SOLUTION (ETHYL ALCOHOL SOLUTION),** packing group II	•2YE		3		33
1170	**ETHANOL (ETHYL ALCOHOL)** or **ETHANOL SOLUTION (ETHYL ALCOHOL SOLUTION),** packing group III	•2Y		3		30
1171	**ETHYLENE GLYCOL MONOETHYL ETHER**	•2Y		3		30
1172	**ETHYLENE GLYCOL MONOETHYL ETHER ACETATE**	•2Y		3		30
1173	**ETHYL ACETATE**	•3YE		3		33
1174	UN No. no longer in use					
1175	**ETHYLBENZENE**	3YE		3		33
1176	**ETHYL BORATE**	•3YE		3		33
1177	**2-ETHYLBUTYL ACETATE**	3Y		3		30
1178	**2-ETHYLBUTYRALDEHYDE**	3YE		3		33
1179	**ETHYL BUTYL ETHER**	3YE		3		33
1180	**ETHYL BUTYRATE**	3Y		3		30
1181	**ETHYL CHLOROACETATE**	2W	A(fl)	6.1	3	63
1182	**ETHYL CHLOROFORMATE**	•3WE	A(fl)	6.1	3, 8	663
1183	**ETHYLDICHLOROSILANE**	4WE	A(fl)	4.3	3, 8	X338
1184	**ETHYLENE DICHLORIDE**	2YE		3	6.1	336
1185	**ETHYLENEIMINE, STABILIZED**	•2WE	A(fl)	6.1	3	663
1186	UN No. no longer in use					
1187	UN No. no longer in use					
1188	**ETHYLENE GLYCOL MONOMETHYL ETHER**	•2Y		3		30
1189	**ETHYLENE GLYCOL MONOMETHYL ETHER ACETATE**	•2Y		3		30

(1) Not applicable to the carriage of dangerous goods under RID or ADR

UN No	Substance	EAC	APP	Hazards Class	Hazards Sub Risks	HIN
1190	ETHYL FORMATE	•2YE		3		33
1191	OCTYL ALDEHYDES	3Y		3		30
1192	ETHYL LACTATE	•2Y		3		30
1193	ETHYL METHYL KETONE (METHYL ETHYL KETONE)	•2YE		3		33
1194	ETHYL NITRITE SOLUTION	•2WE	A(fl)	3	6.1	336
1195	ETHYL PROPIONATE	•3YE		3		33
1196	ETHYLTRICHLOROSILANE	4WE	A(fl)	3	8	X338
1197	EXTRACTS, FLAVOURING, LIQUID, packing group II	3YE		3		33
1197	EXTRACTS, FLAVOURING, LIQUID, packing group III	3Y		3		30
1197	EXTRACTS, FLAVOURING, LIQUID (having a flash point below 23°C and viscous according to ADR 2.2.3.1.4), packing group III	•3YE(1)		3		
1198	FORMALDEHYDE SOLUTION, FLAMMABLE	•2W	A(fl)	3	8	38
1199	FURALDEHYDES	•3Y		6.1	3	63
1200	UN No. no longer in use					
1201	FUSEL OIL, packing group II	•2YE		3		33
1201	FUSEL OIL, packing group III	•2Y		3		30
1202	GAS OIL or DIESEL FUEL or HEATING OIL, LIGHT	3Y		3		30
1203	MOTOR SPIRIT or GASOLINE or PETROL	3YE		3		33
1204	NITROGLYCERIN SOLUTION IN ALCOHOL with not more than 1% nitroglycerin	•2YE(1)		3		
1205	UN No. no longer in use					
1206	HEPTANES	3YE		3		33
1207	HEXALDEHYDE	3Y		3		30
1208	HEXANES	3YE		3		33
1209	UN No. no longer in use					

(1) Not applicable to the carriage of dangerous goods under RID or ADR

UN No	Substance	EAC	APP	Hazards Class	Hazards Sub Risks	HIN
1210	**PRINTING INK,** flammable or **PRINTING INK RELATED MATERIAL** (including printing ink thinning or reducing compound), flammable, packing groups I & II	●3YE		3		33
1210	**PRINTING INK,** flammable or **PRINTING INK RELATED MATERIAL** (including printing ink thinning or reducing compound), flammable, packing group III	●3Y		3		30
1210	**PRINTING INK,** flammable or **PRINTING INK RELATED MATERIAL** (including printing ink thinning or reducing compound), flammable (having a flash point below 23°C and viscous according to ADR 2.2.3.1.4), packing group III	●3YE(1)		3		
1211	UN No. no longer in use					
1212	**ISOBUTANOL (ISOBUTYL ALCOHOL)**	●3Y		3		30
1213	**ISOBUTYL ACETATE**	3YE		3		33
1214	**ISOBUTYLAMINE**	●2WE	A(fl)	3	8	338
1215	UN No. no longer in use					
1216	**ISOOCTENES**	3YE		3		33
1217	UN No. no longer in use					
1218	**ISOPRENE, STABILIZED**	3YE		3		339
1219	**ISOPROPANOL (ISOPROPYL ALCOHOL)**	●2YE		3		33
1220	**ISOPROPYL ACETATE**	●3YE		3		33
1221	**ISOPROPYLAMINE**	●2WE	A(fl)	3	8	338
1222	**ISOPROPYL NITRATE**	3YE(1)		3		
1223	**KEROSENE**	3Y		3		30
1224	**KETONES, LIQUID, N.O.S.,** packing group II	●3YE		3		33
1224	**KETONES, LIQUID, N.O.S.,** packing group III	●3Y		3		30

(1) Not applicable to the carriage of dangerous goods under RID or ADR

UN No	Substance	EAC	APP	Hazards Class	Sub Risks	HIN
1225 to 1227	UN Nos. no longer in use					
1228	MERCAPTANS, LIQUID, FLAMMABLE, TOXIC, N.O.S. or MERCAPTAN MIXTURE, LIQUID, FLAMMABLE, TOXIC, N.O.S.	3WE	A(fl)	3	6.1	336/36
1229	MESITYL OXIDE	•3Y		3		30
1230	METHANOL	•2WE	A(fl)	3	6.1	336
1231	METHYL ACETATE	•2YE		3		33
1232	UN No. no longer in use					
1233	METHYLAMYL ACETATE	3Y		3		30
1234	METHYLAL	•2YE		3		33
1235	METHYLAMINE, AQUEOUS SOLUTION	•2WE	A(fl)	3	8	338
1236	UN No. no longer in use					
1237	METHYL BUTYRATE	•3YE		3		33
1238	METHYL CHLOROFORMATE	2WE	A(fl)	6.1	3, 8	663
1239	METHYL CHLOROMETHYL ETHER	3WE	A(fl)	6.1	3	663
1240	UN No. no longer in use					
1241	UN No. no longer in use					
1242	METHYLDICHLOROSILANE	4WE	A(fl)	4.3	3, 8	X338
1243	METHYL FORMATE	•2YE		3		33
1244	METHYLHYDRAZINE	•2WE	A(fl)	6.1	3, 8	663
1245	METHYL ISOBUTYL KETONE	•3YE		3		33
1246	METHYL ISOPROPENYL KETONE, STABILIZED	3YE		3		339
1247	METHYL METHACRYLATE MONOMER, STABILIZED	3YE		3		339
1248	METHYL PROPIONATE	3YE		3		33
1249	METHYL PROPYL KETONE	•3YE		3		33
1250	METHYLTRICHLOROSILANE	4WE	A(fl)	3	8	X338
1251	METHYL VINYL KETONE, STABILIZED	•2WE	A(fl)	6.1	3, 8	639

UN No	Substance	EAC	APP	Hazards Class	Sub Risks	HIN
1252 to 1258	UN Nos. no longer in use					
1259	**NICKEL CARBONYL**	2WE	A(fl)	6.1	3	663
1260	UN No. no longer in use					
1261	**NITROMETHANE**	●2Y(1)		3		
1262	**OCTANES**	3YE		3		33
1263	**PAINT** (including paint, lacquer, enamel, stain, shellac, varnish, polish, liquid filler and liquid lacquer base) or **PAINT RELATED MATERIAL** (including paint thinning or reducing compound), packing groups I & II	●3YE		3		33
1263	**PAINT** (including paint, lacquer, enamel, stain, shellac, varnish, polish, liquid filler and liquid lacquer base) or **PAINT RELATED MATERIAL** (including paint thinning or reducing compound), packing group III	●3Y		3		30
1263	**PAINT** (including paint, lacquer, enamel, stain, shellac, varnish, polish, liquid filler and liquid lacquer base) or **PAINT RELATED MATERIAL** (including paint thinning or reducing compound) (having a flash point below 23°C and viscous according to ADR 2.2.3.1.4), packing group III	●3YE(1)		3		
1264	**PARALDEHYDE**	●2Y		3		30
1265	**PENTANES,** liquid	3YE		3		33
1266	**PERFUMERY PRODUCTS** with flammable solvents, packing group II	●3YE		3		33
1266	**PERFUMERY PRODUCTS** with flammable solvents, packing group III	●3Y		3		30
1266	**PERFUMERY PRODUCTS** with flammable solvents (having a flash point below 23°C and viscous according to ADR 2.2.3.1.4), packing group III	●3YE(1)		3		
1267	**PETROLEUM CRUDE OIL,** packing groups I & II	3WE	A(fl)	3		33

(1) Not applicable to the carriage of dangerous goods under RID or ADR

UN No	Substance	EAC	APP	Hazards Class	Sub Risks	HIN
1267	**PETROLEUM CRUDE OIL,** packing group III	3W	A(fl)	3		30
1268	**PETROLEUM DISTILLATES, N.O.S.** or **PETROLEUM PRODUCTS, N.O.S.,** packing groups I & II	3YE		3		33
1268	**PETROLEUM DISTILLATES, N.O.S.** or **PETROLEUM PRODUCTS, N.O.S.,** packing group III	3Y		3		30
1269 to 1271	UN Nos. no longer in use					
1272	**PINE OIL**	3Y		3		30
1273	UN No. no longer in use					
1274	**n-PROPANOL (PROPYL ALCOHOL, NORMAL),** packing group II	●2YE		3		33
1274	**n-PROPANOL (PROPYL ALCOHOL, NORMAL),** packing group III	●2Y		3		30
1275	**PROPIONALDEHYDE**	●2YE		3		33
1276	**n-PROPYL ACETATE**	●2YE		3		33
1277	**PROPYLAMINE**	●2WE	A(fl)	3	8	338
1278	**1-CHLOROPROPANE**	3YE		3		33
1279	**1,2-DICHLOROPROPANE**	2YE		3		33
1280	**PROPYLENE OXIDE**	●3YE		3		33
1281	**PROPYL FORMATES**	●3YE		3		33
1282	**PYRIDINE**	●2WE	A(fl)	3		33
1283 to 1285	UN Nos. no longer in use					
1286	**ROSIN OIL,** packing group II	3YE		3		33
1286	**ROSIN OIL,** packing group III	3Y		3		30
1286	**ROSIN OIL** (having a flash point below 23°C and viscous according to ADR 2.2.3.1.4), packing group III	3YE[(1)]		3		
1287	**RUBBER SOLUTION,** packing group II	3YE		3		33
1287	**RUBBER SOLUTION,** packing group III	3Y		3		30

(1) Not applicable to the carriage of dangerous goods under RID or ADR

UN No	Substance	EAC	APP	Hazards Class	Hazards Sub Risks	HIN
1287	**RUBBER SOLUTION** (having a flash point below 23°C and viscous according to ADR 2.2.3.1.4), packing group III	3YE[(1)]		3		
1288	**SHALE OIL,** packing group II	3WE	A(fl)	3		33
1288	**SHALE OIL,** packing group III	3W	A(fl)	3		30
1289	**SODIUM METHYLATE SOLUTION** in alcohol, packing group II	●2WE	A(fl)	3	8	338
1289	**SODIUM METHYLATE SOLUTION** in alcohol, packing group III	●2W	A(fl)	3	8	38
1290	UN No. no longer in use					
1291	UN No. no longer in use					
1292	**TETRAETHYL SILICATE**	3Y		3		30
1293	**TINCTURES, MEDICINAL,** packing group II	●2YE		3		33
1293	**TINCTURES, MEDICINAL,** packing group III	●2Y		3		30
1294	**TOLUENE**	3YE		3		33
1295	**TRICHLOROSILANE**	4WE	A(fl)	4.3	3, 8	X338
1296	**TRIETHYLAMINE**	●2WE	A(fl)	3	8	338
1297	**TRIMETHYLAMINE, AQUEOUS SOLUTION,** not more than 50% trimethylamine, by mass, packing groups I & II	●2WE	A(fl)	3	8	338
1297	**TRIMETHYLAMINE, AQUEOUS SOLUTION,** not more than 50% trimethylamine, by mass, packing group III	●2W	A(fl)	3	8	38
1298	**TRIMETHYLCHLOROSILANE**	4WE	A(fl)	3	8	X338
1299	**TURPENTINE**	3Y		3		30
1300	**TURPENTINE SUBSTITUTE,** packing group II	3YE		3		33
1300	**TURPENTINE SUBSTITUTE,** packing group III	3Y		3		30
1301	**VINYL ACETATE, STABILIZED**	●3YE		3		339
1302	**VINYL ETHYL ETHER, STABILIZED**	3YE		3		339

(1) Not applicable to the carriage of dangerous goods under RID or ADR

UN No	Substance	EAC	APP	Hazards Class	Sub Risks	HIN
1303	**VINYLIDENE CHLORIDE, STABILIZED**	2YE		3		339
1304	**VINYL ISOBUTYL ETHER, STABILIZED**	3YE		3		339
1305	**VINYLTRICHLOROSILANE**	4WE	A(fl)	3	8	X338
1306	**WOOD PRESERVATIVES, LIQUID,** packing group II	●3YE		3		33
1306	**WOOD PRESERVATIVES, LIQUID,** packing group III	●3Y		3		30
1306	**WOOD PRESERVATIVES, LIQUID** (having a flash point below 23°C and viscous according to ADR 2.2.3.1.4), packing group III	●3YE[1]		3		
1307	**XYLENES,** packing group II	3YE		3		33
1307	**XYLENES,** packing group III	3Y		3		30
1308	**ZIRCONIUM SUSPENDED IN A FLAMMABLE LIQUID,** packing groups I & II	3YE		3		33
1308	**ZIRCONIUM SUSPENDED IN A FLAMMABLE LIQUID,** packing group III	3Y		3		30
1309	**ALUMINIUM POWDER, COATED**	4Y		4.1		40
1310	**AMMONIUM PICRATE, WETTED** with not less than 10% water, by mass	1W[1]		4.1		
1311	UN No. no longer in use					
1312	**BORNEOL**	1Z		4.1		40
1313	**CALCIUM RESINATE**	1Z		4.1		40
1314	**CALCIUM RESINATE, FUSED**	1Z		4.1		40
1315 to 1317	UN Nos. no longer in use					
1318	**COBALT RESINATE, PRECIPITATED**	1Z		4.1		40
1319	UN No. no longer in use					
1320	**DINITROPHENOL, WETTED** with not less than 15% water, by mass	1W[1]		4.1	6.1	
1321	**DINITROPHENOLATES, WETTED** with not less than 15% water, by mass	1W[1]		4.1	6.1	

(1) Not applicable to the carriage of dangerous goods under RID or ADR

UN No	Substance	EAC	APP	Hazards		HIN
				Class	Sub Risks	
1322	**DINITRORESORCINOL, WETTED** with not less than 15% water, by mass	1W(1)		4.1		
1323	**FERROCERIUM**	1Z		4.1		40
1324	**FILMS, NITROCELLULOSE BASE,** gelatin coated, except scrap	1Z(1)		4.1		
1325	**FLAMMABLE SOLID, ORGANIC, N.O.S.**	1Z		4.1		40
1326	**HAFNIUM POWDER, WETTED** with not less than 25% water	1Z		4.1		40
1327	**HAY, STRAW** or **BHUSA**	1Z(1)		4.1		
1328	**HEXAMETHYLENETETRAMINE**	1Z		4.1		40
1329	UN No. no longer in use					
1330	**MANGANESE RESINATE**	1Z		4.1		40
1331	**MATCHES, 'STRIKE ANYWHERE'**	1Z(1)		4.1		
1332	**METALDEHYDE**	1Z		4.1		40
1333	**CERIUM,** slabs, ingots or rods	1Z(1)		4.1		
1334	**NAPHTHALENE, CRUDE** or **NAPHTHALENE, REFINED**	1Z		4.1		40
1335	UN No. no longer in use					
1336	**NITROGUANIDINE (PICRITE), WETTED** with not less than 20% water, by mass	1W(1)		4.1		
1337	**NITROSTARCH, WETTED** with not less than 20% water, by mass	1W(1)		4.1		
1338	**PHOSPHORUS, AMORPHOUS**	1Z		4.1		40
1339	**PHOSPHORUS HEPTASULPHIDE,** free from yellow and white phosphorus	4Y		4.1		40
1340	**PHOSPHORUS PENTASULPHIDE,** free from yellow and white phosphorus	4W		4.3	4.1	423
1341	**PHOSPHORUS SESQUISULPHIDE,** free from yellow and white phosphorus	4Y		4.1		40
1342	UN No. no longer in use					
1343	**PHOSPHORUS TRISULPHIDE,** free from yellow and white phosphorus	4Y		4.1		40

(1) Not applicable to the carriage of dangerous goods under RID or ADR

UN No	Substance	EAC	APP	Hazards Class	Sub Risks	HIN
1344	**TRINITROPHENOL (PICRIC ACID), WETTED** with not less than 30% water, by mass	1W[(1)]		4.1		
1345	**RUBBER SCRAP** or **RUBBER SHODDY,** powdered or granulated	1Z		4.1		40
1346	**SILICON POWDER, AMORPHOUS**	1Z		4.1		40
1347	**SILVER PICRATE, WETTED** with not less than 30% water, by mass	1W[(1)]		4.1		
1348	**SODIUM DINITRO-o-CRESOLATE, WETTED** with not less than 15% water, by mass	1W[(1)]		4.1	6.1	
1349	**SODIUM PICRAMATE, WETTED** with not less than 20% water, by mass	1W[(1)]		4.1		
1350	**SULPHUR**	1Z		4.1		40
1351	UN No. no longer in use					
1352	**TITANIUM POWDER, WETTED,** with not less than 25% water	1Z		4.1		40
1353	**FIBRES** or **FABRICS IMPREGNATED WITH WEAKLY NITRATED NITROCELLULOSE, N.O.S.**	1Z[(1)]		4.1		
1354	**TRINITROBENZENE, WETTED** with not less than 30% water, by mass	1W[(1)]		4.1		
1355	**TRINITROBENZOIC ACID, WETTED** with not less than 30% water, by mass	1W[(1)]		4.1		
1356	**TRINITROTOLUENE (TNT), WETTED** with not less than 30% water, by mass	1W[(1)]		4.1		
1357	**UREA NITRATE, WETTED** with not less than 20% water, by mass	1W[(1)]		4.1		
1358	**ZIRCONIUM POWDER, WETTED** with not less than 25% water	1Z		4.1		40
1359	UN No. no longer in use					
1360	**CALCIUM PHOSPHIDE**	4WE[(1)]		4.3	6.1	
1361	**CARBON,** animal or vegetable origin	1Y		4.2		40
1362	**CARBON, ACTIVATED**	1Y		4.2		40
1363	**COPRA**	1Y		4.2		40
1364	**COTTON WASTE, OILY**	1Y		4.2		40

(1) Not applicable to the carriage of dangerous goods under RID or ADR

UN No	Substance	EAC	APP	Hazards Class	Sub Risks	HIN
1365	**COTTON, WET**	1Y		4.2		40
1366 to 1368	UN Nos. no longer in use					
1369	**p-NITROSODIMETHYLANILINE**	1Y		4.2		40
1370	UN No. no longer in use					
1371	UN No. no longer in use					
1372	**FIBRES, ANIMAL** or **FIBRES, VEGETABLE** burnt, wet or damp	1Y[1]		4.2		
1373	**FIBRES** or **FABRICS, ANIMAL** or **VEGETABLE** or **SYNTHETIC, N.O.S.** with oil	1Y		4.2		40
1374	**FISH MEAL (FISH SCRAP), UNSTABILIZED**	1Y		4.2		40
1375	UN No. no longer in use					
1376	**IRON OXIDE, SPENT** or **IRON SPONGE, SPENT** obtained from coal gas purification	1Y		4.2		40
1377	UN No. no longer in use					
1378	**METAL CATALYST, WETTED** with a visible excess of liquid	1Y		4.2		40
1379	**PAPER, UNSATURATED OIL TREATED,** incompletely dried (including carbon paper)	1Y		4.2		40
1380	**PENTABORANE**	4W		4.2	6.1	333
1381	**PHOSPHORUS, WHITE** or **YELLOW, DRY** or **UNDER WATER** or **IN SOLUTION**	1WE		4.2	6.1	46
1382	**POTASSIUM SULPHIDE, ANHYDROUS** or **POTASSIUM SULPHIDE** with less than 30% water of crystallization	1W		4.2		40
1383	**PYROPHORIC METAL, N.O.S.** or **PYROPHORIC ALLOY, N.O.S.**	4Y		4.2		43
1384	**SODIUM DITHIONITE (SODIUM HYDROSULPHITE)**	1S		4.2		40

(1) Not applicable to the carriage of dangerous goods under RID or ADR

UN No	Substance	EAC	APP	Hazards Class	Hazards Sub Risks	HIN
1385	**SODIUM SULPHIDE, ANHYDROUS** or **SODIUM SULPHIDE** with less than 30% water of crystallization	1W		4.2		40
1386	**SEED CAKE** with more than 1.5% oil and not more than 11% moisture	1Y		4.2		40
1387	**WOOL WASTE, WET**	1Y(1)		4.2		
1388	UN No. no longer in use					
1389	**ALKALI METAL AMALGAM, LIQUID**	4W		4.3		X323
1390	**ALKALI METAL AMIDES**	4W		4.3		423
1391	**ALKALI METAL DISPERSION** or **ALKALINE EARTH METAL DISPERSION**	4W		4.3		X323
1392	**ALKALINE EARTH METAL AMALGAM, LIQUID**	4W		4.3		X323
1393	**ALKALINE EARTH METAL ALLOY, N.O.S.**	4W		4.3		423
1394	**ALUMINIUM CARBIDE**	4W		4.3		423
1395	**ALUMINIUM FERROSILICON POWDER**	4W		4.3	6.1	462
1396	**ALUMINIUM POWDER, UNCOATED**	4W		4.3		423
1397	**ALUMINIUM PHOSPHIDE**	4WE(1)		4.3	6.1	
1398	**ALUMINIUM SILICON POWDER, UNCOATED**	4Y		4.3		423
1399	UN No. no longer in use					
1400	**BARIUM**	4W		4.3		423
1401	**CALCIUM**	4W		4.3		423
1402	**CALCIUM CARBIDE**	4W		4.3		X423/ 423
1403	**CALCIUM CYANAMIDE** with more than 0.1% calcium carbide	4W		4.3		423
1404	**CALCIUM HYDRIDE**	4W(1)		4.3		
1405	**CALCIUM SILICIDE**	4W		4.3		423
1406	UN No. no longer in use					
1407	**CAESIUM**	4W		4.3		X423

(1) Not applicable to the carriage of dangerous goods under RID or ADR

UN No	Substance	EAC	APP	Hazards Class	Sub Risks	HIN
1408	**FERROSILICON** with 30% or more but less than 90% silicon	4W		4.3	6.1	462
1409	**METAL HYDRIDES, WATER-REACTIVE, N.O.S.**, packing group I	4W(1)		4.3		
1409	**METAL HYDRIDES, WATER-REACTIVE, N.O.S.**, packing group II	4W		4.3		423
1410	**LITHIUM ALUMINIUM HYDRIDE**	4W(1)		4.3		
1411	**LITHIUM ALUMINIUM HYDRIDE, ETHEREAL**	4WE(1)	A(fl)	4.3	3	
1412	UN No. no longer in use					
1413	**LITHIUM BOROHYDRIDE**	4W(1)		4.3		
1414	**LITHIUM HYDRIDE**	4W(1)		4.3		
1415	**LITHIUM**	4W		4.3		X423
1416	UN No. no longer in use					
1417	**LITHIUM SILICON**	4W		4.3		423
1418	**MAGNESIUM POWDER** or **MAGNESIUM ALLOYS POWDER**, packing group I	4W(1)		4.3	4.2	
1418	**MAGNESIUM POWDER** or **MAGNESIUM ALLOYS POWDER**, packing groups II & III	4W		4.3	4.2	423
1419	**MAGNESIUM ALUMINIUM PHOSPHIDE**	4WE(1)		4.3	6.1	
1420	**POTASSIUM METAL ALLOYS, LIQUID**	4W		4.3		X323
1421	**ALKALI METAL ALLOY, LIQUID, N.O.S.**	4W		4.3		X323
1422	**POTASSIUM SODIUM ALLOYS, LIQUID**	4W		4.3		X323
1423	**RUBIDIUM**	4W		4.3		X423
1424	UN No. no longer in use					
1425	UN No. no longer in use					
1426	**SODIUM BOROHYDRIDE**	4W(1)		4.3		
1427	**SODIUM HYDRIDE**	4W(1)		4.3		
1428	**SODIUM**	4W		4.3		X423

(1) Not applicable to the carriage of dangerous goods under RID or ADR

UN No	Substance	EAC	APP	Hazards Class	Sub Risks	HIN
1429	UN No. no longer in use					
1430	UN No. no longer in use					
1431	**SODIUM METHYLATE**	1W		4.2	8	48
1432	**SODIUM PHOSPHIDE**	4WE(1)		4.3	6.1	
1433	**STANNIC PHOSPHIDES**	4WE(1)		4.3	6.1	
1434	UN No. no longer in use					
1435	**ZINC ASHES**	4Y		4.3		423
1436	**ZINC POWDER** or **ZINC DUST**, packing group I	4W(1)		4.3	4.2	
1436	**ZINC POWDER** or **ZINC DUST**, packing groups II & III	4W		4.3	4.2	423
1437	**ZIRCONIUM HYDRIDE**	4Y		4.1		40
1438	**ALUMINIUM NITRATE**	1Z		5.1		50
1439	**AMMONIUM DICHROMATE**	1Y		5.1		50
1440	UN No. no longer in use					
1441	UN No. no longer in use					
1442	**AMMONIUM PERCHLORATE**	1Y		5.1		50
1443	UN No. no longer in use					
1444	**AMMONIUM PERSULPHATE**	1Z		5.1		50
1445	**BARIUM CHLORATE, SOLID**	1Y		5.1	6.1	56
1446	**BARIUM NITRATE**	1Y		5.1	6.1	56
1447	**BARIUM PERCHLORATE, SOLID**	1Y		5.1	6.1	56
1448	**BARIUM PERMANGANATE**	1Y		5.1	6.1	56
1449	**BARIUM PEROXIDE**	1Y		5.1	6.1	56
1450	**BROMATES, INORGANIC, N.O.S.**	1Y		5.1		50
1451	**CAESIUM NITRATE**	1Z		5.1		50
1452	**CALCIUM CHLORATE**	1Y		5.1		50
1453	**CALCIUM CHLORITE**	1Y		5.1		50
1454	**CALCIUM NITRATE**	1Z		5.1		50
1455	**CALCIUM PERCHLORATE**	1Y		5.1		50
1456	**CALCIUM PERMANGANATE**	1Y		5.1		50

(1) Not applicable to the carriage of dangerous goods under RID or ADR

UN No	Substance	EAC	APP	Hazards Class	Hazards Sub Risks	HIN
1457	CALCIUM PEROXIDE	1Y		5.1		50
1458	CHLORATE AND BORATE MIXTURE	1Y		5.1		50
1459	CHLORATE AND MAGNESIUM CHLORIDE MIXTURE, SOLID	1Y		5.1		50
1460	UN No. no longer in use					
1461	CHLORATES, INORGANIC, N.O.S.	1Y		5.1		50
1462	CHLORITES, INORGANIC, N.O.S.	1Y		5.1		50
1463	CHROMIUM TRIOXIDE, ANHYDROUS	1W		5.1	6.1, 8	568
1464	UN No. no longer in use					
1465	DIDYMIUM NITRATE	1Z		5.1		50
1466	FERRIC NITRATE	1Z		5.1		50
1467	GUANIDINE NITRATE	1Z		5.1		50
1468	UN No. no longer in use					
1469	LEAD NITRATE	1Y		5.1	6.1	56
1470	LEAD PERCHLORATE, SOLID	1Y		5.1	6.1	56
1471	LITHIUM HYPOCHLORITE, DRY or LITHIUM HYPOCHLORITE MIXTURE	1W		5.1		50
1472	LITHIUM PEROXIDE	1Y		5.1		50
1473	MAGNESIUM BROMATE	1Y		5.1		50
1474	MAGNESIUM NITRATE	1Z		5.1		50
1475	MAGNESIUM PERCHLORATE	1Y		5.1		50
1476	MAGNESIUM PEROXIDE	1Y		5.1		50
1477	NITRATES, INORGANIC, N.O.S.	1Y		5.1		50
1478	UN No. no longer in use					
1479	OXIDISING SOLID, N.O.S., packing group I	1Y[1]		5.1		
1479	OXIDISING SOLID, N.O.S., packing groups II & III	1Y		5.1		50
1480	UN No. no longer in use					
1481	PERCHLORATES, INORGANIC, N.O.S.	1Y		5.1		50

[1] Not applicable to the carriage of dangerous goods under RID or ADR

UN No	Substance	EAC	APP	Hazards Class	Hazards Sub Risks	HIN
1482	PERMANGANATES, INORGANIC, N.O.S.	1Y		5.1		50
1483	PEROXIDES, INORGANIC, N.O.S.	1Y		5.1		50
1484	POTASSIUM BROMATE	1Y		5.1		50
1485	POTASSIUM CHLORATE	1Y		5.1		50
1486	POTASSIUM NITRATE	1Z		5.1		50
1487	POTASSIUM NITRATE AND SODIUM NITRITE MIXTURE	1Y		5.1		50
1488	POTASSIUM NITRITE	1Y		5.1		50
1489	POTASSIUM PERCHLORATE	1Y		5.1		50
1490	POTASSIUM PERMANGANATE	1Y		5.1		50
1491	POTASSIUM PEROXIDE	1W[(1)]		5.1		
1492	POTASSIUM PERSULPHATE	1Z		5.1		50
1493	SILVER NITRATE	1Y		5.1		50
1494	SODIUM BROMATE	1Y		5.1		50
1495	SODIUM CHLORATE	1Y		5.1		50
1496	SODIUM CHLORITE	1Y		5.1		50
1497	UN No. no longer in use					
1498	SODIUM NITRATE	1Z		5.1		50
1499	SODIUM NITRATE AND POTASSIUM NITRATE MIXTURE	1Z		5.1		50
1500	SODIUM NITRITE	1Z		5.1	6.1	56
1501	UN No. no longer in use					
1502	SODIUM PERCHLORATE	1Y		5.1		50
1503	SODIUM PERMANGANATE	1Y		5.1		50
1504	SODIUM PEROXIDE	1W[(1)]		5.1		
1505	SODIUM PERSULPHATE	1Z		5.1		50
1506	STRONTIUM CHLORATE	1Y		5.1		50
1507	STRONTIUM NITRATE	1Z		5.1		50
1508	STRONTIUM PERCHLORATE	1Y		5.1		50
1509	STRONTIUM PEROXIDE	1Y		5.1		50
1510	TETRANITROMETHANE	2W		6.1	5.1	665

(1) Not applicable to the carriage of dangerous goods under RID or ADR

UN No	Substance	EAC	APP	Hazards Class	Hazards Sub Risks	HIN
1511	UREA HYDROGEN PEROXIDE	1X		5.1	8	58
1512	ZINC AMMONIUM NITRITE	1Y		5.1		50
1513	ZINC CHLORATE	1Y		5.1		50
1514	ZINC NITRATE	1Y		5.1		50
1515	ZINC PERMANGANATE	1Y		5.1		50
1516	ZINC PEROXIDE	1Y		5.1		50
1517	ZIRCONIUM PICRAMATE, WETTED with not less than 20% water, by mass	1W(1)		4.1		
1518 to 1540	UN Nos. no longer in use					
1541	ACETONE CYANOHYDRIN, STABILIZED	●2X	B	6.1		669
1542	UN No. no longer in use					
1543	UN No. no longer in use					
1544	ALKALOIDS, SOLID, N.O.S. or ALKALOID SALTS, SOLID, N.O.S.	2X		6.1		66/60
1545	ALLYL ISOTHIOCYANATE, STABILIZED	3WE	A(fl)	6.1	3	639
1546	AMMONIUM ARSENATE	2Z		6.1		60
1547	ANILINE	●3X		6.1		60
1548	ANILINE HYDROCHLORIDE	2X		6.1		60
1549	ANTIMONY COMPOUND, INORGANIC, SOLID, N.O.S.	2Z		6.1		60
1550	ANTIMONY LACTATE	2Z		6.1		60
1551	ANTIMONY POTASSIUM TARTRATE	2Z		6.1		60
1552	UN No. no longer in use					
1553	ARSENIC ACID, LIQUID	2X	B	6.1		66
1554	ARSENIC ACID, SOLID	2Z		6.1		60
1555	ARSENIC BROMIDE	2Z		6.1		60
1556	ARSENIC COMPOUND, LIQUID, N.O.S., inorganic, including: Arsenates, n.o.s., Arsenites, n.o.s., Arsenic sulphides, n.o.s., packing group I	2X	B	6.1		66

(1) Not applicable to the carriage of dangerous goods under RID or ADR

UN No	Substance	EAC	APP	Hazards Class	Hazards Sub Risks	HIN
1556	**ARSENIC COMPOUND, LIQUID, N.O.S.,** inorganic, including: Arsenates, n.o.s., Arsenites, n.o.s., Arsenic sulphides, n.o.s., packing groups II & III	2X		6.1		60
1557	**ARSENIC COMPOUND, SOLID, N.O.S.,** inorganic, including: Arsenates, n.o.s., Arsenites, n.o.s., Arsenic sulphides, n.o.s.	2X		6.1		66/60
1558	**ARSENIC**	2Z		6.1		60
1559	**ARSENIC PENTOXIDE**	2Z		6.1		60
1560	**ARSENIC TRICHLORIDE**	2X	B	6.1		66
1561	**ARSENIC TRIOXIDE**	2X		6.1		60
1562	**ARSENICAL DUST**	2Z		6.1		60
1563	UN No. no longer in use					
1564	**BARIUM COMPOUND, N.O.S.**	2Z		6.1		60
1565	**BARIUM CYANIDE**	2X		6.1		66
1566	**BERYLLIUM COMPOUND, N.O.S.**	2Z		6.1		60
1567	**BERYLLIUM POWDER**	2Z		6.1	4.1	64
1568	UN No. no longer in use					
1569	**BROMOACETONE**	2W	A(fl)	6.1	3	63
1570	**BRUCINE**	2X		6.1		66
1571	**BARIUM AZIDE, WETTED** with not less than 50% water, by mass	1W[(1)]		4.1	6.1	
1572	**CACODYLIC ACID**	2Z		6.1		60
1573	**CALCIUM ARSENATE**	2Z		6.1		60
1574	**CALCIUM ARSENATE AND CALCIUM ARSENITE MIXTURE, SOLID**	2Z		6.1		60
1575	**CALCIUM CYANIDE**	2X		6.1		66
1576	UN No. no longer in use					
1577	**CHLORODINITROBENZENES, LIQUID**	2X		6.1		60
1578	**CHLORONITROBENZENES, SOLID**	2X		6.1		60

(1) Not applicable to the carriage of dangerous goods under RID or ADR

UN No	Substance	EAC	APP	Hazards Class	Sub Risks	HIN
1579	4-CHLORO-o-TOLUIDINE HYDROCHLORIDE, SOLID	2X		6.1		60
1580	CHLOROPICRIN	2XE	B	6.1		66
1581	CHLOROPICRIN AND METHYL BROMIDE MIXTURE with more than 2% chloropicrin	2XE	B	2.3		26
1582	CHLOROPICRIN AND METHYL CHLORIDE MIXTURE	2XE	A(c)	2.3		26
1583	CHLOROPICRIN MIXTURE, N.O.S., packing group I	2XE	B	6.1		66
1583	CHLOROPICRIN MIXTURE, N.O.S., packing groups II & III	2X		6.1		60
1584	UN No. no longer in use					
1585	COPPER ACETOARSENITE	2Z		6.1		60
1586	COPPER ARSENITE	2Z		6.1		60
1587	COPPER CYANIDE	2X		6.1		60
1588	CYANIDES, INORGANIC, SOLID, N.O.S.	2X		6.1		66/60
1589	CYANOGEN CHLORIDE, STABILIZED	2XE[1]	B	2.3	8	
1590	DICHLOROANILINES, LIQUID	2X		6.1		60
1591	o-DICHLOROBENZENE	2Z		6.1		60
1592	UN No. no longer in use					
1593	DICHLOROMETHANE	2Z		6.1		60
1594	DIETHYL SULPHATE	2X		6.1		60
1595	DIMETHYL SULPHATE	•3XE	B	6.1	8	668
1596	DINITROANILINES	2X		6.1		60
1597	DINITROBENZENES, LIQUID	2X		6.1		60
1598	DINITRO-o-CRESOL	2X		6.1		60
1599	DINITROPHENOL SOLUTION	2X		6.1		60
1600	DINITROTOLUENES, MOLTEN	2W	A(h)	6.1		60
1601	DISINFECTANT, SOLID, TOXIC, N.O.S.	2X		6.1		66/60

[1] Not applicable to the carriage of dangerous goods under RID or ADR

UN No	Substance	EAC	APP	Hazards Class	Sub Risks	HIN
1602	DYE, LIQUID, TOXIC, N.O.S. or DYE, INTERMEDIATE, LIQUID, TOXIC, N.O.S., packing group I	2X	B	6.1		66
1602	DYE, LIQUID, TOXIC, N.O.S. or DYE, INTERMEDIATE, LIQUID, TOXIC, N.O.S., packing groups II & III	2X		6.1		60
1603	ETHYL BROMOACETATE	2W	A(fl)	6.1	3	63
1604	ETHYLENEDIAMINE	●2W	A(fl)	8	3	83
1605	ETHYLENE DIBROMIDE	2X	B	6.1		66
1606	FERRIC ARSENATE	2X		6.1		60
1607	FERRIC ARSENITE	2X		6.1		60
1608	FERROUS ARSENATE	2X		6.1		60
1609	UN No. no longer in use					
1610	UN No. no longer in use					
1611	HEXAETHYL TETRAPHOSPHATE	2X		6.1		60
1612	HEXAETHYL TETRAPHOSPHATE AND COMPRESSED GAS MIXTURE	2RE	B	2.3		26
1613	HYDROCYANIC ACID, AQUEOUS SOLUTION (HYDROGEN CYANIDE, AQUEOUS SOLUTION) with not more than 20% hydrogen cyanide	●2WE	A(fl)	6.1	3	663
1614	HYDROGEN CYANIDE, STABILIZED, containing less than 3% water and absorbed in a porous inert material	2WE[1]	A(fl)	6.1	3	
1615	UN No. no longer in use					
1616	LEAD ACETATE	2Z		6.1		60
1617	LEAD ARSENATES	2Z		6.1		60
1618	LEAD ARSENITES	2Z		6.1		60
1619	UN No. no longer in use					
1620	LEAD CYANIDE	2Z		6.1		60
1621	LONDON PURPLE	2X		6.1		60
1622	MAGNESIUM ARSENATE	2Z		6.1		60
1623	MERCURIC ARSENATE	2X		6.1		60
1624	MERCURIC CHLORIDE	2X		6.1		60

(1) Not applicable to the carriage of dangerous goods under RID or ADR

UN No	Substance	EAC	APP	Hazards Class	Hazards Sub Risks	HIN
1625	MERCURIC NITRATE	2X		6.1		60
1626	MERCURIC POTASSIUM CYANIDE	2X		6.1		66
1627	MERCUROUS NITRATE	2X		6.1		60
1628	UN No. no longer in use					
1629	MERCURY ACETATE	2X		6.1		60
1630	MERCURY AMMONIUM CHLORIDE	2X		6.1		60
1631	MERCURY BENZOATE	2X		6.1		60
1632	UN No. no longer in use					
1633	UN No. no longer in use					
1634	MERCURY BROMIDES	2X		6.1		60
1635	UN No. no longer in use					
1636	MERCURY CYANIDE	2X		6.1		60
1637	MERCURY GLUCONATE	2X		6.1		60
1638	MERCURY IODIDE	2X		6.1		60
1639	MERCURY NUCLEATE	2X		6.1		60
1640	MERCURY OLEATE	2X		6.1		60
1641	MERCURY OXIDE	2X		6.1		60
1642	MERCURY OXYCYANIDE, DESENSITIZED	2X		6.1		60
1643	MERCURY POTASSIUM IODIDE	2X		6.1		60
1644	MERCURY SALICYLATE	2X		6.1		60
1645	MERCURY SULPHATE	2X		6.1		60
1646	MERCURY THIOCYANATE	2X		6.1		60
1647	METHYL BROMIDE AND ETHYLENE DIBROMIDE MIXTURE, LIQUID	2X	B	6.1		66
1648	ACETONITRILE	●2YE		3		33
1649	MOTOR FUEL ANTI-KNOCK MIXTURE	2WE	B	6.1		66
1650	beta-NAPHTHYLAMINE, SOLID	2Z		6.1		60
1651	NAPHTHYLTHIOUREA	2Z		6.1		60
1652	NAPHTHYLUREA	2X		6.1		60
1653	NICKEL CYANIDE	2X		6.1		60

UN No	Substance	EAC	APP	Hazards Class	Sub Risks	HIN
1654	**NICOTINE**	2X		6.1		60
1655	**NICOTINE COMPOUND, SOLID, N.O.S.** or **NICOTINE PREPARATION, SOLID, N.O.S.**	2X		6.1		66/60
1656	**NICOTINE HYDROCHLORIDE, LIQUID** or **SOLUTION**	2X		6.1		60
1657	**NICOTINE SALICYLATE**	2X		6.1		60
1658	**NICOTINE SULPHATE, SOLUTION**	2X		6.1		60
1659	**NICOTINE TARTRATE**	2X		6.1		60
1660	**NITRIC OXIDE, COMPRESSED**	2PE[(1)]	B	2.3	5.1, 8	
1661	**NITROANILINES (o-,m-,p-)**	2X		6.1		60
1662	**NITROBENZENE**	2X		6.1		60
1663	**NITROPHENOLS (o-,m-,p-)**	2X		6.1		60
1664	**NITROTOLUENES, LIQUID**	2X		6.1		60
1665	**NITROXYLENES, LIQUID**	2X		6.1		60
1666 to 1668	UN Nos. no longer in use					
1669	**PENTACHLOROETHANE**	2Z		6.1		60
1670	**PERCHLOROMETHYL MERCAPTAN**	2XE	B	6.1		66
1671	**PHENOL, SOLID**	2X		6.1		60
1672	**PHENYLCARBYLAMINE CHLORIDE**	2XE	B	6.1		66
1673	**PHENYLENEDIAMINES (o-,m-,p-)**	2X		6.1		60
1674	**PHENYLMERCURIC ACETATE**	2X		6.1		60
1675	UN No. no longer in use					
1676	UN No. no longer in use					
1677	**POTASSIUM ARSENATE**	2X		6.1		60
1678	**POTASSIUM ARSENITE**	2X		6.1		60
1679	**POTASSIUM CUPROCYANIDE**	2X		6.1		60
1680	**POTASSIUM CYANIDE, SOLID**	2X		6.1		66
1681	UN No. no longer in use					
1682	UN No. no longer in use					

(1) Not applicable to the carriage of dangerous goods under RID or ADR

UN No	Substance	EAC	APP	Hazards Class	Sub Risks	HIN
1683	SILVER ARSENITE	2Z		6.1		60
1684	SILVER CYANIDE	2X		6.1		60
1685	SODIUM ARSENATE	2X		6.1		60
1686	SODIUM ARSENITE, AQUEOUS SOLUTION	2X		6.1		60
1687	SODIUM AZIDE	2XE[1]		6.1		
1688	SODIUM CACODYLATE	2X		6.1		60
1689	SODIUM CYANIDE, SOLID	2X		6.1		66
1690	SODIUM FLUORIDE, SOLID	2Z		6.1		60
1691	STRONTIUM ARSENITE	2Z		6.1		60
1692	STRYCHNINE or STRYCHNINE SALTS	2X		6.1		66
1693	TEAR GAS SUBSTANCE, LIQUID, N.O.S., packing group I	2XE	B	6.1		66
1693	TEAR GAS SUBSTANCE, LIQUID, N.O.S., packing group II	2XE		6.1		60
1694	BROMOBENZYL CYANIDES, LIQUID	2XE	B	6.1		66
1695	CHLOROACETONE, STABILIZED	●2WE	A(fl)	6.1	3, 8	663
1696	UN No. no longer in use					
1697	CHLOROACETOPHENONE, SOLID	2Z		6.1		60
1698	DIPHENYLAMINE CHLOROARSINE	2XE		6.1		66
1699	DIPHENYLCHLOROARSINE, LIQUID	2XE	B	6.1		66
1700	TEAR GAS CANDLES	2X[1]		6.1	4.1	
1701	XYLYL BROMIDE, LIQUID	2XE		6.1		60
1702	1,1,2,2-TETRACHLOROETHANE	2X		6.1		60
1703	UN No. no longer in use					
1704	TETRAETHYL DITHIOPYROPHOSPHATE	2X		6.1		60
1705	UN No. no longer in use					
1706	UN No. no longer in use					
1707	THALLIUM COMPOUND, N.O.S.	2Z		6.1		60
1708	TOLUIDINES, LIQUID	●3X		6.1		60
1709	2,4-TOLUYLENEDIAMINE, SOLID	2X		6.1		60

(1) Not applicable to the carriage of dangerous goods under RID or ADR

UN No	Substance	EAC	APP	Hazards Class	Sub Risks	HIN
1710	TRICHLOROETHYLENE	2Z		6.1		60
1711	XYLIDINES, LIQUID	2X		6.1		60
1712	ZINC ARSENATE, ZINC ARSENITE or ZINC ARSENATE AND ZINC ARSENITE MIXTURE	2Z		6.1		60
1713	ZINC CYANIDE	2X		6.1		66
1714	ZINC PHOSPHIDE	4WE[(1)]		4.3	6.1	
1715	ACETIC ANHYDRIDE	●3W	A(fl)	8	3	83
1716	ACETYL BROMIDE	4W		8		80
1717	ACETYL CHLORIDE	4WE	A(fl)	3	8	X338
1718	BUTYL ACID PHOSPHATE	2X		8		80
1719	CAUSTIC ALKALI LIQUID, N.O.S.	2R		8		80
1720	UN No. no longer in use					
1721	UN No. no longer in use					
1722	ALLYL CHLOROFORMATE	●3WE	A(fl)	6.1	3, 8	668
1723	ALLYL IODIDE	2WE	A(fl)	3	8	338
1724	ALLYLTRICHLOROSILANE, STABILIZED	4W	A(fl)	8	3	X839
1725	ALUMINIUM BROMIDE, ANHYDROUS	4W		8		80
1726	ALUMINIUM CHLORIDE, ANHYDROUS	4W		8		80
1727	AMMONIUM HYDROGENDIFLUORIDE, SOLID	2X		8		80
1728	AMYLTRICHLOROSILANE	4W		8		X80
1729	ANISOYL CHLORIDE	4W		8		80
1730	ANTIMONY PENTACHLORIDE, LIQUID	4WE		8		X80
1731	ANTIMONY PENTACHLORIDE SOLUTION	4WE		8		80
1732	ANTIMONY PENTAFLUORIDE	4W		8	6.1	86
1733	ANTIMONY TRICHLORIDE	4W		8		80
1734	UN No. no longer in use					

(1) Not applicable to the carriage of dangerous goods under RID or ADR

UN No	Substance	EAC	APP	Hazards Class	Sub Risks	HIN
1735	UN No. no longer in use					
1736	**BENZOYL CHLORIDE**	4W		8		80
1737	**BENZYL BROMIDE**	2X		6.1	8	68
1738	**BENZYL CHLORIDE**	2X		6.1	8	68
1739	**BENZYL CHLOROFORMATE**	2X	B	8		88
1740	**HYDROGENDIFLUORIDES, SOLID, N.O.S.**	2X		8		80
1741	**BORON TRICHLORIDE**	2WE	B	2.3	8	268
1742	**BORON TRIFLUORIDE ACETIC ACID COMPLEX, LIQUID**	2X		8		80
1743	**BORON TRIFLUORIDE PROPIONIC ACID COMPLEX, LIQUID**	2X		8		80
1744	**BROMINE** or **BROMINE SOLUTION**	2XE	A(!)	8	6.1	886
1745	**BROMINE PENTAFLUORIDE**	4WE	A(!)	5.1	6.1, 8	568
1746	**BROMINE TRIFLUORIDE**	4WE	A(!)	5.1	6.1, 8	568
1747	**BUTYLTRICHLOROSILANE**	4W	A(fl)	8	3	X83
1748	**CALCIUM HYPOCHLORITE, DRY** or **CALCIUM HYPOCHLORITE MIXTURE, DRY** with more than 39% available chlorine (8.8% available oxygen)	1W		5.1		50
1749	**CHLORINE TRIFLUORIDE**	2WE	A(!)	2.3	5.1, 8	265
1750	**CHLOROACETIC ACID SOLUTION**	2X		6.1	8	68
1751	**CHLOROACETIC ACID, SOLID**	2X		6.1	8	68
1752	**CHLOROACETYL CHLORIDE**	2XE	B	6.1	8	668
1753	**CHLOROPHENYLTRICHLOROSILANE**	4W		8		X80
1754	**CHLOROSULPHONIC ACID** (with or without sulphur trioxide)	4WE	B	8		X88
1755	**CHROMIC ACID SOLUTION**	2X		8		80
1756	**CHROMIC FLUORIDE, SOLID**	2X		8		80
1757	**CHROMIC FLUORIDE SOLUTION**	2X		8		80
1758	**CHROMIUM OXYCHLORIDE**	4WE	B	8		X88
1759	**CORROSIVE SOLID, N.O.S.**	2X		8		88/80
1760	**CORROSIVE LIQUID, N.O.S.,** packing group I	2X	B	8		88

UN No	Substance	EAC	APP	Hazards Class	Hazards Sub Risks	HIN
1760	CORROSIVE LIQUID, N.O.S., packing groups II & III	2X		8		80
1761	CUPRIETHYLENEDIAMINE SOLUTION	2X		8	6.1	86
1762	CYCLOHEXENYLTRICHLOROSILANE	4W		8		X80
1763	CYCLOHEXYLTRICHLOROSILANE	4W		8		X80
1764	DICHLOROACETIC ACID	2X		8		80
1765	DICHLOROACETYL CHLORIDE	4W		8		X80
1766	DICHLOROPHENYLTRICHLOROSILANE	4W		8		X80
1767	DIETHYLDICHLOROSILANE	4W	A(fl)	8	3	X83
1768	DIFLUOROPHOSPHORIC ACID, ANHYDROUS	2X		8		80
1769	DIPHENYLDICHLOROSILANE	4W		8		X80
1770	DIPHENYLMETHYL BROMIDE	2X		8		80
1771	DODECYLTRICHLOROSILANE	4W		8		X80
1772	UN No. no longer in use					
1773	FERRIC CHLORIDE, ANHYDROUS	2X		8		80
1774	FIRE EXTINGUISHER CHARGES, corrosive liquid	(1)		8		
1775	FLUOROBORIC ACID	2X		8		80
1776	FLUOROPHOSPHORIC ACID, ANHYDROUS	2X		8		80
1777	FLUOROSULPHONIC ACID	4WE	B	8		88
1778	FLUOROSILICIC ACID	2X		8		80
1779	FORMIC ACID with more than 85% acid by mass	●2W	A(fl)	8	3	83
1780	FUMARYL CHLORIDE	4W		8		80
1781	HEXADECYLTRICHLOROSILANE	4W		8		X80
1782	HEXAFLUOROPHOSPHORIC ACID	2X		8		80
1783	HEXAMETHYLENEDIAMINE SOLUTION	2X		8		80
1784	HEXYLTRICHLOROSILANE	4W		8		X80
1785	UN No. no longer in use					

(1) Not applicable to the carriage of dangerous goods under RID or ADR

UN No	Substance	EAC	APP	Hazards Class	Sub Risks	HIN
1786	HYDROFLUORIC ACID AND SULPHURIC ACID MIXTURE	2W	B	8	6.1	886
1787	HYDRIODIC ACID	2R		8		80
1788	HYDROBROMIC ACID	2R		8		80
1789	HYDROCHLORIC ACID	2R		8		80
1790	HYDROFLUORIC ACID with more than 60% hydrogen fluoride, packing group I	2W	B	8	6.1	886
1790	HYDROFLUORIC ACID with not more than 60% hydrogen fluoride, packing group II	2X		8	6.1	86
1791	HYPOCHLORITE SOLUTION	2X		8		80
1792	IODINE MONOCHLORIDE, SOLID	4WE		8		80
1793	ISOPROPYL ACID PHOSPHATE	2X		8		80
1794	LEAD SULPHATE with more than 3% free acid	2X		8		80
1795	UN No. no longer in use					
1796	NITRATING ACID MIXTURE with more than 50% nitric acid, packing group I	2P	B	8	5.1	885
1796	NITRATING ACID MIXTURE with not more than 50% nitric acid, packing group II	2R		8		80
1797	UN No. no longer in use					
1798	NITROHYDROCHLORIC ACID	2P(1)	B	8		
1799	NONYLTRICHLOROSILANE	4W		8		X80
1800	OCTADECYLTRICHLOROSILANE	4W		8		X80
1801	OCTYLTRICHLOROSILANE	4W		8		X80
1802	PERCHLORIC ACID with not more than 50% acid, by mass	2P		8	5.1	85
1803	PHENOLSULPHONIC ACID, LIQUID	2X		8		80
1804	PHENYLTRICHLOROSILANE	4W		8		X80
1805	PHOSPHORIC ACID, SOLUTION	2R		8		80
1806	PHOSPHORUS PENTACHLORIDE	4W		8		80
1807	PHOSPHORUS PENTOXIDE	2X		8		80

(1) Not applicable to the carriage of dangerous goods under RID or ADR

UN No	Substance	EAC	APP	Hazards Class	Sub Risks	HIN
1808	PHOSPHORUS TRIBROMIDE	4WE		8		X80
1809	PHOSPHORUS TRICHLORIDE	4WE	B	6.1	8	668
1810	PHOSPHORUS OXYCHLORIDE	4WE	B	6.1	8	X668
1811	POTASSIUM HYDROGENDIFLUORIDE, SOLID	2X		8	6.1	86
1812	POTASSIUM FLUORIDE, SOLID	2X		6.1		60
1813	POTASSIUM HYDROXIDE, SOLID	2W		8		80
1814	POTASSIUM HYDROXIDE SOLUTION	2R		8		80
1815	PROPIONYL CHLORIDE	●3WE	A(fl)	3	8	338
1816	PROPYLTRICHLOROSILANE	4W	A(fl)	8	3	X83
1817	PYROSULPHURYL CHLORIDE	4WE		8		X80
1818	SILICON TETRACHLORIDE	4WE		8		X80
1819	SODIUM ALUMINATE SOLUTION	2R		8		80
1820 to 1822	UN Nos. no longer in use					
1823	SODIUM HYDROXIDE, SOLID	2W		8		80
1824	SODIUM HYDROXIDE SOLUTION	2R		8		80
1825	SODIUM MONOXIDE	2W		8		80
1826	NITRATING ACID MIXTURE, SPENT, with more than 50% nitric acid, packing group I	2W	B	8	5.1	885
1826	NITRATING ACID MIXTURE, SPENT, with not more than 50% nitric acid, packing group II	2X		8		80
1827	STANNIC CHLORIDE, ANHYDROUS	4WE		8		X80
1828	SULPHUR CHLORIDES	4WE	B	8		X88
1829	SULPHUR TRIOXIDE, STABILIZED	4WE	B	8		X88
1830	SULPHURIC ACID with more than 51% acid	2P		8		80
1831	SULPHURIC ACID, FUMING	4WE	B	8	6.1	X886
1832	SULPHURIC ACID, SPENT	2W		8		80
1833	SULPHUROUS ACID	2R		8		80

UN No	Substance	EAC	APP	Hazards Class	Sub Risks	HIN
1834	SULPHURYL CHLORIDE	4WE	B	6.1	8	X668
1835	TETRAMETHYLAMMONIUM HYDROXIDE SOLUTION	2X		8		80
1836	THIONYL CHLORIDE	4WE	B	8		X88
1837	THIOPHOSPHORYL CHLORIDE	4WE		8		X80
1838	TITANIUM TETRACHLORIDE	4WE	B	6.1	8	X668
1839	TRICHLOROACETIC ACID	2X		8		80
1840	ZINC CHLORIDE SOLUTION	2X		8		80
1841	ACETALDEHYDE AMMONIA	2Z		9		90
1842	UN No. no longer in use					
1843	AMMONIUM DINITRO-o-CRESOLATE, SOLID	2X		6.1		60
1844	UN No. no longer in use					
1845	CARBON DIOXIDE, SOLID (DRY ICE)	2T(1)		9		
1846	CARBON TETRACHLORIDE	2Z		6.1		60
1847	POTASSIUM SULPHIDE, HYDRATED with not less than 30% water of crystallisation	2X		8		80
1848	PROPIONIC ACID with not less than 10% and less than 90% acid by mass	•2W		8		80
1849	SODIUM SULPHIDE, HYDRATED with not less than 30% water	2X		8		80
1850	UN No. no longer in use					
1851	MEDICINE, LIQUID, TOXIC, N.O.S.	2X		6.1		60
1852	UN No. no longer in use					
1853	UN No. no longer in use					
1854	BARIUM ALLOYS, PYROPHORIC	4Y		4.2		43
1855	CALCIUM, PYROPHORIC or CALCIUM ALLOYS, PYROPHORIC	4W(1)		4.2		
1856	RAGS, OILY	1Y(1)		4.2		
1857	TEXTILE WASTE, WET	1Y(1)		4.2		
1858	HEXAFLUOROPROPYLENE (REFRIGERANT GAS R 1216)	2TE		2.2		20
1859	SILICON TETRAFLUORIDE	2PE	B	2.3	8	268

(1) Not applicable to the carriage of dangerous goods under RID or ADR

UN No	Substance	EAC	APP	Hazards Class	Hazards Sub Risks	HIN
1860	**VINYL FLUORIDE, STABILIZED**	2YE		2.1		239
1861	UN No. no longer in use					
1862	**ETHYL CROTONATE**	3YE		3		33
1863	**FUEL, AVIATION, TURBINE ENGINE,** packing groups I & II	3YE		3		33
1863	**FUEL, AVIATION, TURBINE ENGINE,** packing group III	3Y		3		30
1864	UN No. no longer in use					
1865	**n-PROPYL NITRATE**	3YE[1]		3		
1866	**RESIN SOLUTION,** flammable, packing groups I & II	•3YE		3		33
1866	**RESIN SOLUTION,** flammable, packing group III	•3Y		3		30
1866	**RESIN SOLUTION,** flammable (having a flash point below 23°C and viscous according to ADR 2.2.3.1.4), packing group III	•3YE[1]		3		
1867	UN No. no longer in use					
1868	**DECABORANE**	1X		4.1	6.1	46
1869	**MAGNESIUM** or **MAGNESIUM ALLOYS** with more than 50% magnesium in pellets, turnings or ribbons	1Z		4.1		40
1870	**POTASSIUM BOROHYDRIDE**	4W[1]		4.3		
1871	**TITANIUM HYDRIDE**	1Y		4.1		40
1872	**LEAD DIOXIDE**	1X		5.1	6.1	56
1873	**PERCHLORIC ACID** with more than 50% but not more than 72% acid, by mass	2P		5.1	8	558
1874 to 1883	UN Nos. no longer in use					
1884	**BARIUM OXIDE**	2Z		6.1		60
1885	**BENZIDINE**	2Z		6.1		60
1886	**BENZYLIDENE CHLORIDE**	2Z		6.1		60
1887	**BROMOCHLOROMETHANE**	2X		6.1		60

(1) Not applicable to the carriage of dangerous goods under RID or ADR

UN No	Substance	EAC	APP	Hazards Class	Sub Risks	HIN
1888	CHLOROFORM	2Z		6.1		60
1889	CYANOGEN BROMIDE	2XE	B	6.1	8	668
1890	UN No. no longer in use					
1891	ETHYL BROMIDE	2W		6.1		60
1892	ETHYLDICHLOROARSINE	2XE	B	6.1		66
1893	UN No. no longer in use					
1894	PHENYLMERCURIC HYDROXIDE	2X		6.1		60
1895	PHENYLMERCURIC NITRATE	2X		6.1		60
1896	UN No. no longer in use					
1897	TETRACHLOROETHYLENE	2Z		6.1		60
1898	ACETYL IODIDE	4W		8		80
1899 to 1901	UN Nos. no longer in use					
1902	DIISOOCTYL ACID PHOSPHATE	2X		8		80
1903	DISINFECTANT, LIQUID, CORROSIVE, N.O.S., packing group I	2X	B	8		88
1903	DISINFECTANT, LIQUID, CORROSIVE, N.O.S., packing groups II & III	2X		8		80
1904	UN No. no longer in use					
1905	SELENIC ACID	2X		8		88
1906	SLUDGE ACID	2W		8		80
1907	SODA LIME with more than 4% sodium hydroxide	2X		8		80
1908	CHLORITE SOLUTION	2X		8		80
1909	UN No. no longer in use					
1910	CALCIUM OXIDE	2X[(1)]		8		
1911	DIBORANE	2PE[(1)]	A(fg)	2.3	2.1	
1912	METHYL CHLORIDE AND METHYLENE CHLORIDE MIXTURE	2YE		2.1		23
1913	NEON, REFRIGERATED LIQUID	2T		2.2		22
1914	BUTYL PROPIONATES	3Y		3		30

(1) Not applicable to the carriage of dangerous goods under RID or ADR

UN No	Substance	EAC	APP	Hazards Class	Hazards Sub Risks	HIN
1915	**CYCLOHEXANONE**	●3Y		3		30
1916	**2,2'-DICHLORODIETHYL ETHER**	●3W	A(fl)	6.1	3	63
1917	**ETHYL ACRYLATE, STABILIZED**	●3WE		3		339
1918	**ISOPROPYLBENZENE**	3Y		3		30
1919	**METHYL ACRYLATE, STABILIZED**	3WE		3		339
1920	**NONANES**	3Y		3		30
1921	**PROPYLENEIMINE, STABILIZED**	●2WE	A(fl)	3	6.1	336
1922	**PYRROLIDINE**	●2WE	A(fl)	3	8	338
1923	**CALCIUM DITHIONITE (CALCIUM HYDROSULPHITE)**	1S		4.2		40
1924 to 1927	UN Nos. no longer in use					
1928	**METHYL MAGNESIUM BROMIDE IN ETHYL ETHER**	4WE	A(fl)	4.3	3	X323
1929	**POTASSIUM DITHIONITE (POTASSIUM HYDROSULPHITE)**	1S		4.2		40
1930	UN No. no longer in use					
1931	**ZINC DITHIONITE (ZINC HYDROSULPHITE)**	2Z		9		90
1932	**ZIRCONIUM SCRAP**	1Y		4.2		40
1933	UN No. no longer in use					
1934	UN No. no longer in use					
1935	**CYANIDE SOLUTION, N.O.S.,** packing group I	2X	B	6.1		66
1935	**CYANIDE SOLUTION, N.O.S.,** packing groups II & III	2X		6.1		60
1936	UN No. no longer in use					
1937	UN No. no longer in use					
1938	**BROMOACETIC ACID SOLUTION**	2X		8		80
1939	**PHOSPHORUS OXYBROMIDE**	4W		8		80
1940	**THIOGLYCOLIC ACID**	2X		8		80
1941	**DIBROMODIFLUOROMETHANE**	2Z		9		90

UN No	Substance	EAC	APP	Hazards Class	Hazards Sub Risks	HIN
1942	**AMMONIUM NITRATE** with not more than 0.2% combustible substances, including any organic substance calculated as carbon, to the exclusion of any other added substance	1Y		5.1		50
1943	UN No. no longer in use					
1944	**MATCHES, SAFETY** (book, card or strike on box)	1Z[(1)]		4.1		
1945	**MATCHES, WAX 'VESTA'**	1Z[(1)]		4.1		
1946 to 1949	UN Nos. no longer in use					
1950	**AEROSOLS**	[(1)]		2	[(3)]	
1951	**ARGON, REFRIGERATED LIQUID**	2T		2.2		22
1952	**ETHYLENE OXIDE AND CARBON DIOXIDE MIXTURE** with not more than 9% ethylene oxide	2T		2.2		20
1953	**COMPRESSED GAS, TOXIC, FLAMMABLE, N.O.S.**	2PE	A(fg)	2.3	2.1	263
1954	**COMPRESSED GAS, FLAMMABLE, N.O.S.**	2SE		2.1		23
1955	**COMPRESSED GAS, TOXIC, N.O.S.**	2RE	B	2.3		26
1956	**COMPRESSED GAS, N.O.S.**	2TE		2.2		20
1957	**DEUTERIUM, COMPRESSED**	2SE		2.1		23
1958	**1,2-DICHLORO-1,1,2,2-TETRAFLUOROETHANE (REFRIGERANT GAS R 114)**	2TE		2.2		20
1959	**1,1-DIFLUOROETHYLENE (REFRIGERANT GAS R 1132a)**	2YE		2.1		239
1960	UN No. no longer in use					
1961	**ETHANE, REFRIGERATED LIQUID**	2YE		2.1		223
1962	**ETHYLENE**	2SE		2.1		23
1963	**HELIUM, REFRIGERATED LIQUID**	2T		2.2		22
1964	**HYDROCARBON GAS MIXTURE, COMPRESSED, N.O.S.**	2SE		2.1		23
1965	**HYDROCARBON GAS MIXTURE, LIQUEFIED, N.O.S.**	2YE		2.1		23

(1) Not applicable to the carriage of dangerous goods under RID or ADR   (3) Various

UN No	Substance	EAC	APP	Hazards Class	Hazards Sub Risks	HIN
1966	HYDROGEN, REFRIGERATED LIQUID	2YE		2.1		223
1967	INSECTICIDE GAS, TOXIC, N.O.S.	2XE	A(c)	2.3		26
1968	INSECTICIDE GAS, N.O.S.	2TE		2.2		20
1969	ISOBUTANE	2YE		2.1		23
1970	KRYPTON, REFRIGERATED LIQUID	2TE		2.2		22
1971	METHANE, COMPRESSED or NATURAL GAS, COMPRESSED with high methane content	2SE		2.1		23
1972	METHANE, REFRIGERATED LIQUID or NATURAL GAS, REFRIGERATED LIQUID with high methane content	2YE		2.1		223
1973	CHLORODIFLUOROMETHANE AND CHLOROPENTAFLUOROETHANE MIXTURE with fixed boiling point, with approximately 49% chlorodifluoromethane (REFRIGERANT GAS R502)	2TE		2.2		20
1974	CHLORODIFLUOROBROMOMETHANE (REFRIGERANT GAS R 12B1)	2TE		2.2		20
1975	NITRIC OXIDE AND DINITROGEN TETROXIDE MIXTURE (NITRIC OXIDE AND NITROGEN DIOXIDE MIXTURE)	2PE[(1)]	B	2.3	5.1, 8	
1976	OCTAFLUOROCYCLOBUTANE (REFRIGERANT GAS RC 318)	2TE		2.2		20
1977	NITROGEN, REFRIGERATED LIQUID	2T		2.2		22
1978	PROPANE	2YE		2.1		23
1979 to 1981	UN Nos. no longer in use					
1982	TETRAFLUOROMETHANE (REFRIGERANT GAS R 14)	2TE		2.2		20
1983	1-CHLORO-2,2,2-TRIFLUOROETHANE (REFRIGERANT GAS R 133a)	2TE		2.2		20
1984	TRIFLUOROMETHANE (REFRIGERANT GAS R 23)	2T		2.2		20
1985	UN No. no longer in use					

(1) Not applicable to the carriage of dangerous goods under RID or ADR

UN No	Substance	EAC	APP	Hazards Class	Hazards Sub Risks	HIN
1986	**ALCOHOLS, FLAMMABLE, TOXIC, N.O.S.,** packing groups I & II	●3WE	A(fl)	3	6.1	336
1986	**ALCOHOLS, FLAMMABLE, TOXIC, N.O.S.,** packing group III	●3W	A(fl)	3	6.1	36
1987	**ALCOHOLS, N.O.S.,** packing group II	●3YE		3		33
1987	**ALCOHOLS, N.O.S.,** packing group III	●3Y		3		30
1988	**ALDEHYDES, FLAMMABLE, TOXIC, N.O.S.,** packing groups I & II	●3WE	A(fl)	3	6.1	336
1988	**ALDEHYDES, FLAMMABLE, TOXIC, N.O.S.,** packing group III	●3W	A(fl)	3	6.1	36
1989	**ALDEHYDES, N.O.S.,** packing groups I & II	●3YE		3		33
1989	**ALDEHYDES, N.O.S.,** packing group III	●3Y		3		30
1990	**BENZALDEHYDE**	3Z		9		90
1991	**CHLOROPRENE, STABILIZED**	●3YE		3	6.1	336
1992	**FLAMMABLE LIQUID, TOXIC, N.O.S.,** packing groups I & II	●3WE	A(fl)	3	6.1	336
1992	**FLAMMABLE LIQUID, TOXIC, N.O.S.,** packing group III	●3W	A(fl)	3	6.1	36
1993	**FLAMMABLE LIQUID, N.O.S.,** packing groups I & II	●3YE		3		33
1993	**FLAMMABLE LIQUID, N.O.S.,** packing group III	●3Y		3		30
1993	**FLAMMABLE LIQUID, N.O.S.** (having a flash point below 23°C and viscous according to ADR 2.2.3.1.4), packing group III	●3YE[(1)]		3		
1994	**IRON PENTACARBONYL**	2WE	A(fl)	6.1	3	663
1995 to 1998	UN Nos. no longer in use					
1999	**TARS, LIQUID,** including road oils, and cutback bitumens, packing group II	2WE	A(fl)	3		33
1999	**TARS, LIQUID,** including road oils, and cutback bitumens, packing group III	2W	A(fl)	3		30

(1) Not applicable to the carriage of dangerous goods under RID or ADR

UN No	Substance	EAC	APP	Hazards Class	Hazards Sub Risks	HIN
1999	**TARS, LIQUID,** including road oils, and cutback bitumens (having a flash point below 23°C and viscous according to ADR 2.2.3.1.4), packing group III	2WE[(1)]	A(fl)	3		
2000	**CELLULOID** in block, rods, rolls, sheets, tubes, etc., except scrap	1Z[(1)]		4.1		
2001	**COBALT NAPHTHENATES, POWDER**	1Z		4.1		40
2002	**CELLULOID, SCRAP**	1Y[(1)]		4.2		
2003	UN No. no longer in use					
2004	**MAGNESIUM DIAMIDE**	1Y		4.2		40
2005	UN No. no longer in use					
2006	**PLASTICS, NITROCELLULOSE-BASED, SELF-HEATING, N.O.S.**	1Y[(1)]		4.2		
2007	UN No. no longer in use					
2008	**ZIRCONIUM POWDER, DRY**	4Y		4.2		43/40
2009	**ZIRCONIUM, DRY,** finished sheets, strip or coiled wire	1Y		4.2		40
2010	**MAGNESIUM HYDRIDE**	4WE[(1)]		4.3		
2011	**MAGNESIUM PHOSPHIDE**	4WE[(1)]		4.3	6.1	
2012	**POTASSIUM PHOSPHIDE**	4WE[(1)]		4.3	6.1	
2013	**STRONTIUM PHOSPHIDE**	4WE[(1)]		4.3	6.1	
2014	**HYDROGEN PEROXIDE, AQUEOUS SOLUTION** with not less than 20% but not more than 60% hydrogen peroxide (stabilized as necessary)	2P		5.1	8	58
2015	**HYDROGEN PEROXIDE, AQUEOUS SOLUTION, STABILIZED** with more than 60% hydrogen peroxide	2P		5.1	8	559
2016	**AMMUNITION, TOXIC, NON-EXPLOSIVE**	2X[(1)]		6.1		
2017	**AMMUNITION, TEAR-PRODUCING, NON-EXPLOSIVE**	2XE[(1)]		6.1	8	
2018	**CHLOROANILINES, SOLID**	2X		6.1		60
2019	**CHLOROANILINES, LIQUID**	2X		6.1		60
2020	**CHLOROPHENOLS, SOLID**	2X		6.1		60
2021	**CHLOROPHENOLS, LIQUID**	2X		6.1		60

(1) Not applicable to the carriage of dangerous goods under RID or ADR

UN No	Substance	EAC	APP	Hazards Class	Sub Risks	HIN
2022	CRESYLIC ACID	3X		6.1	8	68
2023	EPICHLOROHYDRIN	●3W	A(fl)	6.1	3	63
2024	MERCURY COMPOUND, LIQUID, N.O.S., packing group I	2X	B	6.1		66
2024	MERCURY COMPOUND, LIQUID, N.O.S., packing groups II & III	2X		6.1		60
2025	MERCURY COMPOUND, SOLID, N.O.S.	2X		6.1		66/60
2026	PHENYLMERCURIC COMPOUND, N.O.S.	2X		6.1		66/60
2027	SODIUM ARSENITE, SOLID	2Z		6.1		60
2028	BOMBS, SMOKE, NON-EXPLOSIVE with corrosive liquid, without initiating device	2X(1)		8		
2029	HYDRAZINE, ANHYDROUS	●2WE(1)	A(fl)	8	3, 6.1	
2030	HYDRAZINE AQUEOUS SOLUTION with more than 37% hydrazine by mass, packing group I	●2X	B	8	6.1	886
2030	HYDRAZINE AQUEOUS SOLUTION with more than 37% hydrazine by mass, packing groups II & III	●2X		8	6.1	86
2031	NITRIC ACID, other than red fuming, with more than 70% nitric acid	2P	B	8	5.1	885
2031	NITRIC ACID, other than red fuming, with at least 65%, but not more than 70% nitric acid	2R		8	5.1	85
2031	NITRIC ACID, other than red fuming, with less than 65% nitric acid	2R		8		80
2032	NITRIC ACID, RED FUMING	2PE	B	8	5.1, 6.1	856
2033	POTASSIUM MONOXIDE	2W		8		80
2034	HYDROGEN AND METHANE MIXTURE, COMPRESSED	2SE		2.1		23
2035	1,1,1-TRIFLUOROETHANE (REFRIGERANT GAS R 143a)	2YE		2.1		23
2036	XENON	2TE		2.2		20

(1) Not applicable to the carriage of dangerous goods under RID or ADR

UN No	Substance	EAC	APP	Hazards Class	Hazards Sub Risks	HIN
2037	RECEPTACLES, SMALL, CONTAINING GAS (GAS CARTRIDGES)	(1)		2	(3)	
2038	DINITROTOLUENES, LIQUID	2X		6.1		60
2039 to 2043	UN Nos. no longer in use					
2044	2,2-DIMETHYLPROPANE	2YE		2.1		23
2045	ISOBUTYRALDEHYDE (ISOBUTYL ALDEHYDE)	●2YE		3		33
2046	CYMENES	3Y		3		30
2047	DICHLOROPROPENES, packing group II	2YE		3		33
2047	DICHLOROPROPENES, packing group III	2Y		3		30
2048	DICYCLOPENTADIENE	3Y		3		30
2049	DIETHYLBENZENE	3Y		3		30
2050	DIISOBUTYLENE, ISOMERIC COMPOUNDS	3YE		3		33
2051	2-DIMETHYLAMINOETHANOL	●2W	A(fl)	8	3	83
2052	DIPENTENE	3Y		3		30
2053	METHYL ISOBUTYL CARBINOL	●3Y		3		30
2054	MORPHOLINE	●2W	A(fl)	8	3	883
2055	STYRENE MONOMER, STABILIZED	3Y		3		39
2056	TETRAHYDROFURAN	●2YE		3		33
2057	TRIPROPYLENE, packing group II	3YE		3		33
2057	TRIPROPYLENE, packing group III	3Y		3		30
2058	VALERALDEHYDE	3YE		3		33
2059	NITROCELLULOSE SOLUTION, FLAMMABLE, packing groups I & II	●2YE		3		33
2059	NITROCELLULOSE SOLUTION, FLAMMABLE, packing group III	●2Y		3		30
2060 to 2066	UN Nos. no longer in use					

(1) Not applicable to the carriage of dangerous goods under RID or ADR   (3) Various

UN No	Substance	EAC	APP	Hazards Class	Sub Risks	HIN
2067	AMMONIUM NITRATE BASED FERTILIZER	1Y		5.1		50
2068 to 2070	UN Nos. no longer in use					
2071	AMMONIUM NITRATE BASED FERTILIZER	1Y[1]		9		
2072	UN No. no longer in use					
2073	AMMONIA SOLUTION, relative density less than 0.880 at 15°C in water, with more than 35% but not more than 50% ammonia	2XE		2.2		20
2074	ACRYLAMIDE, SOLID	2X		6.1		60
2075	CHLORAL, ANHYDROUS, STABILIZED	2X		6.1		69
2076	CRESOLS, LIQUID	●2X		6.1	8	68
2077	alpha-NAPHTHYLAMINE	2Z		6.1		60
2078	TOLUENE DIISOCYANATE	2Z		6.1		60
2079	DIETHYLENETRIAMINE	2X		8		80
2080 to 2185	UN Nos. no longer in use					
2186	HYDROGEN CHLORIDE, REFRIGERATED LIQUID	2RE[1]	A(c)	2.3	8	
2187	CARBON DIOXIDE, REFRIGERATED LIQUID	2T		2.2		22
2188	ARSINE	2PE[1]	A(cf)	2.3	2.1	
2189	DICHLOROSILANE	2WE	A(fg)	2.3	2.1, 8	263
2190	OXYGEN DIFLUORIDE, COMPRESSED	2PE[1]	B	2.3	5.1, 8	
2191	SULPHURYL FLUORIDE	2XE	A(c)	2.3		26
2192	GERMANE	2PE	A(cf)	2.3	2.1	263
2193	HEXAFLUOROETHANE (REFRIGERANT GAS R 116)	2TE		2.2		20
2194	SELENIUM HEXAFLUORIDE	2RE[1]	A(c)	2.3	8	
2195	TELLURIUM HEXAFLUORIDE	2RE[1]	A(c)	2.3	8	

(1) Not applicable to the carriage of dangerous goods under RID or ADR

UN No	Substance	EAC	APP	Hazards Class	Hazards Sub Risks	HIN
2196	**TUNGSTEN HEXAFLUORIDE**	2WE[(1)]	B	2.3	8	
2197	**HYDROGEN IODIDE, ANHYDROUS**	2RE	A(c)	2.3	8	268
2198	**PHOSPHORUS PENTAFLUORIDE**	2RE[(1)]	B	2.3	8	
2199	**PHOSPHINE**	2PE[(1)]	A(cf)	2.3	2.1	
2200	**PROPADIENE, STABILIZED**	2YE		2.1		239
2201	**NITROUS OXIDE, REFRIGERATED LIQUID**	2P	A(co)	2.2	5.1	225
2202	**HYDROGEN SELENIDE, ANHYDROUS**	2WE[(1)]	A(cf)	2.3	2.1	
2203	**SILANE**	2SE		2.1		23
2204	**CARBONYL SULPHIDE**	2PE	A(cf)	2.3	2.1	263
2205	**ADIPONITRILE**	●3X		6.1		60
2206	**ISOCYANATES, TOXIC, N.O.S.** or **ISOCYANATE SOLUTION, TOXIC, N.O.S.**	2X		6.1		60
2207	UN No. no longer in use					
2208	**CALCIUM HYPOCHLORITE MIXTURE, DRY** with more than 10% but not more than 39% available chlorine	1X		5.1		50
2209	**FORMALDEHYDE SOLUTION** with not less than 25% formaldehyde	●2X		8		80
2210	**MANEB** or **MANEB PREPARATION** with not less than 60% maneb	1Y		4.2	4.3	40
2211	**POLYMERIC BEADS, EXPANDABLE,** evolving flammable vapour	2Y		9		90
2212	**ASBESTOS, AMPHIBOLE** (amosite, tremolite, actinolite, anthophyllite, crocidolite)	2X		9		90
2213	**PARAFORMALDEHYDE**	1Z		4.1		40
2214	**PHTHALIC ANHYDRIDE** with more than 0.05% of maleic anhydride	2X		8		80
2215	**MALEIC ANHYDRIDE**	2X		8		80
2216	**FISH MEAL (FISH SCRAP), STABILIZED**	1Z[(1)]		9		

(1) Not applicable to the carriage of dangerous goods under RID or ADR

UN No	Substance	EAC	APP	Hazards Class	Sub Risks	HIN
2217	**SEED CAKE** with not more than 1.5% oil and not more than 11% moisture	1Y		4.2		40
2218	**ACRYLIC ACID, STABILIZED**	•2W	A(fl)	8	3	839
2219	**ALLYL GLYCIDYL ETHER**	•2Y		3		30
2220	UN No. no longer in use					
2221	UN No. no longer in use					
2222	**ANISOLE**	3Y		3		30
2223	UN No. no longer in use					
2224	**BENZONITRILE**	3Z		6.1		60
2225	**BENZENESULPHONYL CHLORIDE**	2X		8		80
2226	**BENZOTRICHLORIDE**	2X		8		80
2227	**n-BUTYL METHACRYLATE, STABILIZED**	3W	A(fl)	3		39
2228 to 2231	UN Nos. no longer in use					
2232	**2-CHLOROETHANAL**	•2XE	B	6.1		66
2233	**CHLOROANISIDINES**	2X		6.1		60
2234	**CHLOROBENZOTRIFLUORIDES**	2Y		3		30
2235	**CHLOROBENZYL CHLORIDES, LIQUID**	2Z		6.1		60
2236	**3-CHLORO-4-METHYLPHENYL ISOCYANATE, LIQUID**	2X		6.1		60
2237	**CHLORONITROANILINES**	2X		6.1		60
2238	**CHLOROTOLUENES**	3Y		3		30
2239	**CHLOROTOLUIDINES, SOLID**	2X		6.1		60
2240	**CHROMOSULPHURIC ACID**	2W		8		88
2241	**CYCLOHEPTANE**	3YE		3		33
2242	**CYCLOHEPTENE**	3YE		3		33
2243	**CYCLOHEXYL ACETATE**	3Y		3		30
2244	**CYCLOPENTANOL**	3Y		3		30
2245	**CYCLOPENTANONE**	•3Y		3		30
2246	**CYCLOPENTENE**	3YE		3		33

UN No	Substance	EAC	APP	Hazards Class	Hazards Sub Risks	HIN
2247	n-DECANE	3Y		3		30
2248	DI-n-BUTYLAMINE	•3W	A(fl)	8	3	83
2249	DICHLORODIMETHYL ETHER, SYMMETRICAL	•3WE[1]	A(fl)	6.1	3	
2250	DICHLOROPHENYL ISOCYANATES	2X		6.1		60
2251	BICYCLO[2.2.1] HEPTA-2, 5-DIENE, STABILIZED (2,5-NORBORNADIENE, STABILIZED)	3YE		3		339
2252	1,2-DIMETHOXYETHANE	•2YE		3		33
2253	N,N-DIMETHYLANILINE	3Z		6.1		60
2254	MATCHES, FUSEE	1Z[1]		4.1		
2255	UN No. no longer in use					
2256	CYCLOHEXENE	3YE		3		33
2257	POTASSIUM	4W		4.3		X423
2258	1,2-PROPYLENEDIAMINE	•2W	A(fl)	8	3	83
2259	TRIETHYLENETETRAMINE	2X		8		80
2260	TRIPROPYLAMINE	3W	A(fl)	3	8	38
2261	XYLENOLS, SOLID	2X		6.1		60
2262	DIMETHYLCARBAMOYL CHLORIDE	4W		8		80
2263	DIMETHYLCYCLOHEXANES	3YE		3		33
2264	N,N-DIMETHYLCYCLOHEXYLAMINE	•3W	A(fl)	8	3	83
2265	N,N-DIMETHYLFORMAMIDE	•2Y		3		30
2266	DIMETHYL-N-PROPYLAMINE	•2WE	A(fl)	3	8	338
2267	DIMETHYL THIOPHOSPHORYL CHLORIDE	2X		6.1	8	68
2268	UN No. no longer in use					
2269	3,3'-IMINODIPROPYLAMINE	•2X		8		80
2270	ETHYLAMINE, AQUEOUS SOLUTION with not less than 50% but not more than 70% ethylamine	•2PE	A(fl)	3	8	338
2271	ETHYL AMYL KETONE	3Y		3		30
2272	N-ETHYLANILINE	3Z		6.1		60
2273	2-ETHYLANILINE	3X		6.1		60

(1) Not applicable to the carriage of dangerous goods under RID or ADR

UN No	Substance	EAC	APP	Hazards Class	Sub Risks	HIN
2274	N-ETHYL-N-BENZYLANILINE	2X		6.1		60
2275	2-ETHYLBUTANOL	3Y		3		30
2276	2-ETHYLHEXYLAMINE	•2W	A(fl)	3	8	38
2277	ETHYL METHACRYLATE, STABILIZED	3WE	A(fl)	3		339
2278	n-HEPTENE	3YE		3		33
2279	HEXACHLOROBUTADIENE	2X		6.1		60
2280	HEXAMETHYLENEDIAMINE, SOLID	2X		8		80
2281	HEXAMETHYLENE DIISOCYANATE	2Z		6.1		60
2282	HEXANOLS	3Y		3		30
2283	ISOBUTYL METHACRYLATE, STABILIZED	3W	A(fl)	3		39
2284	ISOBUTYRONITRILE	•3WE	A(fl)	3	6.1	336
2285	ISOCYANATOBENZOTRIFLUORIDES	•3W	A(fl)	6.1	3	63
2286	PENTAMETHYLHEPTANE	3Y		3		30
2287	ISOHEPTENE	3YE		3		33
2288	ISOHEXENE	3YE		3		33
2289	ISOPHORONEDIAMINE	2X		8		80
2290	ISOPHORONE DIISOCYANATE	2Z		6.1		60
2291	LEAD COMPOUND, SOLUBLE, N.O.S.	2Z		6.1		60
2292	UN No. no longer in use					
2293	4-METHOXY-4-METHYLPENTAN-2-ONE	3Y		3		30
2294	N-METHYLANILINE	3X		6.1		60
2295	METHYL CHLOROACETATE	2W	A(fl)	6.1	3	663
2296	METHYLCYCLOHEXANE	3YE		3		33
2297	METHYLCYCLOHEXANONE	•3Y		3		30
2298	METHYLCYCLOPENTANE	3YE		3		33
2299	METHYL DICHLOROACETATE	2X		6.1		60
2300	2-METHYL-5-ETHYLPYRIDINE	3Z		6.1		60
2301	2-METHYLFURAN	3YE		3		33

UN No	Substance	EAC	APP	Hazards Class	Sub Risks	HIN
2302	5-METHYLHEXAN-2-ONE	●3Y		3		30
2303	ISOPROPENYLBENZENE	3Y		3		30
2304	NAPHTHALENE, MOLTEN	1Y		4.1		44
2305	NITROBENZENESULPHONIC ACID	2X		8		80
2306	NITROBENZOTRIFLUORIDES, LIQUID	2X		6.1		60
2307	3-NITRO-4-CHLOROBENZOTRIFLUORIDE	2X		6.1		60
2308	NITROSYLSULPHURIC ACID, LIQUID	2X		8		X80
2309	OCTADIENES	3YE		3		33
2310	PENTANE-2,4-DIONE	●2Y		3	6.1	36
2311	PHENETIDINES	2X		6.1		60
2312	PHENOL, MOLTEN	●3X		6.1		60
2313	PICOLINES	●2W	A(fl)	3		30
2314	UN No. no longer in use					
2315	POLYCHLORINATED BIPHENYLS, LIQUID	2X		9		90
2316	SODIUM CUPROCYANIDE, SOLID	2X		6.1		66
2317	SODIUM CUPROCYANIDE SOLUTION	2X	B	6.1		66
2318	SODIUM HYDROSULPHIDE with less than 25% water of crystallization	1Y		4.2		40
2319	TERPENE HYDROCARBONS, N.O.S.	3Y		3		30
2320	TETRAETHYLENEPENTAMINE	2X		8		80
2321	TRICHLOROBENZENES, LIQUID	2X		6.1		60
2322	TRICHLOROBUTENE	2Z		6.1		60
2323	TRIETHYL PHOSPHITE	3Y		3		30
2324	TRIISOBUTYLENE	3Y		3		30
2325	1,3,5-TRIMETHYLBENZENE	3Y		3		30
2326	TRIMETHYLCYCLOHEXYLAMINE	2X		8		80
2327	TRIMETHYLHEXAMETHYLENEDIAMINES	2X		8		80
2328	TRIMETHYLHEXAMETHYLENE DIISOCYANATE	2Z		6.1		60

UN No	Substance	EAC	APP	Hazards Class	Sub Risks	HIN
2329	TRIMETHYL PHOSPHITE	3Y		3		30
2330	UNDECANE	3Y		3		30
2331	ZINC CHLORIDE, ANHYDROUS	2X		8		80
2332	ACETALDEHYDE OXIME	•2Y		3		30
2333	ALLYL ACETATE	•3YE		3	6.1	336
2334	ALLYLAMINE	•2WE	A(fl)	6.1	3	663
2335	ALLYL ETHYL ETHER	3WE	A(fl)	3	6.1	336
2336	ALLYL FORMATE	3WE	A(fl)	3	6.1	336
2337	PHENYL MERCAPTAN	3WE	A(fl)	6.1	3	663
2338	BENZOTRIFLUORIDE	2YE		3		33
2339	2-BROMOBUTANE	2YE		3		33
2340	2-BROMOETHYL ETHYL ETHER	•2YE		3		33
2341	1-BROMO-3-METHYLBUTANE	2Y		3		30
2342	BROMOMETHYLPROPANES	2YE		3		33
2343	2-BROMOPENTANE	2YE		3		33
2344	BROMOPROPANES, packing group II	2YE		3		33
2344	BROMOPROPANES, packing group III	2Y		3		30
2345	3-BROMOPROPYNE	2YE		3		33
2346	BUTANEDIONE	•2YE		3		33
2347	BUTYL MERCAPTAN	•3WE	A(fl)	3		33
2348	BUTYL ACRYLATES, STABILIZED	3W	A(fl)	3		39
2349	UN No. no longer in use					
2350	BUTYL METHYL ETHER	3YE		3		33
2351	BUTYL NITRITES, packing group II	•3YE		3		33
2351	BUTYL NITRITES, packing group III	•3Y		3		30
2352	BUTYL VINYL ETHER, STABILIZED	•3YE		3		339
2353	BUTYRYL CHLORIDE	•3WE	A(fl)	3	8	338
2354	CHLOROMETHYL ETHYL ETHER	•3WE	A(fl)	3	6.1	336
2355	UN No. no longer in use					
2356	2-CHLOROPROPANE	3YE		3		33

UN No	Substance	EAC	APP	Hazards Class	Sub Risks	HIN
2357	CYCLOHEXYLAMINE	•2W	A(fl)	8	3	83
2358	CYCLOOCTATETRAENE	3YE		3		33
2359	DIALLYLAMINE	•2WE	A(fl)	3	6.1, 8	338
2360	DIALLYL ETHER	•3WE	A(fl)	3	6.1	336
2361	DIISOBUTYLAMINE	3WE	A(fl)	3	8	38
2362	1,1-DICHLOROETHANE	2YE		3		33
2363	ETHYL MERCAPTAN	3WE	A(fl)	3		33
2364	n-PROPYLBENZENE	3Y		3		30
2365	UN No. no longer in use					
2366	DIETHYL CARBONATE	3Y		3		30
2367	alpha-METHYLVALERALDEHYDE	3YE		3		33
2368	alpha-PINENE	3Y		3		30
2369	UN No. no longer in use					
2370	1-HEXENE	3YE		3		33
2371	ISOPENTENES	3YE		3		33
2372	1,2-DI-(DIMETHYLAMINO) ETHANE	•2YE		3		33
2373	DIETHOXYMETHANE	•2YE		3		33
2374	3,3-DIETHOXYPROPENE	•3YE		3		33
2375	DIETHYL SULPHIDE	3WE	A(fl)	3		33
2376	2,3-DIHYDROPYRAN	•2YE		3		33
2377	1,1-DIMETHOXYETHANE	•2YE		3		33
2378	2-DIMETHYLAMINOACETONITRILE	3WE	A(fl)	3	6.1	336
2379	1,3-DIMETHYLBUTYLAMINE	3WE	A(fl)	3	8	338
2380	DIMETHYLDIETHOXYSILANE	•2YE		3		33
2381	DIMETHYL DISULPHIDE	3WE	A(fl)	3	6.1	336
2382	DIMETHYLHYDRAZINE, SYMMETRICAL	•2WE	A(fl)	6.1	3	663
2383	DIPROPYLAMINE	•2WE	A(fl)	3	8	338
2384	DI-n-PROPYL ETHER	3YE		3		33
2385	ETHYL ISOBUTYRATE	•3YE		3		33
2386	1-ETHYLPIPERIDINE	3WE	A(fl)	3	8	338

NUMERICAL LIST OF DANGEROUS GOODS

UN No	Substance	EAC	APP	Hazards Class	Hazards Sub Risks	HIN
2387	FLUOROBENZENE	3YE		3		33
2388	FLUOROTOLUENES	3YE		3		33
2389	FURAN	3YE		3		33
2390	2-IODOBUTANE	2YE		3		33
2391	IODOMETHYLPROPANES	2YE		3		33
2392	IODOPROPANES	2Y		3		30
2393	ISOBUTYL FORMATE	●3YE		3		33
2394	ISOBUTYL PROPIONATE	3Y		3		30
2395	ISOBUTYRYL CHLORIDE	●3WE	A(fl)	3	8	338
2396	METHACRYLALDEHYDE, STABILIZED	●2WE	A(fl)	3	6.1	336
2397	3-METHYLBUTAN-2-ONE	●3YE		3		33
2398	METHYL tert-BUTYL ETHER	●3YE		3		33
2399	1-METHYLPIPERIDINE	●2WE	A(fl)	3	8	338
2400	METHYL ISOVALERATE	●3YE		3		33
2401	PIPERIDINE	●2WE	A(fl)	8	3	883
2402	PROPANETHIOLS	●3WE	A(fl)	3		33
2403	ISOPROPENYL ACETATE	●3YE		3		33
2404	PROPIONITRILE	●2WE	A(fl)	3	6.1	336
2405	ISOPROPYL BUTYRATE	3Y		3		30
2406	ISOPROPYL ISOBUTYRATE	3YE		3		33
2407	ISOPROPYL CHLOROFORMATE	●3WE(1)	A(fl)	6.1	3, 8	
2408	UN No. no longer in use					
2409	ISOPROPYL PROPIONATE	3YE		3		33
2410	1,2,3,6-TETRAHYDROPYRIDINE	●2WE	A(fl)	3		33
2411	BUTYRONITRILE	●3WE	A(fl)	3	6.1	336
2412	TETRAHYDROTHIOPHENE	3WE	A(fl)	3		33
2413	TETRAPROPYL ORTHOTITANATE	●2Y		3		30
2414	THIOPHENE	3WE	A(fl)	3		33
2415	UN No. no longer in use					
2416	TRIMETHYL BORATE	●3YE		3		33

(1) Not applicable to the carriage of dangerous goods under RID or ADR

UN No	Substance	EAC	APP	Hazards Class	Hazards Sub Risks	HIN
2417	CARBONYL FLUORIDE	2PE	B	2.3	8	268
2418	SULPHUR TETRAFLUORIDE	2PE[(1)]	A(c)	2.3	8	
2419	BROMOTRIFLUOROETHYLENE	2YE		2.1		23
2420	HEXAFLUOROACETONE	2WE	A(c)	2.3	8	268
2421	NITROGEN TRIOXIDE	2PE[(1)]	B	2.3	5.1, 8	
2422	OCTAFLUOROBUT-2-ENE (REFRIGERANT GAS R 1318)	2TE		2.2		20
2423	UN No. no longer in use					
2424	OCTAFLUOROPROPANE (REFRIGERANT GAS R 218)	2TE		2.2		20
2425	UN No. no longer in use					
2426	AMMONIUM NITRATE, LIQUID (hot concentrated solution)	1Y		5.1		59
2427	POTASSIUM CHLORATE, AQUEOUS SOLUTION	2Y		5.1		50
2428	SODIUM CHLORATE, AQUEOUS SOLUTION	2Y		5.1		50
2429	CALCIUM CHLORATE, AQUEOUS SOLUTION	2Y		5.1		50
2430	ALKYL PHENOLS, SOLID, N.O.S. (including C2-C12 homologues)	2X		8		88/80
2431	ANISIDINES	2Z		6.1		60
2432	N, N-DIETHYLANILINE	●3X		6.1		60
2433	CHLORONITROTOLUENES, LIQUID	2X		6.1		60
2434	DIBENZYLDICHLOROSILANE	4W		8		X80
2435	ETHYLPHENYLDICHLOROSILANE	4W		8		X80
2436	THIOACETIC ACID	●2WE	A(fl)	3		33
2437	METHYLPHENYLDICHLOROSILANE	4W		8		X80
2438	TRIMETHYLACETYL CHLORIDE	●3WE	A(fl)	6.1	3, 8	663
2439	SODIUM HYDROGENDIFLUORIDE	2X		8		80
2440	STANNIC CHLORIDE PENTAHYDRATE	2X		8		80

(1) Not applicable to the carriage of dangerous goods under RID or ADR

UN No	Substance	EAC	APP	Hazards Class	Hazards Sub Risks	HIN
2441	TITANIUM TRICHLORIDE, PYROPHORIC or TITANIUM TRICHLORIDE MIXTURE, PYROPHORIC	4WE(1)		4.2	8	
2442	TRICHLOROACETYL CHLORIDE	4W		8		X80
2443	VANADIUM OXYTRICHLORIDE	4WE		8		80
2444	VANADIUM TETRACHLORIDE	4WE	B	8		X88
2445	UN No. no longer in use					
2446	NITROCRESOLS, SOLID	2X		6.1		60
2447	PHOSPHORUS, WHITE, MOLTEN	1WE	A(h)	4.2	6.1	446
2448	SULPHUR, MOLTEN	1Y		4.1		44
2449	UN No. no longer in use					
2450	UN No. no longer in use					
2451	NITROGEN TRIFLUORIDE	2S		2.2	5.1	25
2452	ETHYL ACETYLENE, STABILIZED	2YE		2.1		239
2453	ETHYL FLUORIDE (REFRIGERANT GAS R 161)	2YE		2.1		23
2454	METHYL FLUORIDE (REFRIGERANT GAS R 41)	2YE		2.1		23
2455	METHYL NITRITE	2PE(1)		2.2		
2456	2-CHLOROPROPENE	3YE		3		33
2457	2,3-DIMETHYLBUTANE	3YE		3		33
2458	HEXADIENES	3YE		3		33
2459	2-METHYL-1-BUTENE	3YE		3		33
2460	2-METHYL-2-BUTENE	3YE		3		33
2461	METHYLPENTADIENE	3YE		3		33
2462	UN No. no longer in use					
2463	ALUMINIUM HYDRIDE	4WE(1)		4.3		
2464	BERYLLIUM NITRATE	1Y		5.1	6.1	56
2465	DICHLOROISOCYANURIC ACID, DRY or DICHLOROISOCYANURIC ACID SALTS	1W		5.1		50
2466	POTASSIUM SUPEROXIDE	1W(1)		5.1		

(1) Not applicable to the carriage of dangerous goods under RID or ADR

UN No	Substance	EAC	APP	Hazards Class	Sub Risks	HIN
2467	UN No. no longer in use					
2468	TRICHLOROISOCYANURIC ACID, DRY	1W		5.1		50
2469	ZINC BROMATE	1Z		5.1		50
2470	PHENYLACETONITRILE, LIQUID	2X		6.1		60
2471	OSMIUM TETROXIDE	2X		6.1		66
2472	UN No. no longer in use					
2473	SODIUM ARSANILATE	2Z		6.1		60
2474	THIOPHOSGENE	2X		6.1		66
2475	VANADIUM TRICHLORIDE	2X		8		80
2476	UN No. no longer in use					
2477	METHYL ISOTHIOCYANATE	●3WE	A(fl)	6.1	3	663
2478	ISOCYANATES, FLAMMABLE, TOXIC, N.O.S. or ISOCYANATE SOLUTION, FLAMMABLE, TOXIC, N.O.S., packing group II	●3WE	A(fl)	3	6.1	336
2478	ISOCYANATES, FLAMMABLE, TOXIC, N.O.S. or ISOCYANATE SOLUTION, FLAMMABLE, TOXIC, N.O.S., packing group III	●3W	A(fl)	3	6.1	36
2479	UN No. no longer in use					
2480	METHYL ISOCYANATE	●3WE	A(fl)	6.1	3	663
2481	ETHYL ISOCYANATE	●3WE	A(fl)	6.1	3	663
2482	n-PROPYL ISOCYANATE	●3WE	A(fl)	6.1	3	663
2483	ISOPROPYL ISOCYANATE	●3WE	A(fl)	6.1	3	663
2484	tert-BUTYL ISOCYANATE	●3WE	A(fl)	6.1	3	663
2485	n-BUTYL ISOCYANATE	●3W	A(fl)	6.1	3	663
2486	ISOBUTYL ISOCYANATE	●3WE	A(fl)	6.1	3	663
2487	PHENYL ISOCYANATE	●3W	A(fl)	6.1	3	663
2488	CYCLOHEXYL ISOCYANATE	●3W	A(fl)	6.1	3	663
2489	UN No. no longer in use					
2490	DICHLOROISOPROPYL ETHER	2Z		6.1		60
2491	ETHANOLAMINE or ETHANOLAMINE SOLUTION	2X		8		80

UN No	Substance	EAC	APP	Hazards Class	Hazards Sub Risks	HIN
2492	UN No. no longer in use					
2493	HEXAMETHYLENEIMINE	•2WE	A(fl)	3	8	338
2494	UN No. no longer in use					
2495	IODINE PENTAFLUORIDE	4WE	A(!)	5.1	6.1, 8	568
2496	PROPIONIC ANHYDRIDE	•3X		8		80
2497	UN No. no longer in use					
2498	1,2,3,6-TETRAHYDROBENZALDEHYDE	•3Y		3		30
2499	UN No. no longer in use					
2500	UN No. no longer in use					
2501	TRIS(1-AZIRIDINYL) PHOSPHINE OXIDE SOLUTION	2X		6.1		60
2502	VALERYL CHLORIDE	4W	A(fl)	8	3	83
2503	ZIRCONIUM TETRACHLORIDE	2X		8		80
2504	TETRABROMOETHANE	2Z		6.1		60
2505	AMMONIUM FLUORIDE	2X		6.1		60
2506	AMMONIUM HYDROGEN SULPHATE	2X		8		80
2507	CHLOROPLATINIC ACID, SOLID	2X		8		80
2508	MOLYBDENUM PENTACHLORIDE	2X		8		80
2509	POTASSIUM HYDROGEN SULPHATE	2X		8		80
2510	UN No. no longer in use					
2511	2-CHLOROPROPIONIC ACID	2X		8		80
2512	AMINOPHENOLS (o-,m-,p-)	2X		6.1		60
2513	BROMOACETYL BROMIDE	4W		8		X80
2514	BROMOBENZENE	2Y		3		30
2515	BROMOFORM	2X		6.1		60
2516	CARBON TETRABROMIDE	2Z		6.1		60
2517	1-CHLORO-1, 1-DIFLUOROETHANE (REFRIGERANT GAS R 142b)	2YE		2.1		23
2518	1,5,9-CYCLODODECATRIENE	3Z		6.1		60
2519	UN No. no longer in use					
2520	CYCLOOCTADIENES	3Y		3		30

UN No	Substance	EAC	APP	Hazards Class	Hazards Sub Risks	HIN
2521	DIKETENE, STABILIZED	●3W	A(fl)	6.1	3	663
2522	2-DIMETHYLAMINOETHYL METHACRYLATE	●2W		6.1		69
2523	UN No. no longer in use					
2524	ETHYL ORTHOFORMATE	●3Y		3		30
2525	ETHYL OXALATE	●3Z		6.1		60
2526	FURFURYLAMINE	●2W	A(fl)	3	8	38
2527	ISOBUTYL ACRYLATE, STABILIZED	3W	A(fl)	3		39
2528	ISOBUTYL ISOBUTYRATE	3Y		3		30
2529	ISOBUTYRIC ACID	●2W	A(fl)	3	8	38
2530	UN No. no longer in use					
2531	METHACRYLIC ACID, STABILIZED	3W		8		89
2532	UN No. no longer in use					
2533	METHYL TRICHLOROACETATE	2Z		6.1		60
2534	METHYLCHLOROSILANE	2WE	A(fg)	2.3	2.1, 8	263
2535	4-METHYLMORPHOLINE (N-METHYLMORPHOLINE)	●2WE	A(fl)	3	8	338
2536	METHYLTETRAHYDROFURAN	●2YE		3		33
2537	UN No. no longer in use					
2538	NITRONAPHTHALENE	1Z		4.1		40
2539	UN No. no longer in use					
2540	UN No. no longer in use					
2541	TERPINOLENE	3Y		3		30
2542	TRIBUTYLAMINE	3X		6.1		60
2543	UN No. no longer in use					
2544	UN No. no longer in use					
2545	HAFNIUM POWDER, DRY, packing group I	1Y[1]		4.2		
2545	HAFNIUM POWDER, DRY, packing groups II & III	1Y		4.2		40
2546	TITANIUM POWDER, DRY, packing group I	1Y[1]		4.2		

(1) Not applicable to the carriage of dangerous goods under RID or ADR

UN No	Substance	EAC	APP	Hazards Class	Hazards Sub Risks	HIN
2546	**TITANIUM POWDER, DRY,** packing groups II & III	1Y		4.2		40
2547	**SODIUM SUPEROXIDE**	1W(1)		5.1		
2548	**CHLORINE PENTAFLUORIDE**	2WE(1)	A(!)	2.3	5.1, 8	
2549 to 2551	UN Nos. no longer in use					
2552	**HEXAFLUOROACETONE HYDRATE, LIQUID**	2X		6.1		60
2553	UN No. no longer in use					
2554	**METHYLALLYL CHLORIDE**	3WE		3		33
2555	**NITROCELLULOSE WITH WATER** (not less than 25% water, by mass)	1Z(1)		4.1		
2556	**NITROCELLULOSE WITH ALCOHOL** (not less than 25% alcohol, by mass, and not more than 12.6% nitrogen, by dry mass)	1Y(1)		4.1		
2557	**NITROCELLULOSE,** with not more than 12.6% nitrogen, by dry mass, **MIXTURE WITH** or **WITHOUT PLASTICIZER, WITH** or **WITHOUT PIGMENT**	1Z(1)		4.1		
2558	**EPIBROMOHYDRIN**	●2W	A(fl)	6.1	3	663
2559	UN No. no longer in use					
2560	**2-METHYLPENTAN-2-OL**	●3Y		3		30
2561	**3-METHYL-1-BUTENE**	3YE		3		33
2562	UN No. no longer in use					
2563	UN No. no longer in use					
2564	**TRICHLOROACETIC ACID SOLUTION**	2X		8		80
2565	**DICYCLOHEXYLAMINE**	2X		8		80
2566	UN No. no longer in use					
2567	**SODIUM PENTACHLOROPHENATE**	2X		6.1		60
2568	UN No. no longer in use					
2569	UN No. no longer in use					
2570	**CADMIUM COMPOUND**	2X		6.1		66/60

(1) Not applicable to the carriage of dangerous goods under RID or ADR

UN No	Substance	EAC	APP	Hazards Class	Hazards Sub Risks	HIN
2571	**ALKYLSULPHURIC ACIDS**	2X		8		80
2572	**PHENYLHYDRAZINE**	●3X		6.1		60
2573	**THALLIUM CHLORATE**	1Y		5.1	6.1	56
2574	**TRICRESYL PHOSPHATE** with more than 3% ortho isomer	2X		6.1		60
2575	UN No. no longer in use					
2576	**PHOSPHORUS OXYBROMIDE, MOLTEN**	1X		8		80
2577	**PHENYLACETYL CHLORIDE**	4W		8		80
2578	**PHOSPHORUS TRIOXIDE**	2X		8		80
2579	**PIPERAZINE**	2X		8		80
2580	**ALUMINIUM BROMIDE SOLUTION**	2X		8		80
2581	**ALUMINIUM CHLORIDE SOLUTION**	2X		8		80
2582	**FERRIC CHLORIDE SOLUTION**	2X		8		80
2583	**ALKYLSULPHONIC ACIDS, SOLID** or **ARYLSULPHONIC ACIDS, SOLID** with more than 5% free sulphuric acid	2X		8		80
2584	**ALKYLSULPHONIC ACIDS, LIQUID** or **ARYLSULPHONIC ACIDS, LIQUID** with more than 5% free sulphuric acid	2X		8		80
2585	**ALKYLSULPHONIC ACIDS, SOLID** or **ARYLSULPHONIC ACIDS, SOLID** with not more than 5% free sulphuric acid	2X		8		80
2586	**ALKYLSULPHONIC ACIDS, LIQUID** or **ARYLSULPHONIC ACIDS, LIQUID** with not more than 5% free sulphuric acid	2X		8		80
2587	**BENZOQUINONE**	2Z		6.1		60
2588	**PESTICIDE, SOLID, TOXIC, N.O.S.**	2X		6.1		66/60
2589	**VINYL CHLOROACETATE**	3W	A(fl)	6.1	3	63
2590	**ASBESTOS, CHRYSOTILE**	2X		9		90
2591	**XENON, REFRIGERATED LIQUID**	2TE		2.2		22
2592 to 2598	UN Nos. no longer in use					

UN No	Substance	EAC	APP	Hazards Class	Sub Risks	HIN
2599	**CHLOROTRIFLUOROMETHANE AND TRIFLUOROMETHANE AZEOTROPIC MIXTURE** with approximately 60% chlorotrifluoromethane **(REFRIGERANT GAS R 503)**	2TE		2.2		20
2600	UN No. no longer in use					
2601	**CYCLOBUTANE**	2YE		2.1		23
2602	**DICHLORODIFLUOROMETHANE AND 1,1-DIFLUOROETHANE AZEOTROPIC MIXTURE** with approximately 74% dichlorodifluoromethane **(REFRIGERANT GAS R 500)**	2TE		2.2		20
2603	**CYCLOHEPTATRIENE**	3WE	A(fl)	3	6.1	336
2604	**BORON TRIFLUORIDE DIETHYL ETHERATE**	4WE	A(fl)	8	3	883
2605	**METHOXYMETHYL ISOCYANATE**	3WE	A(fl)	6.1	3	663
2606	**METHYL ORTHOSILICATE**	3WE	A(fl)	6.1	3	663
2607	**ACROLEIN DIMER, STABILIZED**	●2Y		3		39
2608	**NITROPROPANES**	●3Y		3		30
2609	**TRIALLYL BORATE**	2X		6.1		60
2610	**TRIALLYLAMINE**	3W	A(fl)	3	8	38
2611	**PROPYLENE CHLOROHYDRIN**	●2W	A(fl)	6.1	3	63
2612	**METHYL PROPYL ETHER**	●3YE		3		33
2613	UN No. no longer in use					
2614	**METHALLYL ALCOHOL**	●2Y		3		30
2615	**ETHYL PROPYL ETHER**	●3YE		3		33
2616	**TRIISOPROPYL BORATE,** packing group II	●3YE		3		33
2616	**TRIISOPROPYL BORATE,** packing group III	●3Y		3		30
2617	**METHYLCYCLOHEXANOLS,** flammable	●3Y		3		30
2618	**VINYLTOLUENES, STABILIZED**	3Y		3		39
2619	**BENZYLDIMETHYLAMINE**	3W	A(fl)	8	3	83

UN No	Substance	EAC	APP	Hazards Class	Hazards Sub Risks	HIN
2620	**AMYL BUTYRATES**	●3Y		3		30
2621	**ACETYL METHYL CARBINOL**	●2Y		3		30
2622	**GLYCIDALDEHYDE**	●2WE	A(fl)	3	6.1	336
2623	**FIRELIGHTERS, SOLID** with flammable liquid	1Z[(1)]		4.1		
2624	**MAGNESIUM SILICIDE**	4W		4.3		423
2625	UN No. no longer in use					
2626	**CHLORIC ACID, AQUEOUS SOLUTION** with not more than 10% chloric acid	2P		5.1		50
2627	**NITRITES, INORGANIC, N.O.S.**	1Y		5.1		50
2628	**POTASSIUM FLUOROACETATE**	2X		6.1		66
2629	**SODIUM FLUOROACETATE**	2X		6.1		66
2630	**SELENATES** or **SELENITES**	2X		6.1		66
2631 to 2641	UN Nos. no longer in use					
2642	**FLUOROACETIC ACID**	2X		6.1		66
2643	**METHYL BROMOACETATE**	2X		6.1		60
2644	**METHYL IODIDE**	2X	B	6.1		66
2645	**PHENACYL BROMIDE**	2X		6.1		60
2646	**HEXACHLOROCYCLOPENTADIENE**	2X	B	6.1		66
2647	**MALONONITRILE**	2X		6.1		60
2648	**1,2-DIBROMOBUTAN-3-ONE**	2X		6.1		60
2649	**1,3-DICHLOROACETONE**	2X		6.1		60
2650	**1,1-DICHLORO-1-NITROETHANE**	2X		6.1		60
2651	**4,4'-DIAMINODIPHENYLMETHANE**	2Z		6.1		60
2652	UN No. no longer in use					
2653	**BENZYL IODIDE**	2X		6.1		60
2654	UN No. no longer in use					
2655	**POTASSIUM FLUOROSILICATE**	2X		6.1		60
2656	**QUINOLINE**	2X		6.1		60

(1) Not applicable to the carriage of dangerous goods under RID or ADR

UN No	Substance	EAC	APP	Hazards Class	Sub Risks	HIN
2657	SELENIUM DISULPHIDE	2Z		6.1		60
2658	UN No. no longer in use					
2659	SODIUM CHLOROACETATE	2Z		6.1		60
2660	NITROTOLUIDINES (MONO)	2X		6.1		60
2661	HEXACHLOROACETONE	2Z		6.1		60
2662	UN No. no longer in use					
2663	UN No. no longer in use					
2664	DIBROMOMETHANE	2Z		6.1		60
2665	UN No. no longer in use					
2666	UN No. no longer in use					
2667	BUTYLTOLUENES	3X		6.1		60
2668	CHLOROACETONITRILE	2W	A(fl)	6.1	3	663
2669	CHLOROCRESOLS SOLUTION	2Z		6.1		60
2670	CYANURIC CHLORIDE	2X		8		80
2671	AMINOPYRIDINES (o-,m-,p-)	2X		6.1		60
2672	AMMONIA SOLUTION, relative density between 0.880 and 0.957 at 15°C in water, with more than 10% but not more than 35% ammonia	2X		8		80
2673	2-AMINO-4-CHLOROPHENOL	2X		6.1		60
2674	SODIUM FLUOROSILICATE	2X		6.1		60
2675	UN No. no longer in use					
2676	STIBINE	2PE[(1)]	A(fg)	2.3	2.1	
2677	RUBIDIUM HYDROXIDE SOLUTION	2R		8		80
2678	RUBIDIUM HYDROXIDE	2W		8		80
2679	LITHIUM HYDROXIDE SOLUTION	2R		8		80
2680	LITHIUM HYDROXIDE	2X		8		80
2681	CAESIUM HYDROXIDE SOLUTION	2R		8		80
2682	CAESIUM HYDROXIDE	2W		8		80
2683	AMMONIUM SULPHIDE SOLUTION	●2W	A(fl)	8	3, 6.1	86
2684	3-DIETHYLAMINOPROPYLAMINE	●2W	A(fl)	3	8	38
2685	N,N-DIETHYLETHYLENEDIAMINE	●2W	A(fl)	8	3	83

(1) Not applicable to the carriage of dangerous goods under RID or ADR

UN No	Substance	EAC	APP	Hazards Class	Hazards Sub Risks	HIN
2686	2-DIETHYLAMINOETHANOL	●2W	A(fl)	8	3	83
2687	DICYCLOHEXYLAMMONIUM NITRITE	1Z		4.1		40
2688	1-BROMO-3-CHLOROPROPANE	2X		6.1		60
2689	GLYCEROL alpha-MONOCHLOROHYDRIN	2X		6.1		60
2690	N,n-BUTYLIMIDAZOLE	2X		6.1		60
2691	PHOSPHORUS PENTABROMIDE	4W		8		80
2692	BORON TRIBROMIDE	4WE	B	8		X88
2693	BISULPHITES, AQUEOUS SOLUTION, N.O.S.	2X		8		80
2694 to 2697	UN Nos. no longer in use					
2698	TETRAHYDROPHTHALIC ANHYDRIDES with more than 0.05% of maleic anhydride	2X		8		80
2699	TRIFLUOROACETIC ACID	2X	B	8		88
2700 to 2704	UN Nos. no longer in use					
2705	1-PENTOL	2X		8		80
2706	UN No. no longer in use					
2707	DIMETHYLDIOXANES, packing group II	●3YE		3		33
2707	DIMETHYLDIOXANES, packing group III	●3Y		3		30
2708	UN No. no longer in use					
2709	BUTYLBENZENES	3Y		3		30
2710	DIPROPYL KETONE	3Y		3		30
2711	UN No. no longer in use					
2712	UN No. no longer in use					
2713	ACRIDINE	2X		6.1		60
2714	ZINC RESINATE	1Z		4.1		40
2715	ALUMINIUM RESINATE	1Z		4.1		40

UN No	Substance	EAC	APP	Hazards Class	Hazards Sub Risks	HIN
2716	1,4-BUTYNEDIOL	2X		6.1		60
2717	CAMPHOR, synthetic	1Z		4.1		40
2718	UN No. no longer in use					
2719	BARIUM BROMATE	1W		5.1	6.1	56
2720	CHROMIUM NITRATE	1Z		5.1		50
2721	COPPER CHLORATE	1Y		5.1		50
2722	LITHIUM NITRATE	1Z		5.1		50
2723	MAGNESIUM CHLORATE	1Y		5.1		50
2724	MANGANESE NITRATE	1Z		5.1		50
2725	NICKEL NITRATE	1Z		5.1		50
2726	NICKEL NITRITE	1Z		5.1		50
2727	THALLIUM NITRATE	1Y		6.1	5.1	65
2728	ZIRCONIUM NITRATE	1Z		5.1		50
2729	HEXACHLOROBENZENE	2Z		6.1		60
2730	NITROANISOLES, LIQUID	2Z		6.1		60
2731	UN No. no longer in use					
2732	NITROBROMOBENZENES, LIQUID	2X		6.1		60
2733	AMINES, FLAMMABLE, CORROSIVE, N.O.S. or POLYAMINES, FLAMMABLE, CORROSIVE, N.O.S., packing groups I & II	•2WE	A(fl)	3	8	338
2733	AMINES, FLAMMABLE, CORROSIVE, N.O.S. or POLYAMINES, FLAMMABLE, CORROSIVE, N.O.S., packing group III	•2W	A(fl)	3	8	38
2734	AMINES, LIQUID, CORROSIVE, FLAMMABLE, N.O.S. or POLYAMINES, LIQUID, CORROSIVE, FLAMMABLE, N.O.S.	•2W	A(fl)	8	3	883/83
2735	AMINES, LIQUID, CORROSIVE, N.O.S. or POLYAMINES, LIQUID, CORROSIVE, N.O.S., packing group I	2X	B	8		88
2735	AMINES, LIQUID, CORROSIVE, N.O.S. or POLYAMINES, LIQUID, CORROSIVE, N.O.S., packing groups II & III	2X		8		80

UN No	Substance	EAC	APP	Hazards Class	Sub Risks	HIN
2736	UN No. no longer in use					
2737	UN No. no longer in use					
2738	N-BUTYLANILINE	2Z		6.1		60
2739	BUTYRIC ANHYDRIDE	●3X		8		80
2740	n-PROPYL CHLOROFORMATE	●3WE	A(fl)	6.1	3, 8	668
2741	BARIUM HYPOCHLORITE with more than 22% available chlorine	1Y		5.1	6.1	56
2742	CHLOROFORMATES, TOXIC, CORROSIVE, FLAMMABLE, N.O.S.	●3W	A(fl)	6.1	3, 8	638
2743	n-BUTYL CHLOROFORMATE	●3W	A(fl)	6.1	3, 8	638
2744	CYCLOBUTYL CHLOROFORMATE	●3W	A(fl)	6.1	3, 8	638
2745	CHLOROMETHYL CHLOROFORMATE	2X		6.1	8	68
2746	PHENYL CHLOROFORMATE	2X		6.1	8	68
2747	tert-BUTYLCYCLOHEXYL CHLOROFORMATE	2X		6.1		60
2748	2-ETHYLHEXYL CHLOROFORMATE	2X		6.1	8	68
2749	TETRAMETHYLSILANE	3YE		3		33
2750	1,3-DICHLOROPROPANOL-2	2X		6.1		60
2751	DIETHYLTHIOPHOSPHORYL CHLORIDE	4W		8		80
2752	1,2-EPOXY-3-ETHOXYPROPANE	3Y		3		30
2753	N-ETHYLBENZYLTOLUIDINES, LIQUID	2X		6.1		60
2754	N-ETHYLTOLUIDINES	3X		6.1		60
2755	UN No. no longer in use					
2756	UN No. no longer in use					
2757	CARBAMATE PESTICIDE, SOLID, TOXIC	2X		6.1		66/60
2758	CARBAMATE PESTICIDE, LIQUID, FLAMMABLE, TOXIC, flash point less than 23°C	●3WE	A(fl)	3	6.1	336
2759	ARSENICAL PESTICIDE, SOLID, TOXIC	2X		6.1		66/60

UN No	Substance	EAC	APP	Hazards Class	Sub Risks	HIN
2760	ARSENICAL PESTICIDE, LIQUID, FLAMMABLE, TOXIC, flash point less than 23°C	●3WE	A(fl)	3	6.1	336
2761	ORGANOCHLORINE PESTICIDE, SOLID, TOXIC	2X		6.1		66/60
2762	ORGANOCHLORINE PESTICIDE, LIQUID, FLAMMABLE, TOXIC, flash point less than 23°C	●3WE	A(fl)	3	6.1	336
2763	TRIAZINE PESTICIDE, SOLID, TOXIC	2X		6.1		66/60
2764	TRIAZINE PESTICIDE, LIQUID, FLAMMABLE, TOXIC, flash point less than 23°C	●3WE	A(fl)	3	6.1	336
2765 to 2770	UN Nos. no longer in use					
2771	THIOCARBAMATE PESTICIDE, SOLID, TOXIC	2X		6.1		66/60
2772	THIOCARBAMATE PESTICIDE, LIQUID, FLAMMABLE, TOXIC, flash point less than 23°C	●3WE	A(fl)	3	6.1	336
2773	UN No. no longer in use					
2774	UN No. no longer in use					
2775	COPPER BASED PESTICIDE, SOLID, TOXIC	2X		6.1		66/60
2776	COPPER BASED PESTICIDE, LIQUID, FLAMMABLE, TOXIC, flash point less than 23°C	●3WE	A(fl)	3	6.1	336
2777	MERCURY BASED PESTICIDE, SOLID, TOXIC	2X		6.1		66/60
2778	MERCURY BASED PESTICIDE, LIQUID, FLAMMABLE, TOXIC, flash point less than 23°C	●3WE	A(fl)	3	6.1	336
2779	SUBSTITUTED NITROPHENOL PESTICIDE, SOLID, TOXIC	2X		6.1		66/60
2780	SUBSTITUTED NITROPHENOL PESTICIDE, LIQUID, FLAMMABLE, TOXIC, flash point less than 23°C	●3WE	A(fl)	3	6.1	336
2781	BIPYRIDILIUM PESTICIDE, SOLID, TOXIC	2X		6.1		66/60

UN No	Substance	EAC	APP	Hazards Class	Hazards Sub Risks	HIN
2782	**BIPYRIDILIUM PESTICIDE, LIQUID, FLAMMABLE, TOXIC,** flash point less than 23°C	●3WE	A(fl)	3	6.1	336
2783	**ORGANOPHOSPHORUS PESTICIDE, SOLID, TOXIC**	2X		6.1		66/60
2784	**ORGANOPHOSPHORUS PESTICIDE, LIQUID, FLAMMABLE, TOXIC,** flash point less than 23°C	●3WE	A(fl)	3	6.1	336
2785	**4-THIAPENTANAL**	2X		6.1		60
2786	**ORGANOTIN PESTICIDE, SOLID, TOXIC**	2X		6.1		66/60
2787	**ORGANOTIN PESTICIDE, LIQUID, FLAMMABLE, TOXIC,** flash point less than 23°C	●3WE	A(fl)	3	6.1	336
2788	**ORGANOTIN COMPOUND, LIQUID, N.O.S.,** packing group I	2X	B	6.1		66
2788	**ORGANOTIN COMPOUND, LIQUID, N.O.S.,** packing groups II & III	2X		6.1		60
2789	**ACETIC ACID, GLACIAL** or **ACETIC ACID SOLUTION,** more than 80% acid, by mass	●2P	A(fl)	8	3	83
2790	**ACETIC ACID SOLUTION,** more than 10% but not more than 80% acid, by mass	●2R		8		80
2791	UN No. no longer in use					
2792	UN No. no longer in use					
2793	**FERROUS METAL BORINGS, SHAVINGS, TURNINGS** or **CUTTINGS** in a form liable to self-heating	1Y		4.2		40
2794	**BATTERIES, WET, FILLED WITH ACID,** electric storage	2R		8		80
2795	**BATTERIES, WET, FILLED WITH ALKALI,** electric storage	2R		8		80
2796	**SULPHURIC ACID** with not more than 51% acid or **BATTERY FLUID, ACID**	2R		8		80
2797	**BATTERY FLUID, ALKALI**	2R		8		80
2798	**PHENYLPHOSPHORUS DICHLORIDE**	2X		8		80

UN No	Substance	EAC	APP	Hazards Class	Sub Risks	HIN
2799	PHENYLPHOSPHORUS THIODICHLORIDE	2W		8		80
2800	BATTERIES, WET, NON-SPILLABLE, electric storage	2R		8		80
2801	DYE, LIQUID, CORROSIVE, N.O.S. or DYE INTERMEDIATE, LIQUID, CORROSIVE, N.O.S., packing group I	2X	B	8		88
2801	DYE, LIQUID, CORROSIVE, N.O.S. or DYE INTERMEDIATE, LIQUID, CORROSIVE, N.O.S., packing groups II & III	2X		8		80
2802	COPPER CHLORIDE	2X		8		80
2803	GALLIUM	2Z		8		80
2804	UN No. no longer in use					
2805	LITHIUM HYDRIDE, FUSED SOLID	4W		4.3		423
2806	LITHIUM NITRIDE	4W[1]		4.3		
2807	MAGNETIZED MATERIAL	2Z[1]		9		
2808	UN No. no longer in use					
2809	MERCURY	2X		8	6.1	86
2810	TOXIC LIQUID, ORGANIC, N.O.S., packing group I	2X	B	6.1		66
2810	TOXIC LIQUID, ORGANIC, N.O.S., packing groups II & III	2X		6.1		60
2811	TOXIC SOLID, ORGANIC, N.O.S.	2X		6.1		66/60
2812	SODIUM ALUMINATE, SOLID	2X[1]		8		
2813	WATER-REACTIVE SOLID, N.O.S.	4W		4.3		X423/ 423
2814	INFECTIOUS SUBSTANCE, AFFECTING HUMANS	2XE[1]		6.2		
2814	INFECTIOUS SUBSTANCE, AFFECTING HUMANS, in refrigerated nitrogen	2XE[1]	A(c)	6.2	2.2	
2814	INFECTIOUS SUBSTANCE, AFFECTING HUMANS (animal material only)	2XE		6.2		606
2815	N-AMINOETHYLPIPERAZINE	●2X		8	6.1	86

(1) Not applicable to the carriage of dangerous goods under RID or ADR

UN No	Substance	EAC	APP	Hazards Class	Sub Risks	HIN
2816	UN No. no longer in use					
2817	**AMMONIUM HYDROGENDIFLUORIDE SOLUTION**	2X		8	6.1	86
2818	**AMMONIUM POLYSULPHIDE SOLUTION**	2X		8	6.1	86
2819	**AMYL ACID PHOSPHATE**	2X		8		80
2820	**BUTYRIC ACID**	●2X		8		80
2821	**PHENOL SOLUTION**	2X		6.1		60
2822	**2-CHLOROPYRIDINE**	2X		6.1		60
2823	**CROTONIC ACID, SOLID**	2X		8		80
2824	UN No. no longer in use					
2825	UN No. no longer in use					
2826	**ETHYL CHLOROTHIOFORMATE**	2W	A(fl)	8	3	83
2827	UN No. no longer in use					
2828	UN No. no longer in use					
2829	**CAPROIC ACID**	2X		8		80
2830	**LITHIUM FERROSILICON**	4W		4.3		423
2831	**1,1,1-TRICHLOROETHANE**	2Z		6.1		60
2832	UN No. no longer in use					
2833	UN No. no longer in use					
2834	**PHOSPHOROUS ACID**	2X		8		80
2835	**SODIUM ALUMINIUM HYDRIDE**	4W		4.3		423
2836	UN No. no longer in use					
2837	**BISULPHATES, AQUEOUS SOLUTION**	2R		8		80
2838	**VINYL BUTYRATE, STABILIZED**	3YE		3		339
2839	**ALDOL**	●2X		6.1		60
2840	**BUTYRALDOXIME**	●3W	A(fl)	3		30
2841	**DI-n-AMYLAMINE**	●3W	A(fl)	3	6.1	36
2842	**NITROETHANE**	●3Y		3		30
2843	UN No. no longer in use					
2844	**CALCIUM MANGANESE SILICON**	4Y		4.3		423

UN No	Substance	EAC	APP	Hazards Class	Sub Risks	HIN
2845	PYROPHORIC LIQUID, ORGANIC, N.O.S.	●3W		4.2		333
2846	PYROPHORIC SOLID, ORGANIC, N.O.S.	4Y[(1)]		4.2		
2847	UN No. no longer in use					
2848	UN No. no longer in use					
2849	3-CHLOROPROPANOL-1	●2X		6.1		60
2850	PROPYLENE TETRAMER	3Y		3		30
2851	BORON TRIFLUORIDE DIHYDRATE	4W		8		80
2852	DIPICRYL SULPHIDE, WETTED with not less than 10% water, by mass	1W[(1)]		4.1		
2853	MAGNESIUM FLUOROSILICATE	2Z		6.1		60
2854	AMMONIUM FLUOROSILICATE	2Z		6.1		60
2855	ZINC FLUOROSILICATE	2Z		6.1		60
2856	FLUOROSILICATES, N.O.S.	2Z		6.1		60
2857	REFRIGERATING MACHINES containing non-flammable, non-toxic gases or ammonia solutions (UN 2672)	2Z[(1)]		2.2		
2858	ZIRCONIUM, DRY, coiled wire, finished metal sheets, strip (thinner than 254 microns but not thinner than 18 microns)	1Z		4.1		40
2859	AMMONIUM METAVANADATE	2Z		6.1		60
2860	UN No. no longer in use					
2861	AMMONIUM POLYVANADATE	2X		6.1		60
2862	VANADIUM PENTOXIDE, non-fused form	2X		6.1		60
2863	SODIUM AMMONIUM VANADATE	2X		6.1		60
2864	POTASSIUM METAVANADATE	2X		6.1		60
2865	HYDROXYLAMINE SULPHATE	2X		8		80
2866 to 2868	UN Nos. no longer in use					
2869	TITANIUM TRICHLORIDE MIXTURE	4W		8		80
2870	ALUMINIUM BOROHYDRIDE	4W		4.2	4.3	X333

(1) Not applicable to the carriage of dangerous goods under RID or ADR

UN No	Substance	EAC	APP	Hazards Class	Hazards Sub Risks	HIN
2870	**ALUMINIUM BOROHYDRIDE IN DEVICES**	4W⁽¹⁾		4.2	4.3	
2871	**ANTIMONY POWDER**	2X		6.1		60
2872	**DIBROMOCHLOROPROPANES**	2X		6.1		60
2873	**DIBUTYLAMINOETHANOL**	2Z		6.1		60
2874	**FURFURYL ALCOHOL**	●2X		6.1		60
2875	**HEXACHLOROPHENE**	2X		6.1		60
2876	**RESORCINOL**	2Z		6.1		60
2877	UN No. no longer in use					
2878	**TITANIUM SPONGE GRANULES** or **TITANIUM SPONGE POWDERS**	4Y		4.1		40
2879	**SELENIUM OXYCHLORIDE**	4WE	B	8	6.1	X886
2880	**CALCIUM HYPOCHLORITE, HYDRATED,** or **CALCIUM HYPOCHLORITE, HYDRATED MIXTURE** with not less than 5.5% but not more than 16% water	1W		5.1		50
2881	**METAL CATALYST, DRY**	4Y		4.2		43/40
2882 to 2899	UN Nos. no longer in use					
2900	**INFECTIOUS SUBSTANCE, AFFECTING ANIMALS** only	2X⁽¹⁾		6.2		
2900	**INFECTIOUS SUBSTANCE, AFFECTING ANIMALS** only (animal material only)	2X		6.2		606
2900	**INFECTIOUS SUBSTANCE, AFFECTING ANIMALS** only, in refrigerated liquid nitrogen	2X⁽¹⁾	A(c)	6.2	2.2	
2901	**BROMINE CHLORIDE**	2WE	B	2.3	5.1, 8	265
2902	**PESTICIDE, LIQUID, TOXIC, N.O.S.,** packing group I	2X	B	6.1		66
2902	**PESTICIDE, LIQUID, TOXIC, N.O.S.,** packing groups II & III	2X		6.1		60
2903	**PESTICIDE, LIQUID, TOXIC, FLAMMABLE, N.O.S.**	●3W	A(fl)	6.1	3	663/63

(1) Not applicable to the carriage of dangerous goods under RID or ADR

UN No	Substance	EAC	APP	Hazards Class	Sub Risks	HIN
2904	**CHLOROPHENOLATES, LIQUID** or **PHENOLATES, LIQUID**	2X		8		80
2905	**CHLOROPHENOLATES, SOLID** or **PHENOLATES, SOLID**	2X		8		80
2906	UN No. no longer in use					
2907	**ISOSORBIDE DINITRATE MIXTURE** with not less than 60% lactose, mannose, starch or calcium hydrogen phosphate	1Z[(1)]		4.1		
2908	**RADIOACTIVE MATERIAL, EXCEPTED PACKAGE – EMPTY PACKAGING**	[(2)]		7		
2909	**RADIOACTIVE MATERIAL, EXCEPTED PACKAGE – ARTICLES MANUFACTURED FROM NATURAL URANIUM** or **DEPLETED URANIUM** or **NATURAL THORIUM**	[(2)]		7		
2910	**RADIOACTIVE MATERIAL, EXCEPTED PACKAGE – LIMITED QUANTITY OF MATERIAL**	[(2)]		7		
2911	**RADIOACTIVE MATERIAL, EXCEPTED PACKAGE – INSTRUMENTS** or **ARTICLES**	[(2)]		7		
2912	**RADIOACTIVE MATERIAL, LOW SPECIFIC ACTIVITY (LSA-I),** non-fissile or fissile excepted	[(2)]		7		70
2913	**RADIOACTIVE MATERIAL, SURFACE CONTAMINATED OBJECTS (SCO-I** or **SCO-II),** non-fissile or fissile excepted	[(2)]		7		70
2914	UN No. no longer in use					
2915	**RADIOACTIVE MATERIAL, TYPE A PACKAGE,** non-special form, non-fissile or fissile excepted	[(2)]		7		70
2916	**RADIOACTIVE MATERIAL, TYPE B (U) PACKAGE,** non-fissile or fissile excepted	[(2)]		7		70
2917	**RADIOACTIVE MATERIAL, TYPE B (M) PACKAGE,** non-fissile or fissile excepted	[(2)]		7		70
2918	UN No. no longer in use					

(1) Not applicable to the carriage of dangerous goods under RID or ADR   (2) Radioactive material

UN No	Substance	EAC	APP	Hazards Class	Hazards Sub Risks	HIN
2919	**RADIOACTIVE MATERIAL, TRANSPORTED UNDER SPECIAL ARRANGEMENT,** non-fissile or fissile excepted	(2)		7		70
2920	**CORROSIVE LIQUID, FLAMMABLE, N.O.S.**	•3W	A(fl)	8	3	883/83
2921	**CORROSIVE SOLID, FLAMMABLE, N.O.S.**	2X		8	4.1	884/84
2922	**CORROSIVE LIQUID, TOXIC, N.O.S.,** packing group I	2X	B	8	6.1	886
2922	**CORROSIVE LIQUID, TOXIC, N.O.S.,** packing groups II & III	2X		8	6.1	86
2923	**CORROSIVE SOLID, TOXIC, N.O.S.**	2X		8	6.1	886/86
2924	**FLAMMABLE LIQUID, CORROSIVE, N.O.S.,** packing groups I & II	•3WE	A(fl)	3	8	338
2924	**FLAMMABLE LIQUID, CORROSIVE, N.O.S.,** packing group III	•3W	A(fl)	3	8	38
2925	**FLAMMABLE SOLID, CORROSIVE, ORGANIC, N.O.S.**	1W		4.1	8	48
2926	**FLAMMABLE SOLID, TOXIC, ORGANIC, N.O.S.**	1X		4.1	6.1	46
2927	**TOXIC LIQUID, CORROSIVE, ORGANIC, N.O.S.,** packing group I	2XE	B	6.1	8	668
2927	**TOXIC LIQUID, CORROSIVE, ORGANIC, N.O.S.,** packing group II	2X		6.1	8	68
2928	**TOXIC SOLID, CORROSIVE, ORGANIC, N.O.S.**	2X		6.1	8	668/68
2929	**TOXIC LIQUID, FLAMMABLE, ORGANIC, N.O.S.**	•3W	A(fl)	6.1	3	663/63
2930	**TOXIC SOLID, FLAMMABLE, ORGANIC, N.O.S.**	2X		6.1	4.1	664/64
2931	**VANADYL SULPHATE**	2Z		6.1		60
2932	UN No. no longer in use					
2933	**METHYL 2-CHLOROPROPIONATE**	•3Y		3		30
2934	**ISOPROPYL 2-CHLOROPROPIONATE**	3Y		3		30
2935	**ETHYL 2-CHLOROPROPIONATE**	3Y		3		30
2936	**THIOLACTIC ACID**	•2X		6.1		60

(2) Radioactive material

UN No	Substance	EAC	APP	Hazards Class	Sub Risks	HIN
2937	alpha-METHYLBENZYL ALCOHOL, LIQUID	2Z		6.1		60
2938	UN No. no longer in use					
2939	UN No. no longer in use					
2940	9-PHOSPHABICYCLONONANES (CYCLOOCTADIENE PHOSPHINES)	1Y		4.2		40
2941	FLUOROANILINES	2X		6.1		60
2942	2-TRIFLUOROMETHYLANILINE	2X		6.1		60
2943	TETRAHYDROFURFURYLAMINE	●2Y		3		30
2944	UN No. no longer in use					
2945	N-METHYLBUTYLAMINE	●2WE	A(fl)	3	8	338
2946	2-AMINO-5-DIETHYLAMINOPENTANE	2X		6.1		60
2947	ISOPROPYL CHLOROACETATE	3Y		3		30
2948	3-TRIFLUOROMETHYLANILINE	2X		6.1		60
2949	SODIUM HYDROSULPHIDE, HYDRATED with not less than 25% water of crystallization	2X		8		80
2950	MAGNESIUM GRANULES, COATED	4Y		4.3		423
2951 to 2955	UN Nos. no longer in use					
2956	5-tert-BUTYL-2,4,6-TRINITRO-m-XYLENE (MUSK XYLENE)	1Y[(1)]		4.1		
2957 to 2964	UN Nos. no longer in use					
2965	BORON TRIFLUORIDE DIMETHYL ETHERATE	4WE	A(fl)	4.3	3, 8	382
2966	THIOGLYCOL	2X		6.1		60
2967	SULPHAMIC ACID	2X		8		80
2968	MANEB, STABILIZED or MANEB PREPARATION, STABILIZED against self-heating	4Y		4.3		423

(1) Not applicable to the carriage of dangerous goods under RID or ADR

UN No	Substance	EAC	APP	Hazards Class	Hazards Sub Risks	HIN
2969	**CASTOR BEANS** or **CASTOR MEAL** or **CASTOR POMACE** or **CASTOR FLAKE**	2Z		9		90
2970 to 2976	UN Nos. no longer in use					
2977	**RADIOACTIVE MATERIAL, URANIUM HEXAFLUORIDE, FISSILE**	(2)		7	6.1, 8	768
2978	**RADIOACTIVE MATERIAL, URANIUM HEXAFLUORIDE,** non-fissile or fissile excepted	(2)		7	6.1, 8	768
2979 to 2982	UN Nos. no longer in use					
2983	**ETHYLENE OXIDE AND PROPYLENE OXIDE MIXTURE,** not more than 30% ethylene oxide	●2WE	A(fl)	3	6.1	336
2984	**HYDROGEN PEROXIDE, AQUEOUS SOLUTION** with not less than 8% but less than 20% hydrogen peroxide (stabilized as necessary)	2R		5.1		50
2985	**CHLOROSILANES, FLAMMABLE, CORROSIVE, N.O.S.**	4WE	A(fl)	3	8	X338
2986	**CHLOROSILANES, CORROSIVE, FLAMMABLE, N.O.S.**	4W	A(fl)	8	3	X83
2987	**CHLOROSILANES, CORROSIVE, N.O.S.**	4W		8		X80
2988	**CHLOROSILANES, WATER-REACTIVE, FLAMMABLE, CORROSIVE, N.O.S.**	4WE	A(fl)	4.3	3, 8	X338
2989	**LEAD PHOSPHITE, DIBASIC**	1Z		4.1		40
2990	**LIFE-SAVING APPLIANCES, SELF-INFLATING**	2Z[(1)]		9		
2991	**CARBAMATE PESTICIDE, LIQUID, TOXIC, FLAMMABLE,** flash point not less than 23°C	●3W	A(fl)	6.1	3	663/63
2992	**CARBAMATE PESTICIDE, LIQUID, TOXIC,** packing group I	2X	B	6.1		66
2992	**CARBAMATE PESTICIDE, LIQUID, TOXIC,** packing groups II & III	2X		6.1		60

(1) Not applicable to the carriage of dangerous goods under RID or ADR   (2) Radioactive material

NUMERICAL LIST OF DANGEROUS GOODS

UN No	Substance	EAC	APP	Hazards Class	Hazards Sub Risks	HIN
2993	**ARSENICAL PESTICIDE, LIQUID, TOXIC, FLAMMABLE,** flash point not less than 23°C	●3W	A(fl)	6.1	3	663/63
2994	**ARSENICAL PESTICIDE, LIQUID, TOXIC,** packing group I	2X	B	6.1		66
2994	**ARSENICAL PESTICIDE, LIQUID, TOXIC,** packing groups II & III	2X		6.1		60
2995	**ORGANOCHLORINE PESTICIDE, LIQUID, TOXIC, FLAMMABLE,** flash point not less than 23°C	●3W	A(fl)	6.1	3	663/63
2996	**ORGANOCHLORINE PESTICIDE, LIQUID, TOXIC,** packing group I	2X	B	6.1		66
2996	**ORGANOCHLORINE PESTICIDE, LIQUID, TOXIC,** packing groups II & III	2X		6.1		60
2997	**TRIAZINE PESTICIDE, LIQUID, TOXIC, FLAMMABLE,** flash point not less than 23°C	●3W	A(fl)	6.1	3	663/63
2998	**TRIAZINE PESTICIDE, LIQUID, TOXIC,** packing group I	2X	B	6.1		66
2998	**TRIAZINE PESTICIDE, LIQUID, TOXIC,** packing groups II & III	2X		6.1		60
2999 to 3004	UN Nos. no longer in use					
3005	**THIOCARBAMATE PESTICIDE, LIQUID, TOXIC, FLAMMABLE,** flash point not less than 23°C	●3W	A(fl)	6.1	3	663/63
3006	**THIOCARBAMATE PESTICIDE, LIQUID, TOXIC,** packing group I	2X	B	6.1		66
3006	**THIOCARBAMATE PESTICIDE, LIQUID, TOXIC,** packing groups II & III	2X		6.1		60
3007	UN No. no longer in use					
3008	UN No. no longer in use					
3009	**COPPER BASED PESTICIDE, LIQUID, TOXIC, FLAMMABLE,** flash point not less than 23°C	●3W	A(fl)	6.1	3	663/63
3010	**COPPER BASED PESTICIDE, LIQUID, TOXIC,** packing group I	2X	B	6.1		66

UN No	Substance	EAC	APP	Hazards Class	Sub Risks	HIN
3010	**COPPER BASED PESTICIDE, LIQUID, TOXIC,** packing groups II & III	2X		6.1		60
3011	**MERCURY BASED PESTICIDE, LIQUID, TOXIC, FLAMMABLE,** flash point not less than 23°C	•3W	A(fl)	6.1	3	663/63
3012	**MERCURY BASED PESTICIDE, LIQUID, TOXIC,** packing group I	2X	B	6.1		66
3012	**MERCURY BASED PESTICIDE, LIQUID, TOXIC,** packing groups II & III	2X		6.1		60
3013	**SUBSTITUTED NITROPHENOL PESTICIDE, LIQUID, TOXIC, FLAMMABLE,** flash point not less than 23°C	•3W	A(fl)	6.1	3	663/63
3014	**SUBSTITUTED NITROPHENOL PESTICIDE, LIQUID, TOXIC,** packing group I	2X	B	6.1		66
3014	**SUBSTITUTED NITROPHENOL PESTICIDE, LIQUID, TOXIC,** packing groups II & III	2X		6.1		60
3015	**BIPYRIDILIUM PESTICIDE, LIQUID, TOXIC, FLAMMABLE,** flash point not less than 23°C	•3W	A(fl)	6.1	3	663/63
3016	**BIPYRIDILIUM PESTICIDE, LIQUID, TOXIC,** packing group I	2X	B	6.1		66
3016	**BIPYRIDILIUM PESTICIDE, LIQUID, TOXIC,** packing groups II & III	2X		6.1		60
3017	**ORGANOPHOSPHORUS PESTICIDE, LIQUID, TOXIC, FLAMMABLE,** flash point not less than 23°C	•3W	A(fl)	6.1	3	663/63
3018	**ORGANOPHOSPHORUS PESTICIDE, LIQUID, TOXIC,** packing group I	2X	B	6.1		66
3018	**ORGANOPHOSPHORUS PESTICIDE, LIQUID, TOXIC,** packing groups II & III	2X		6.1		60
3019	**ORGANOTIN PESTICIDE, LIQUID, TOXIC, FLAMMABLE,** flash point not less than 23°C	•3W	A(fl)	6.1	3	663/63
3020	**ORGANOTIN PESTICIDE, LIQUID, TOXIC,** packing group I	2X	B	6.1		66
3020	**ORGANOTIN PESTICIDE, LIQUID, TOXIC,** packing groups II & III	2X		6.1		60

UN No	Substance	EAC	APP	Hazards Class	Sub Risks	HIN
3021	PESTICIDE, LIQUID, FLAMMABLE, TOXIC, N.O.S., flash point less than 23°C	●3WE	A(fl)	3	6.1	336
3022	1,2-BUTYLENE OXIDE, STABILIZED	●2YE		3		339
3023	2-METHYL-2-HEPTANETHIOL	3WE	A(fl)	6.1	3	663
3024	COUMARIN DERIVATIVE PESTICIDE, LIQUID, FLAMMABLE, TOXIC, flash point less than 23°C	●3WE	A(fl)	3	6.1	336
3025	COUMARIN DERIVATIVE PESTICIDE, LIQUID, TOXIC, FLAMMABLE, flash point not less than 23°C	●3W	A(fl)	6.1	3	663/63
3026	COUMARIN DERIVATIVE PESTICIDE, LIQUID, TOXIC, packing group I	2X	B	6.1		66
3026	COUMARIN DERIVATIVE PESTICIDE, LIQUID, TOXIC, packing groups II & III	2X		6.1		60
3027	COUMARIN DERIVATIVE PESTICIDE, SOLID, TOXIC	2X		6.1		66/60
3028	BATTERIES, DRY, CONTAINING POTASSIUM HYDROXIDE SOLID, electric storage	2X		8		80
3029 to 3047	UN Nos. no longer in use					
3048	ALUMINIUM PHOSPHIDE PESTICIDE	4W		6.1		642
3049 to 3053	UN Nos. no longer in use					
3054	CYCLOHEXYL MERCAPTAN	3WE		3		30
3055	2-(2-AMINOETHOXY)ETHANOL	2X		8		80
3056	n-HEPTALDEHYDE	3Y		3		30
3057	TRIFLUOROACETYL CHLORIDE	2XE	A(c)	2.3	8	268
3058 to 3063	UN Nos. no longer in use					
3064	NITROGLYCERIN, SOLUTION IN ALCOHOL with more than 1% but not more than 5% nitroglycerin	●2YE[1]		3		

(1) Not applicable to the carriage of dangerous goods under RID or ADR

UN No	Substance	EAC	APP	Hazards Class	Hazards Sub Risks	HIN
3065	**ALCOHOLIC BEVERAGES,** with more than 70% alcohol by volume	●2YE		3		33
3065	**ALCOHOLIC BEVERAGES,** with more than 24% but not more than 70% alcohol by volume	●2Y		3		30
3066	**PAINT** (including paint, lacquer, enamel, stain, shellac, varnish, polish, liquid filler and liquid lacquer base) or **PAINT RELATED MATERIAL** (including paint-thinning or reducing compound)	2X		8		80
3067 to 3069	UN Nos. no longer in use					
3070	**ETHYLENE OXIDE AND DICHLORODIFLUOROMETHANE MIXTURE** with not more than 12.5% ethylene oxide	2TE		2.2		20
3071	**MERCAPTANS, LIQUID, TOXIC, FLAMMABLE, N.O.S.** or **MERCAPTAN MIXTURE, LIQUID, TOXIC, FLAMMABLE, N.O.S.**	●3WE	A(fl)	6.1	3	63
3072	**LIFE-SAVING APPLIANCES NOT SELF-INFLATING** containing dangerous goods as equipment	2Z(1)		9		
3073	**VINYLPYRIDINES, STABILIZED**	●3W	A(fl)	6.1	3, 8	638
3074 to 3076	UN Nos. no longer in use					
3077	**ENVIRONMENTALLY HAZARDOUS SUBSTANCE, SOLID, N.O.S.**	2Z		9		90
3078	**CERIUM,** turnings or gritty powder	4W		4.3		423
3079	**METHACRYLONITRILE, STABILIZED**	●3WE	A(fl)	6.1	3	663
3080	**ISOCYANATES, TOXIC, FLAMMABLE, N.O.S.** or **ISOCYANATE SOLUTION, TOXIC, FLAMMABLE, N.O.S.**	●3W	A(fl)	6.1	3	63
3081	UN No. no longer in use					
3082	**ENVIRONMENTALLY HAZARDOUS SUBSTANCE, LIQUID, N.O.S.**	●3Z		9		90

UN No	Substance	EAC	APP	Hazards Class	Hazards Sub Risks	HIN
3083	PERCHLORYL FLUORIDE	2WE	A(co)	2.3	5.1	265
3084	CORROSIVE SOLID, OXIDISING, N.O.S.	2W		8	5.1	885/85
3085	OXIDISING SOLID, CORROSIVE, N.O.S., packing group I	1W(1)		5.1	8	
3085	OXIDISING SOLID, CORROSIVE, N.O.S., packing groups II & III	1W		5.1	8	58
3086	TOXIC SOLID, OXIDISING, N.O.S.	2W		6.1	5.1	665/65
3087	OXIDISING SOLID, TOXIC, N.O.S., packing group I	1W(1)		5.1	6.1	
3087	OXIDISING SOLID, TOXIC, N.O.S., packing groups II & III	1W		5.1	6.1	56
3088	SELF-HEATING SOLID, ORGANIC, N.O.S.	1Y		4.2		40
3089	METAL POWDER, FLAMMABLE, N.O.S.	4Y		4.1		40
3090	LITHIUM METAL BATTERIES (including lithium alloy batteries)	4W(1)		9		
3091	LITHIUM METAL BATTERIES CONTAINED IN EQUIPMENT or LITHIUM METAL BATTERIES PACKED WITH EQUIPMENT	4W(1)		9		
3092	1-METHOXY-2-PROPANOL	•2Y		3		30
3093	CORROSIVE LIQUID, OXIDISING, N.O.S., packing group I	2W	B	8	5.1	885
3093	CORROSIVE LIQUID, OXIDISING, N.O.S., packing group II	2W		8	5.1	85
3094	CORROSIVE LIQUID, WATER-REACTIVE, N.O.S.	4W		8	4.3	823
3095	CORROSIVE SOLID, SELF-HEATING, N.O.S.	2W		8	4.2	884/84
3096	CORROSIVE SOLID, WATER-REACTIVE, N.O.S.	4W		8	4.3	842
3097	FLAMMABLE SOLID, OXIDISING, N.O.S.	1Y(1)		4.1	5.1	
3098	OXIDISING LIQUID, CORROSIVE, N.O.S.	2W(1)		5.1	8	

(1) Not applicable to the carriage of dangerous goods under RID or ADR

UN No	Substance	EAC	APP	Hazards Class	Hazards Sub Risks	HIN
3099	OXIDISING LIQUID, TOXIC, N.O.S.	2W[(1)]		5.1	6.1	
3100	OXIDISING SOLID, SELF-HEATING, N.O.S.	1W[(1)]		5.1	4.2	
3101	ORGANIC PEROXIDE TYPE B, LIQUID	2WE[(1)]		5.2	1	
3102	ORGANIC PEROXIDE TYPE B, SOLID	1WE[(1)]		5.2	1	
3103	ORGANIC PEROXIDE TYPE C, LIQUID	2WE[(1)]		5.2		
3104	ORGANIC PEROXIDE TYPE C, SOLID	1WE[(1)]		5.2		
3105	ORGANIC PEROXIDE TYPE D, LIQUID	2WE[(1)]		5.2		
3106	ORGANIC PEROXIDE TYPE D, SOLID	1WE[(1)]		5.2		
3107	ORGANIC PEROXIDE TYPE E, LIQUID	2W[(1)]		5.2		
3108	ORGANIC PEROXIDE TYPE E, SOLID	1W[(1)]		5.2		
3109	ORGANIC PEROXIDE TYPE F, LIQUID	2W		5.2		539
3110	ORGANIC PEROXIDE TYPE F, SOLID	1W		5.2		539
3111	ORGANIC PEROXIDE TYPE B, LIQUID, TEMPERATURE CONTROLLED	2WE[(1)]		5.2	1	
3112	ORGANIC PEROXIDE TYPE B, SOLID, TEMPERATURE CONTROLLED	1WE[(1)]		5.2	1	
3113	ORGANIC PEROXIDE TYPE C, LIQUID, TEMPERATURE CONTROLLED	2WE[(1)]		5.2		
3114	ORGANIC PEROXIDE TYPE C, SOLID, TEMPERATURE CONTROLLED	1WE[(1)]		5.2		
3115	ORGANIC PEROXIDE TYPE D, LIQUID, TEMPERATURE CONTROLLED	2WE[(1)]		5.2		
3116	ORGANIC PEROXIDE TYPE D, SOLID, TEMPERATURE CONTROLLED	1WE[(1)]		5.2		
3117	ORGANIC PEROXIDE TYPE E, LIQUID, TEMPERATURE CONTROLLED	2W[(1)]		5.2		
3118	ORGANIC PEROXIDE TYPE E, SOLID, TEMPERATURE CONTROLLED	1W[(1)]		5.2		

(1) Not applicable to the carriage of dangerous goods under RID or ADR

UN No	Substance	EAC	APP	Hazards Class	Sub Risks	HIN
3119	ORGANIC PEROXIDE TYPE F, LIQUID, TEMPERATURE CONTROLLED	2W		5.2		539
3120	ORGANIC PEROXIDE TYPE F, SOLID, TEMPERATURE CONTROLLED	1W		5.2		539
3121	OXIDISING SOLID, WATER-REACTIVE, N.O.S.	4W(1)		5.1	4.3	
3122	TOXIC LIQUID, OXIDISING, N.O.S., packing group I	2WE	B	6.1	5.1	665
3122	TOXIC LIQUID, OXIDISING, N.O.S., packing group II	2WE		6.1	5.1	65
3123	TOXIC LIQUID, WATER-REACTIVE, N.O.S.	4W		6.1	4.3	623
3124	TOXIC SOLID, SELF-HEATING, N.O.S.	2W		6.1	4.2	664/64
3125	TOXIC SOLID, WATER-REACTIVE, N.O.S.	4W		6.1	4.3	642
3126	SELF-HEATING SOLID, CORROSIVE, ORGANIC, N.O.S.	1W		4.2	8	48
3127	SELF-HEATING SOLID, OXIDISING, N.O.S.	1W(1)		4.2	5.1	
3128	SELF-HEATING SOLID, TOXIC, ORGANIC, N.O.S.	1W		4.2	6.1	46
3129	WATER-REACTIVE LIQUID, CORROSIVE, N.O.S.	4W		4.3	8	X382/382
3130	WATER-REACTIVE LIQUID, TOXIC, N.O.S.	4W		4.3	6.1	X362/362
3131	WATER-REACTIVE SOLID, CORROSIVE, N.O.S.	4W		4.3	8	X482/482
3132	WATER-REACTIVE SOLID, FLAMMABLE, N.O.S., packing group I	4W(1)		4.3	4.1	
3132	WATER-REACTIVE SOLID, FLAMMABLE, N.O.S., packing groups II & III	4W		4.3	4.1	423
3133	WATER-REACTIVE SOLID, OXIDISING, N.O.S.	4W(1)		4.3	5.1	
3134	WATER-REACTIVE SOLID, TOXIC, N.O.S., packing group I	4W(1)		4.3	6.1	

(1) Not applicable to the carriage of dangerous goods under RID or ADR

UN No	Substance	EAC	APP	Hazards Class	Hazards Sub Risks	HIN
3134	WATER-REACTIVE SOLID, TOXIC, N.O.S., packing groups II & III	4W		4.3	6.1	462
3135	WATER-REACTIVE SOLID, SELF-HEATING, N.O.S., packing group I	4W[1]		4.3	4.2	
3135	WATER-REACTIVE SOLID, SELF-HEATING, N.O.S., packing groups II & III	4W		4.3	4.2	423
3136	TRIFLUOROMETHANE, REFRIGERATED LIQUID	2T		2.2		22
3137	OXIDISING SOLID, FLAMMABLE, N.O.S.	1W[1]		5.1	4.1	
3138	ETHYLENE, ACETYLENE AND PROPYLENE MIXTURE, REFRIGERATED LIQUID containing at least 71.5% ethylene with not more than 22.5% acetylene and not more than 6% propylene	2YE		2.1		223
3139	OXIDISING LIQUID, N.O.S.	2Y[1]		5.1		
3140	ALKALOIDS, LIQUID, N.O.S. or ALKALOID SALTS, LIQUID, N.O.S., packing group I	2X	B	6.1		66
3140	ALKALOIDS, LIQUID, N.O.S. or ALKALOID SALTS, LIQUID, N.O.S., packing groups II & III	2X		6.1		60
3141	ANTIMONY COMPOUND, INORGANIC, LIQUID, N.O.S.	2Z		6.1		60
3142	DISINFECTANT, LIQUID, TOXIC, N.O.S., packing group I	2X	B	6.1		66
3142	DISINFECTANT, LIQUID, TOXIC, N.O.S., packing groups II & III	2X		6.1		60
3143	DYE, SOLID, TOXIC, N.O.S. or DYE INTERMEDIATE, SOLID, TOXIC, N.O.S.	2X		6.1		66/60
3144	NICOTINE COMPOUND, LIQUID, N.O.S. or NICOTINE PREPARATION, LIQUID, N.O.S., packing group I	2X	B	6.1		66
3144	NICOTINE COMPOUND, LIQUID, N.O.S. or NICOTINE PREPARATION, LIQUID, N.O.S., packing groups II & III	2X		6.1		60

[1] Not applicable to the carriage of dangerous goods under RID or ADR

UN No	Substance	EAC	APP	Hazards Class	Hazards Sub Risks	HIN
3145	**ALKYLPHENOLS, LIQUID, N.O.S.** (including C2-C12 homologues), packing group I	2X	B	8		88
3145	**ALKYLPHENOLS, LIQUID, N.O.S.** (including C2-C12 homologues), packing groups II & III	2X		8		80
3146	**ORGANOTIN COMPOUND, SOLID, N.O.S.**	2X		6.1		66/60
3147	**DYE, SOLID, CORROSIVE, N.O.S.** or **DYE INTERMEDIATE, SOLID, CORROSIVE, N.O.S.**	2X		8		88/80
3148	**WATER-REACTIVE LIQUID, N.O.S.**	4W		4.3		X323/323
3149	**HYDROGEN PEROXIDE AND PEROXYACETIC ACID MIXTURE** with acid(s), water and not more than 5% peroxyacetic acid, **STABILIZED**	2P		5.1	8	58
3150	**DEVICES, SMALL, HYDROCARBON GAS POWERED** or **HYDROCARBON GAS REFILLS FOR SMALL DEVICES** with release device	2YE[1]		2.1		
3151	**POLYHALOGENATED BIPHENYLS, LIQUID** or **HALOGENATED MONOMETHYLDIPHENYLMETHANES, LIQUID** or **POLYHALOGENATED TERPHENYLS, LIQUID**	2X		9		90
3152	**POLYHALOGENATED BIPHENYLS, SOLID** or **HALOGENATED MONOMETHYLDIPHENYLMETHANES, SOLID** or **POLYHALOGENATED TERPHENYLS, SOLID**	2X		9		90
3153	**PERFLUORO (METHYL VINYL ETHER)**	2YE		2.1		23
3154	**PERFLUORO (ETHYL VINYL ETHER)**	2YE		2.1		23
3155	**PENTACHLOROPHENOL**	2X		6.1		60
3156	**COMPRESSED GAS, OXIDISING, N.O.S.**	2S		2.2	5.1	25
3157	**LIQUEFIED GAS, OXIDISING, N.O.S.**	2PE	A(co)	2.2	5.1	25
3158	**GAS, REFRIGERATED LIQUID, N.O.S.**	2TE		2.2		22

(1) Not applicable to the carriage of dangerous goods under RID or ADR

UN No	Substance	EAC	APP	Hazards Class	Sub Risks	HIN
3159	1,1,1,2-TETRAFLUOROETHANE (REFRIGERANT GAS R 134a)	2TE		2.2		20
3160	LIQUEFIED GAS, TOXIC, FLAMMABLE, N.O.S.	2WE	A(cf)	2.3	2.1	263
3161	LIQUEFIED GAS, FLAMMABLE, N.O.S.	2YE		2.1		23
3162	LIQUEFIED GAS, TOXIC, N.O.S.	2XE	A(c)	2.3		26
3163	LIQUEFIED GAS, N.O.S.	2TE		2.2		20
3164	ARTICLES, PRESSURISED, PNEUMATIC or HYDRAULIC (containing non-flammable gas)	2T[1]		2.2		
3165	AIRCRAFT HYDRAULIC POWER UNIT FUEL TANK (containing a mixture of anhydrous hydrazine and methylhydrazine) (M86 fuel)	●2WE[1]	A(fl)	3	6.1, 8	
3166	VEHICLE, FLAMMABLE GAS POWERED or VEHICLE, FLAMMABLE LIQUID POWERED or VEHICLE, FUEL CELL, FLAMMABLE GAS POWERED or VEHICLE, FUEL CELL, FLAMMABLE LIQUID POWERED	2YE[1]		9		
3167	GAS SAMPLE, NON-PRESSURISED, FLAMMABLE, N.O.S., not refrigerated liquid	2YE[1]		2.1		
3168	GAS SAMPLE, NON-PRESSURISED, TOXIC, FLAMMABLE, N.O.S., not refrigerated liquid	2WE[1]	A(fg)	2.3	2.1	
3169	GAS SAMPLE, NON-PRESSURISED, TOXIC, N.O.S., not refrigerated liquid	2XE[1]	B	2.3		
3170	ALUMINIUM SMELTING BY-PRODUCTS or ALUMINIUM REMELTING BY-PRODUCTS	4W		4.3		423
3171	BATTERY POWERED VEHICLE or BATTERY POWERED EQUIPMENT	4W[1]		9		
3172	TOXINS, EXTRACTED FROM LIVING SOURCES, LIQUID, N.O.S., packing group I	2X	B	6.1		66
3172	TOXINS, EXTRACTED FROM LIVING SOURCES, LIQUID, N.O.S., packing groups II & III	2X		6.1		60

(1) Not applicable to the carriage of dangerous goods under RID or ADR

UN No	Substance	EAC	APP	Hazards		HIN
				Class	Sub Risks	
3173	UN No. no longer in use					
3174	TITANIUM DISULPHIDE	1Y		4.2		40
3175	SOLIDS CONTAINING FLAMMABLE LIQUID, N.O.S.	1Z		4.1		40
3176	FLAMMABLE SOLID, ORGANIC, MOLTEN, N.O.S.	1Y		4.1		44
3177	UN No. no longer in use					
3178	FLAMMABLE SOLID, INORGANIC, N.O.S.	1Z		4.1		40
3179	FLAMMABLE SOLID, TOXIC, INORGANIC, N.O.S.	1X		4.1	6.1	46
3180	FLAMMABLE SOLID, CORROSIVE, INORGANIC, N.O.S.	1X		4.1	8	48
3181	METAL SALTS OF ORGANIC COMPOUNDS, FLAMMABLE, N.O.S.	1Z		4.1		40
3182	METAL HYDRIDES, FLAMMABLE, N.O.S.	1Z		4.1		40
3183	SELF-HEATING LIQUID, ORGANIC, N.O.S.	●3W		4.2		30
3184	SELF-HEATING LIQUID, TOXIC, ORGANIC, N.O.S.	●3W		4.2	6.1	36
3185	SELF-HEATING LIQUID, CORROSIVE, ORGANIC, N.O.S.	●3W		4.2	8	38
3186	SELF-HEATING LIQUID, INORGANIC, N.O.S.	●3W		4.2		30
3187	SELF-HEATING LIQUID, TOXIC, INORGANIC, N.O.S.	●3W		4.2	6.1	36
3188	SELF-HEATING LIQUID, CORROSIVE, INORGANIC, N.O.S.	●3W		4.2	8	38
3189	METAL POWDER, SELF-HEATING, N.O.S.	1Y		4.2		40
3190	SELF-HEATING SOLID, INORGANIC, N.O.S.	1Y		4.2		40
3191	SELF-HEATING SOLID, TOXIC, INORGANIC, N.O.S.	1W		4.2	6.1	46
3192	SELF-HEATING SOLID, CORROSIVE, INORGANIC, N.O.S.	1W		4.2	8	48

UN No	Substance	EAC	APP	Hazards Class	Hazards Sub Risks	HIN
3193	UN No. no longer in use					
3194	PYROPHORIC LIQUID, INORGANIC, N.O.S.	2W		4.2		333
3195 to 3199	UN Nos. no longer in use					
3200	PYROPHORIC SOLID, INORGANIC, N.O.S.	4W		4.2		43
3201 to 3204	UN Nos. no longer in use					
3205	ALKALINE EARTH METAL ALCOHOLATES, N.O.S.	1Y		4.2		40
3206	ALKALI METAL ALCOHOLATES, SELF-HEATING, CORROSIVE, N.O.S.	1W		4.2	8	48
3207	UN No. no longer in use					
3208	METALLIC SUBSTANCE, WATER-REACTIVE, N.O.S., packing group I	4W[(1)]		4.3		
3208	METALLIC SUBSTANCE, WATER-REACTIVE, N.O.S., packing groups II & III	4W		4.3		423
3209	METALLIC SUBSTANCE, WATER-REACTIVE, SELF-HEATING, N.O.S., packing group I	4W[(1)]		4.3	4.2	
3209	METALLIC SUBSTANCE, WATER-REACTIVE, SELF-HEATING, N.O.S., packing groups II & III	4W		4.3	4.2	423
3210	CHLORATES, INORGANIC, AQUEOUS SOLUTION, N.O.S.	2Y		5.1		50
3211	PERCHLORATES, INORGANIC, AQUEOUS SOLUTION, N.O.S.	2Y		5.1		50
3212	HYPOCHLORITES, INORGANIC, N.O.S.	1W		5.1		50
3213	BROMATES, INORGANIC, AQUEOUS SOLUTION, N.O.S.	2Y		5.1		50
3214	PERMANGANATES, INORGANIC, AQUEOUS SOLUTION, N.O.S.	2Y		5.1		50
3215	PERSULPHATES, INORGANIC, N.O.S.	1Z		5.1		50

(1) Not applicable to the carriage of dangerous goods under RID or ADR

UN No	Substance	EAC	APP	Hazards Class	Sub Risks	HIN
3216	PERSULPHATES, INORGANIC, AQUEOUS SOLUTION, N.O.S.	2Z		5.1		50
3217	UN No. no longer in use					
3218	NITRATES, INORGANIC, AQUEOUS SOLUTION, N.O.S.	2Y		5.1		50
3219	NITRITES, INORGANIC, AQUEOUS SOLUTION, N.O.S.	2Y		5.1		50
3220	PENTAFLUOROETHANE (REFRIGERANT GAS R 125)	2TE		2.2		20
3221	SELF-REACTIVE LIQUID TYPE B	2WE(1)		4.1	1	
3222	SELF-REACTIVE SOLID TYPE B	1WE(1)		4.1	1	
3223	SELF-REACTIVE LIQUID TYPE C	2WE(1)		4.1		
3224	SELF-REACTIVE SOLID TYPE C	1WE(1)		4.1		
3225	SELF-REACTIVE LIQUID TYPE D	2WE(1)		4.1		
3226	SELF-REACTIVE SOLID TYPE D	1WE(1)		4.1		
3227	SELF-REACTIVE LIQUID TYPE E	2W(1)		4.1		
3228	SELF-REACTIVE SOLID TYPE E	1W(1)		4.1		
3229	SELF-REACTIVE LIQUID TYPE F	2W		4.1		40
3230	SELF-REACTIVE SOLID TYPE F	1W		4.1		40
3231	SELF-REACTIVE LIQUID TYPE B, TEMPERATURE CONTROLLED	2WE(1)		4.1	1	
3232	SELF-REACTIVE SOLID TYPE B, TEMPERATURE CONTROLLED	1WE(1)		4.1	1	
3233	SELF-REACTIVE LIQUID TYPE C, TEMPERATURE CONTROLLED	2WE(1)		4.1		
3234	SELF-REACTIVE SOLID TYPE C, TEMPERATURE CONTROLLED	1WE(1)		4.1		
3235	SELF-REACTIVE LIQUID TYPE D, TEMPERATURE CONTROLLED	2WE(1)		4.1		
3236	SELF-REACTIVE SOLID TYPE D, TEMPERATURE CONTROLLED	1WE(1)		4.1		
3237	SELF-REACTIVE LIQUID TYPE E, TEMPERATURE CONTROLLED	2W(1)		4.1		
3238	SELF-REACTIVE SOLID TYPE E, TEMPERATURE CONTROLLED	1W(1)		4.1		

(1) Not applicable to the carriage of dangerous goods under RID or ADR

UN No	Substance	EAC	APP	Hazards Class	Sub Risks	HIN
3239	SELF-REACTIVE LIQUID TYPE F, TEMPERATURE CONTROLLED	2W		4.1		40
3240	SELF-REACTIVE SOLID TYPE F, TEMPERATURE CONTROLLED	1W		4.1		40
3241	2-BROMO-2-NITROPROPANE-1,3-DIOL	1Y(1)		4.1		
3242	AZODICARBONAMIDE	1Y		4.1		40
3243	SOLIDS CONTAINING TOXIC LIQUID, N.O.S.	2X		6.1		60
3244	SOLIDS CONTAINING CORROSIVE LIQUID, N.O.S.	2X		8		80
3245	GENETICALLY MODIFIED MICROORGANISMS or GENETICALLY MODIFIED ORGANISMS	2Z(1)		9		
3245	GENETICALLY MODIFIED MICROORGANISMS or GENETICALLY MODIFIED ORGANISMS, in refrigerated liquid nitrogen	2Z(1)		9	2.2	
3246	METHANESULPHONYL CHLORIDE	2XE	B	6.1	8	668
3247	SODIUM PEROXOBORATE, ANHYDROUS	1Y		5.1		50
3248	MEDICINE, LIQUID, FLAMMABLE, TOXIC, N.O.S., packing group II	●3WE	A(fl)	3	6.1	336
3248	MEDICINE, LIQUID, FLAMMABLE, TOXIC, N.O.S., packing group III	●3W	A(fl)	3	6.1	36
3249	MEDICINE, SOLID, TOXIC, N.O.S.	2X		6.1		60
3250	CHLOROACETIC ACID, MOLTEN	2W	A(h)	6.1	8	68
3251	ISOSORBIDE-5-MONONITRATE	1Y(1)		4.1		
3252	DIFLUOROMETHANE (REFRIGERANT GAS R 32)	2YE		2.1		23
3253	DISODIUM TRIOXOSILICATE	2X		8		80
3254	TRIBUTYLPHOSPHANE	3W		4.2		333
3255	tert-BUTYL HYPOCHLORITE	2WE(1)		4.2	8	

(1) Not applicable to the carriage of dangerous goods under RID or ADR

UN No	Substance	EAC	APP	Hazards Class	Sub Risks	HIN
3256	**ELEVATED TEMPERATURE LIQUID, FLAMMABLE, N.O.S.** with flash point above 60°C, at or above its flash point	2Y		3		30
3257	**ELEVATED TEMPERATURE LIQUID, N.O.S.,** at or above 100°C and below its flash point (including molten metals, molten salts, etc.), filled at a temperature higher than 190°C	2Y		9		99
3257	**ELEVATED TEMPERATURE LIQUID, N.O.S.,** at or above 100°C and below its flash point (including molten metals, molten salts, etc.), filled at or below 190°C	2Y		9		99
3258	**ELEVATED TEMPERATURE SOLID, N.O.S.,** at or above 240°C	1Y		9		99
3259	**AMINES, SOLID, CORROSIVE, N.O.S.** or **POLYAMINES, SOLID, CORROSIVE, N.O.S.**	2X		8		88/80
3260	**CORROSIVE SOLID, ACIDIC, INORGANIC, N.O.S.**	2X		8		88/80
3261	**CORROSIVE SOLID, ACIDIC, ORGANIC, N.O.S.**	2X		8		88/80
3262	**CORROSIVE SOLID, BASIC, INORGANIC, N.O.S.**	2X		8		88/80
3263	**CORROSIVE SOLID, BASIC, ORGANIC, N.O.S.**	2X		8		88/80
3264	**CORROSIVE LIQUID, ACIDIC, INORGANIC, N.O.S.,** packing group I	2X	B	8		88
3264	**CORROSIVE LIQUID, ACIDIC, INORGANIC, N.O.S.,** packing groups II & III	2X		8		80
3265	**CORROSIVE LIQUID, ACIDIC, ORGANIC, N.O.S.,** packing group I	2X	B	8		88
3265	**CORROSIVE LIQUID, ACIDIC, ORGANIC, N.O.S.,** packing groups II & III	2X		8		80
3266	**CORROSIVE LIQUID, BASIC, INORGANIC, N.O.S.,** packing group I	2X	B	8		88

UN No	Substance	EAC	APP	Hazards Class	Hazards Sub Risks	HIN
3266	**CORROSIVE LIQUID, BASIC, INORGANIC, N.O.S.,** packing groups II & III	2X		8		80
3267	**CORROSIVE LIQUID, BASIC, ORGANIC, N.O.S.,** packing group I	2X	B	8		88
3267	**CORROSIVE LIQUID, BASIC, ORGANIC, N.O.S.,** packing groups II & III	2X		8		80
3268	**SAFETY DEVICES,** electrically initiated	2Z[(1)]		9		
3269	**POLYESTER RESIN KIT,** liquid base material	●2YE[(1)]		3		
3270	**NITROCELLULOSE MEMBRANE FILTERS**	1Z[(1)]		4.1		
3271	**ETHERS, N.O.S.,** packing group II	3YE		3		33
3271	**ETHERS, N.O.S.,** packing group III	3Y		3		30
3272	**ESTERS, N.O.S.,** packing group II	●3YE		3		33
3272	**ESTERS, N.O.S.,** packing group III	●3Y		3		30
3273	**NITRILES, FLAMMABLE, TOXIC, N.O.S.**	3WE	A(fl)	3	6.1	336
3274	**ALCOHOLATES SOLUTION, N.O.S.,** in alcohol	●3WE	A(fl)	3	8	338
3275	**NITRILES, TOXIC, FLAMMABLE, N.O.S.**	3W	A(fl)	6.1	3	663/63
3276	**NITRILES, LIQUID, TOXIC, N.O.S.,** packing group I	2X	B	6.1		66
3276	**NITRILES, LIQUID, TOXIC, N.O.S.,** packing groups II & III	2X		6.1		60
3277	**CHLOROFORMATES, TOXIC, CORROSIVE, N.O.S.**	2X		6.1	8	68
3278	**ORGANOPHOSPHORUS COMPOUND, LIQUID, TOXIC, N.O.S.,** packing group I	2X	B	6.1		66
3278	**ORGANOPHOSPHORUS COMPOUND, LIQUID, TOXIC, N.O.S.,** packing groups II & III	2X		6.1		60
3279	**ORGANOPHOSPHORUS COMPOUND, TOXIC, FLAMMABLE, N.O.S.**	●3W	A(fl)	6.1	3	663/63

(1) Not applicable to the carriage of dangerous goods under RID or ADR

UN No	Substance	EAC	APP	Hazards Class	Sub Risks	HIN
3280	ORGANOARSENIC COMPOUND, LIQUID, N.O.S., packing group I	2X	B	6.1		66
3280	ORGANOARSENIC COMPOUND, LIQUID, N.O.S., packing groups II & III	2X		6.1		60
3281	METAL CARBONYLS, LIQUID, N.O.S., packing group I	2X	B	6.1		66
3281	METAL CARBONYLS, LIQUID, N.O.S., packing groups II & III	2X		6.1		60
3282	ORGANOMETALLIC COMPOUND, LIQUID, TOXIC, N.O.S., packing group I	2X	B	6.1		66
3282	ORGANOMETALLIC COMPOUND, LIQUID, TOXIC, N.O.S., packing groups II & III	2X		6.1		60
3283	SELENIUM COMPOUND, SOLID, N.O.S.	2X		6.1		66/60
3284	TELLURIUM COMPOUND, N.O.S.	2X		6.1		66/60
3285	VANADIUM COMPOUND, N.O.S.	2X		6.1		66/60
3286	FLAMMABLE LIQUID, TOXIC, CORROSIVE, N.O.S.	•3WE	A(fl)	3	6.1, 8	368
3287	TOXIC LIQUID, INORGANIC, N.O.S., packing group I	2X	B	6.1		66
3287	TOXIC LIQUID, INORGANIC, N.O.S., packing groups II & III	2X		6.1		60
3288	TOXIC SOLID, INORGANIC, N.O.S.	2X		6.1		66/60
3289	TOXIC LIQUID, CORROSIVE, INORGANIC, N.O.S., packing group I	2X	B	6.1	8	668
3289	TOXIC LIQUID, CORROSIVE, INORGANIC, N.O.S., packing group II	2X		6.1	8	68
3290	TOXIC SOLID, CORROSIVE, INORGANIC, N.O.S.	2X		6.1	8	668/68
3291	CLINICAL WASTE, UNSPECIFIED, N.O.S. or (BIO) MEDICAL WASTE, N.O.S. or REGULATED MEDICAL WASTE, N.O.S.	2X		6.2		606

UN No	Substance	EAC	APP	Hazards Class	Hazards Sub Risks	HIN
3291	**CLINICAL WASTE, UNSPECIFIED, N.O.S.** or **(BIO) MEDICAL WASTE, N.O.S.** or **REGULATED MEDICAL WASTE, N.O.S.**, in refrigerated liquid nitrogen	2X⁽¹⁾	A(c)	6.2	2.2	
3292	**BATTERIES, CONTAINING SODIUM,** or **CELLS, CONTAINING SODIUM**	4W⁽¹⁾		4.3		
3293	**HYDRAZINE, AQUEOUS SOLUTION** with not more than 37% hydrazine, by mass	•2X		6.1		60
3294	**HYDROGEN CYANIDE, SOLUTION IN ALCOHOL** with not more than 45% hydrogen cyanide	•2WE	A(fl)	6.1	3	663
3295	**HYDROCARBONS, LIQUID, N.O.S.,** packing groups I & II	3YE		3		33
3295	**HYDROCARBONS, LIQUID, N.O.S.,** packing group III	3Y		3		30
3296	**HEPTAFLUOROPROPANE (REFRIGERANT GAS R 227)**	2T		2.2		20
3297	**ETHYLENE OXIDE AND CHLOROTETRAFLUOROETHANE MIXTURE** with not more than 8.8% ethylene oxide	2TE		2.2		20
3298	**ETHYLENE OXIDE AND PENTAFLUOROETHANE MIXTURE** with not more than 7.9% ethylene oxide	2TE		2.2		20
3299	**ETHYLENE OXIDE AND TETRAFLUOROETHANE MIXTURE** with not more than 5.6% ethylene oxide	2TE		2.2		20
3300	**ETHYLENE OXIDE AND CARBON DIOXIDE MIXTURE** with more than 87% ethylene oxide	2PE	A(cf)	2.3	2.1	263
3301	**CORROSIVE LIQUID, SELF-HEATING, N.O.S.,** packing group I	2W	B	8	4.2	884
3301	**CORROSIVE LIQUID, SELF-HEATING, N.O.S.,** packing group II	2W		8	4.2	84
3302	**2-DIMETHYLAMINOETHYL ACRYLATE**	2X		6.1		60

(1) Not applicable to the carriage of dangerous goods under RID or ADR

UN No	Substance	EAC	APP	Hazards Class	Hazards Sub Risks	HIN
3303	COMPRESSED GAS, TOXIC, OXIDISING, N.O.S.	2PE	B	2.3	5.1	265
3304	COMPRESSED GAS, TOXIC, CORROSIVE, N.O.S.	2RE	B	2.3	8	268
3305	COMPRESSED GAS, TOXIC, FLAMMABLE, CORROSIVE, N.O.S.	2PE	A(fg)	2.3	2.1, 8	263
3306	COMPRESSED GAS, TOXIC, OXIDISING, CORROSIVE, N.O.S.	2PE	B	2.3	5.1, 8	265
3307	LIQUEFIED GAS, TOXIC, OXIDISING, N.O.S.	2WE	A(co)	2.3	5.1	265
3308	LIQUEFIED GAS, TOXIC, CORROSIVE, N.O.S.	2XE	A(c)	2.3	8	268
3309	LIQUEFIED GAS, TOXIC, FLAMMABLE, CORROSIVE, N.O.S.	2WE	A(cf)	2.3	2.1, 8	263
3310	LIQUEFIED GAS, TOXIC, OXIDISING, CORROSIVE, N.O.S.	2WE	A(co)	2.3	5.1, 8	265
3311	GAS, REFRIGERATED LIQUID, OXIDISING, N.O.S.	2PE	A(co)	2.2	5.1	225
3312	GAS, REFRIGERATED LIQUID, FLAMMABLE, N.O.S.	2YE		2.1		223
3313	ORGANIC PIGMENTS, SELF-HEATING	1Y		4.2		40
3314	PLASTICS MOULDING COMPOUND in dough, sheet or extruded rope form, evolving flammable vapour	2Y[(1)]		9		90
3315	CHEMICAL SAMPLE, TOXIC	2X[(1)]	B	6.1		
3316	CHEMICAL KIT or FIRST AID KIT	2Z[(1)]		9		
3317	2-AMINO-4,6-DINITROPHENOL, WETTED with not less than 20% water, by mass	1W[(1)]		4.1		
3318	AMMONIA SOLUTION, relative density less than 0.880 at 15°C in water, with more than 50% ammonia	2XE	B	2.3	8	268
3319	NITROGLYCERIN MIXTURE, DESENSITIZED, SOLID, N.O.S. with more than 2% but not more than 10% nitroglycerin, by mass	1Y[(1)]		4.1		

(1) Not applicable to the carriage of dangerous goods under RID or ADR

UN No	Substance	EAC	APP	Hazards		HIN
				Class	Sub Risks	
3320	**SODIUM BOROHYDRIDE AND SODIUM HYDROXIDE SOLUTION,** with not more than 12% sodium borohydride and not more than 40% sodium hydroxide by mass	2X		8		80
3321	**RADIOACTIVE MATERIAL, LOW SPECIFIC ACTIVITY (LSA-II),** non-fissile or fissile-excepted	(2)		7		70
3322	**RADIOACTIVE MATERIAL, LOW SPECIFIC ACTIVITY (LSA-III),** non-fissile or fissile-excepted	(2)		7		70
3323	**RADIOACTIVE MATERIAL, TYPE C PACKAGE,** non-fissile or fissile-excepted	(2)		7		70
3324	**RADIOACTIVE MATERIAL, LOW SPECIFIC ACTIVITY (LSA-II), FISSILE**	(2)		7		70
3325	**RADIOACTIVE MATERIAL, LOW SPECIFIC ACTIVITY, (LSA-III), FISSILE**	(2)		7		70
3326	**RADIOACTIVE MATERIAL, SURFACE CONTAMINATED OBJECTS (SCO-I or SCO-II), FISSILE**	(2)		7		70
3327	**RADIOACTIVE MATERIAL, TYPE A PACKAGE, FISSILE,** non-special form	(2)		7		70
3328	**RADIOACTIVE MATERIAL, TYPE B(U) PACKAGE, FISSILE**	(2)		7		70
3329	**RADIOACTIVE MATERIAL, TYPE B(M) PACKAGE, FISSILE**	(2)		7		70
3330	**RADIOACTIVE MATERIAL, TYPE C PACKAGE, FISSILE**	(2)		7		70
3331	**RADIOACTIVE MATERIAL, TRANSPORTED UNDER SPECIAL ARRANGEMENT, FISSILE**	(2)		7		70
3332	**RADIOACTIVE MATERIAL, TYPE A PACKAGE, SPECIAL FORM,** non-fissile or fissile excepted	(2)		7		70
3333	**RADIOACTIVE MATERIAL, TYPE A PACKAGE, SPECIAL FORM, FISSILE**	(2)		7		70
3334	**AVIATION REGULATED LIQUID, N.O.S.**	2Z(1)		9		

(1) Not applicable to the carriage of dangerous goods under RID or ADR (2) Radioactive material

UN No	Substance	EAC	APP	Hazards Class	Hazards Sub Risks	HIN
3335	**AVIATION REGULATED SOLID, N.O.S.**	2Z⁽¹⁾		9		
3336	**MERCAPTANS, LIQUID, FLAMMABLE, N.O.S.** or **MERCAPTAN MIXTURE, LIQUID, FLAMMABLE, N.O.S.**	3WE	A(fl)	3		33/30
3337	**REFRIGERANT GAS R 404A**	2TE		2.2		20
3338	**REFRIGERANT GAS R 407A**	2TE		2.2		20
3339	**REFRIGERANT GAS R 407B**	2TE		2.2		20
3340	**REFRIGERANT GAS R 407C**	2TE		2.2		20
3341	**THIOUREA DIOXIDE**	1Y		4.2		40
3342	**XANTHATES**	1Y		4.2		40
3343	**NITROGLYCERIN MIXTURE, DESENSITIZED, LIQUID, FLAMMABLE, N.O.S.** with not more than 30% nitroglycerin, by mass	●2Y⁽¹⁾		3		
3344	**PENTAERYTHRITE TETRANITRATE (PENTAERYTHRITOL TETRANITRATE; PETN) MIXTURE, DESENSITIZED, SOLID, N.O.S.** with more than 10% but not more than 20% PETN, by mass	1Y⁽¹⁾		4.1		
3345	**PHENOXYACETIC ACID DERIVATIVE PESTICIDE, SOLID, TOXIC**	2X		6.1		66/60
3346	**PHENOXYACETIC ACID DERIVATIVE PESTICIDE, LIQUID, FLAMMABLE, TOXIC,** flash point less than 23°C	●3WE	A(fl)	3	6.1	336
3347	**PHENOXYACETIC ACID DERIVATIVE PESTICIDE, LIQUID, TOXIC, FLAMMABLE,** flash point not less than 23°C	●3W	A(fl)	6.1	3	663/63
3348	**PHENOXYACETIC ACID DERIVATIVE PESTICIDE, LIQUID, TOXIC,** packing group I	2X	B	6.1		66
3348	**PHENOXYACETIC ACID DERIVATIVE PESTICIDE, LIQUID, TOXIC,** packing groups II & III	2X		6.1		60
3349	**PYRETHROID PESTICIDE, SOLID, TOXIC**	2X		6.1		66/60

(1) Not applicable to the carriage of dangerous goods under RID or ADR

UN No	Substance	EAC	APP	Hazards Class	Hazards Sub Risks	HIN
3350	**PYRETHROID PESTICIDE, LIQUID, FLAMMABLE, TOXIC,** flash point less than 23°C	●3WE	A(fl)	3	6.1	336
3351	**PYRETHROID PESTICIDE, LIQUID, TOXIC, FLAMMABLE,** flash point not less than 23°C	●3W	A(fl)	6.1	3	663/63
3352	**PYRETHROID PESTICIDE, LIQUID, TOXIC,** packing group I	2X	B	6.1		66
3352	**PYRETHROID PESTICIDE, LIQUID, TOXIC,** packing groups II & III	2X		6.1		60
3353	UN No. no longer in use					
3354	**INSECTICIDE GAS, FLAMMABLE, N.O.S.**	2YE		2.1		23
3355	**INSECTICIDE GAS, TOXIC, FLAMMABLE, N.O.S.**	2WE	A(cf)	2.3	2.1	263
3356	**OXYGEN GENERATOR, CHEMICAL**	1Y[(1)]		5.1		
3357	**NITROGLYCERIN MIXTURE, DESENSITIZED, LIQUID, N.O.S.** with not more than 30% nitroglycerin, by mass	●2Y[(1)]		3		
3358	**REFRIGERATING MACHINES** containing flammable, non-toxic, liquefied gas	2YE[(1)]		2.1		
3359	**FUMIGATED CARGO TRANSPORT UNIT**	2Z[(1)]		9		
3360	**FIBRES, VEGETABLE, DRY**	1Z[(1)]		4.1		
3361	**CHLOROSILANES, TOXIC, CORROSIVE, N.O.S.**	4W	B	6.1	8	68
3362	**CHLOROSILANES, TOXIC, CORROSIVE, FLAMMABLE, N.O.S.**	4WE	A(fl)	6.1	3, 8	638
3363	**DANGEROUS GOODS IN MACHINERY** or **DANGEROUS GOODS IN APPARATUS**	1Z[(1)]		9		
3364	**TRINITROPHENOL (PICRIC ACID), WETTED,** with not less than 10% water by mass	1W[(1)]		4.1		
3365	**TRINITROCHLOROBENZENE (PICRYL CHLORIDE), WETTED,** with not less than 10% water by mass	1W[(1)]		4.1		

(1) Not applicable to the carriage of dangerous goods under RID or ADR

UN No	Substance	EAC	APP	Hazards Class	Sub Risks	HIN
3366	TRINITROTOLUENE (TNT), WETTED, with not less than 10% water by mass	1W(1)		4.1		
3367	TRINITROBENZENE, WETTED, with not less than 10% water by mass	1W(1)		4.1		
3368	TRINITROBENZOIC ACID, WETTED, with not less than 10% water by mass	1W(1)		4.1		
3369	SODIUM DINITRO-o-CRESOLATE, WETTED, with not less than 10% water by mass	1W(1)		4.1	6.1	
3370	UREA NITRATE, WETTED, with not less than 10% water by mass	1W(1)		4.1		
3371	2-METHYLBUTANAL	3YE		3		33
3372	UN No. no longer in use					
3373	BIOLOGICAL SUBSTANCE, CATEGORY B	2X		6.2		606
3374	ACETYLENE, SOLVENT FREE	2SE(1)		2.1		
3375	AMMONIUM NITRATE EMULSION or SUSPENSION or GEL, intermediate for blasting explosives	1Y		5.1		50
3376	4-NITROPHENYLHYDRAZINE, with not less than 30% water, by mass	1W(1)		4.1		
3377	SODIUM PERBORATE MONOHYDRATE	1Z		5.1		50
3378	SODIUM CARBONATE PEROXYHYDRATE	1Y		5.1		50
3379	DESENSITIZED EXPLOSIVE, LIQUID, N.O.S.	●3YE(1)		3		
3380	DESENSITIZED EXPLOSIVE, SOLID, N.O.S.	1W(1)		4.1		
3381	TOXIC BY INHALATION LIQUID, N.O.S. with an LC_{50} lower than or equal to 200ml/m^3 and saturated vapour concentration greater than or equal to 500 LC_{50}	2XE	B	6.1		66
3382	TOXIC BY INHALATION LIQUID, N.O.S. with an LC_{50} lower than or equal to 1000ml/m^3 and saturated vapour concentration greater than or equal to 10 LC_{50}	2XE	B	6.1		66

(1) Not applicable to the carriage of dangerous goods under RID or ADR

UN No	Substance	EAC	APP	Hazards Class	Hazards Sub Risks	HIN
3383	**TOXIC BY INHALATION LIQUID, FLAMMABLE, N.O.S.** with an LC_{50} lower than or equal to 200ml/m³ and saturated vapour concentration greater than or equal to 500 LC_{50}	●3WE	A(fl)	6.1	3	663
3384	**TOXIC BY INHALATION LIQUID, FLAMMABLE, N.O.S.** with an LC_{50} lower than or equal to 1000ml/m³ and saturated vapour concentration greater than or equal to 10 LC_{50}	●3WE	A(fl)	6.1	3	663
3385	**TOXIC BY INHALATION LIQUID, WATER-REACTIVE, N.O.S.** with an LC_{50} lower than or equal to 200ml/m³ and saturated vapour concentration greater than or equal to 500 LC_{50}	4WE	B	6.1	4.3	623
3386	**TOXIC BY INHALATION LIQUID, WATER-REACTIVE, N.O.S.** with an LC_{50} lower than or equal to 1000ml/m³ and saturated vapour concentration greater than or equal to 10 LC_{50}	4WE	B	6.1	4.3	623
3387	**TOXIC BY INHALATION LIQUID, OXIDISING, N.O.S.** with an LC_{50} lower than or equal to 200ml/m³ and saturated vapour concentration greater than or equal to 500 LC_{50}	2WE	B	6.1	5.1	665
3388	**TOXIC BY INHALATION LIQUID, OXIDISING, N.O.S.** with an LC_{50} lower than or equal to 1000ml/m³ and saturated vapour concentration greater than or equal to 10 LC_{50}	2WE	B	6.1	5.1	665
3389	**TOXIC BY INHALATION LIQUID, CORROSIVE, N.O.S.** with an LC_{50} lower than or equal to 200ml/m³ and saturated vapour concentration greater than or equal to 500 LC_{50}	2XE	B	6.1	8	668
3390	**TOXIC BY INHALATION LIQUID, CORROSIVE, N.O.S.** with an LC_{50} lower than or equal to 1000ml/m³ and saturated vapour concentration greater than or equal to 10 LC_{50}	2XE	B	6.1	8	668
3391	**ORGANOMETALLIC SUBSTANCE, SOLID, PYROPHORIC**	4Y		4.2		43
3392	**ORGANOMETALLIC SUBSTANCE, LIQUID, PYROPHORIC**	4Y		4.2		333

UN No	Substance	EAC	APP	Hazards Class	Sub Risks	HIN
3393	ORGANOMETALLIC SUBSTANCE, SOLID, PYROPHORIC, WATER-REACTIVE	4W		4.2	4.3	X432
3394	ORGANOMETALLIC SUBSTANCE, LIQUID, PYROPHORIC, WATER-REACTIVE	4W		4.2	4.3	X333
3395	ORGANOMETALLIC SUBSTANCE, SOLID, WATER-REACTIVE	4W		4.3		X423/ 423
3396	ORGANOMETALLIC SUBSTANCE, SOLID, WATER-REACTIVE, FLAMMABLE	4W		4.3	4.1	X423/ 423
3397	ORGANOMETALLIC SUBSTANCE, SOLID, WATER-REACTIVE, SELF-HEATING	4W		4.3	4.2	X423/ 423
3398	ORGANOMETALLIC SUBSTANCE, LIQUID, WATER-REACTIVE	4W		4.3		X323/ 323
3399	ORGANOMETALLIC SUBSTANCE, LIQUID, WATER-REACTIVE, FLAMMABLE	4W	A(fl)	4.3	3	X323/ 323
3400	ORGANOMETALLIC SUBSTANCE, SOLID, SELF-HEATING	2Y		4.2		40
3401	ALKALI METAL AMALGAM, SOLID	4W		4.3		X423
3402	ALKALINE EARTH METAL AMALGAM, SOLID	4W		4.3		X423
3403	POTASSIUM METAL ALLOYS, SOLID	4W		4.3		X423
3404	POTASSIUM SODIUM ALLOYS, SOLID	4W		4.3		X423
3405	BARIUM CHLORATE SOLUTION	2Y		5.1	6.1	56
3406	BARIUM PERCHLORATE SOLUTION	2Y		5.1	6.1	56
3407	CHLORATE AND MAGNESIUM CHLORIDE MIXTURE SOLUTION	2Y		5.1		50
3408	LEAD PERCHLORATE SOLUTION	2Y		5.1	6.1	56
3409	CHLORONITROBENZENES, LIQUID	2X		6.1		60
3410	4-CHLORO-o-TOLUIDINE HYDROCHLORIDE SOLUTION	2X		6.1		60
3411	beta-NAPHTHYLAMINE SOLUTION	2Z		6.1		60

UN No	Substance	EAC	APP	Hazards Class	Hazards Sub Risks	HIN
3412	**FORMIC ACID** with not less than 10% but not more than 85% acid by mass	•2X		8		80
3412	**FORMIC ACID** with not less than 5% but less than 10% acid by mass	2X		8		80
3413	**POTASSIUM CYANIDE SOLUTION,** packing group I	2X	B	6.1		66
3413	**POTASSIUM CYANIDE SOLUTION,** packing groups II & III	2X		6.1		60
3414	**SODIUM CYANIDE SOLUTION,** packing group I	2X	B	6.1		66
3414	**SODIUM CYANIDE SOLUTION,** packing groups II & III	2X		6.1		60
3415	**SODIUM FLUORIDE SOLUTION**	2Z		6.1		60
3416	**CHLOROACETOPHENONE, LIQUID**	2Z		6.1		60
3417	**XYLYL BROMIDE, SOLID**	2X		6.1		60
3418	**2,4-TOLUYLENEDIAMINE SOLUTION**	2X		6.1		60
3419	**BORON TRIFLUORIDE ACETIC ACID COMPLEX, SOLID**	2X		8		80
3420	**BORON TRIFLUORIDE PROPIONIC ACID COMPLEX, SOLID**	2X		8		80
3421	**POTASSIUM HYDROGEN DIFLUORIDE SOLUTION**	2X		8	6.1	86
3422	**POTASSIUM FLUORIDE SOLUTION**	2X		6.1		60
3423	**TETRAMETHYLAMMONIUM HYDROXIDE, SOLID**	2X		8		80
3424	**AMMONIUM DINITRO-o-CRESOLATE, SOLUTION**	2X		6.1		60
3425	**BROMOACETIC ACID, SOLID**	2X		8		80
3426	**ACRYLAMIDE SOLUTION**	2X		6.1		60
3427	**CHLOROBENZYL CHLORIDES, SOLID**	2X		6.1		60
3428	**3-CHLORO-4-METHYLPHENYL ISOCYANATE, SOLID**	2X		6.1		60
3429	**CHLOROTOLUIDINES, LIQUID**	2X		6.1		60
3430	**XYLENOLS, LIQUID**	2X		6.1		60

UN No	Substance	EAC	APP	Hazards Class	Sub Risks	HIN
3431	NITROBENZOTRIFLUORIDES, SOLID	2X		6.1		60
3432	POLYCHLORINATED BIPHENYLS, SOLID	2X		9		90
3433	UN No. no longer in use					
3434	NITROCRESOLS, LIQUID	2X		6.1		60
3435	UN No. no longer in use					
3436	HEXAFLUOROACETONE HYDRATE, SOLID	2X		6.1		60
3437	CHLOROCRESOLS, SOLID	2Z		6.1		60
3438	alpha-METHYLBENZYL ALCOHOL, SOLID	2Z		6.1		60
3439	NITRILES, SOLID, TOXIC, N.O.S.	2X		6.1		66/60
3440	SELENIUM COMPOUND, LIQUID, N.O.S., packing group I	2X	B	6.1		66
3440	SELENIUM COMPOUND, LIQUID, N.O.S., packing groups II & III	2X		6.1		60
3441	CHLORODINITROBENZENES, SOLID	2X		6.1		60
3442	DICHLOROANILINES, SOLID	2X		6.1		60
3443	DINITROBENZENES, SOLID	2X		6.1		60
3444	NICOTINE HYDROCHLORIDE, SOLID	2X		6.1		60
3445	NICOTINE SULPHATE, SOLID	2X		6.1		60
3446	NITROTOLUENES, SOLID	2X		6.1		60
3447	NITROXYLENES, SOLID	2X		6.1		60
3448	TEAR GAS SUBSTANCE, SOLID, N.O.S.	2X		6.1		66/60
3449	BROMOBENZYL CYANIDES, SOLID	2X		6.1		66
3450	DIPHENYLCHLOROARSINE, SOLID	2X		6.1		66
3451	TOLUIDINES, SOLID	2X		6.1		60
3452	XYLIDINES, SOLID	2X		6.1		60
3453	PHOSPHORIC ACID, SOLID	2X		8		80
3454	DINITROTOLUENES, SOLID	2X		6.1		60
3455	CRESOLS, SOLID	2X		6.1	8	68
3456	NITROSYLSULPHURIC ACID, SOLID	2X		8		X80

UN No	Substance	EAC	APP	Hazards Class	Hazards Sub Risks	HIN
3457	**CHLORONITROTOLUENES, SOLID**	2X		6.1		60
3458	**NITROANISOLES, SOLID**	2Z		6.1		60
3459	**NITROBROMOBENZENES, SOLID**	2X		6.1		60
3460	**N-ETHYLBENZYLTOLUIDINES, SOLID**	2X		6.1		60
3461	UN No. no longer in use					
3462	**TOXINS, EXTRACTED FROM LIVING SOURCES, SOLID, N.O.S.**	2X		6.1		66/60
3463	**PROPIONIC ACID** with not less than 90% acid by mass	●2W	A(fl)	8	3	83
3464	**ORGANOPHOSPHORUS COMPOUND, SOLID, TOXIC, N.O.S.**	2X		6.1		66/60
3465	**ORGANOARSENIC COMPOUND, SOLID, N.O.S.**	2X		6.1		66/60
3466	**METAL CARBONYLS, SOLID, N.O.S.**	2X		6.1		66/60
3467	**ORGANOMETALLIC COMPOUND, SOLID, TOXIC, N.O.S.**	2X		6.1		66/60
3468	**HYDROGEN IN A METAL HYDRIDE STORAGE SYSTEM** or **HYDROGEN IN A METAL HYDRIDE STORAGE SYSTEM CONTAINED IN EQUIPMENT** or **HYDROGEN IN A METAL HYDRIDE STORAGE SYSTEM PACKED WITH EQUIPMENT**	2SE[1]		2.1		
3469	**PAINT, FLAMMABLE, CORROSIVE** (including paint, lacquer, enamel, stain, shellac, varnish, polish, liquid filler and liquid lacquer base) or **PAINT RELATED MATERIAL, FLAMMABLE, CORROSIVE** (including paint thinning or reducing compound), packing groups I & II	●3WE	A(fl)	3	8	338
3469	**PAINT, FLAMMABLE, CORROSIVE** (including paint, lacquer, enamel, stain, shellac, varnish, polish, liquid filler and liquid lacquer base) or **PAINT RELATED MATERIAL, FLAMMABLE, CORROSIVE** (including paint thinning or reducing compound), packing group III	●3W	A(fl)	3	8	38

[1] Not applicable to the carriage of dangerous goods under RID or ADR

UN No	Substance	EAC	APP	Hazards Class	Sub Risks	HIN
3470	**PAINT, CORROSIVE, FLAMMABLE** (including paint, lacquer, enamel, stain, shellac, varnish, polish, liquid filler and liquid lacquer base) or **PAINT RELATED MATERIAL, CORROSIVE, FLAMMABLE** (including paint thinning or reducing compound)	●3W	A(fl)	8	3	83
3471	**HYDROGENDIFLUORIDES SOLUTION, N.O.S.**	2X		8	6.1	86
3472	**CROTONIC ACID, LIQUID**	●2X		8		80
3473	**FUEL CELL CARTRIDGES** or **FUEL CELL CARTRIDGES CONTAINED IN EQUIPMENT** or **FUEL CELL CARTRIDGES PACKED WITH EQUIPMENT,** containing flammable liquids	●2WE[(1)]	A(fl)	3		
3474	**1-HYDROXYBENZOTRIAZOLE MONOHYDRATE**	1W[(1)]		4.1		
3475	**ETHANOL AND GASOLINE MIXTURE** or **ETHANOL AND MOTOR SPIRIT MIXTURE** or **ETHANOL AND PETROL MIXTURE,** with more than 10% ethanol	●3YE		3		33
3476	**FUEL CELL CARTRIDGES** or **FUEL CELL CARTRIDGES CONTAINED IN EQUIPMENT** or **FUEL CELL CARTRIDGES PACKED WITH EQUIPMENT,** containing water-reactive substances	4W[(1)]		4.3		
3477	**FUEL CELL CARTRIDGES** or **FUEL CELL CARTRIDGES CONTAINED IN EQUIPMENT** or **FUEL CELL CARTRIDGES PACKED WITH EQUIPMENT,** containing corrosive substances	2X[(1)]		8		
3478	**FUEL CELL CARTRIDGES** or **FUEL CELL CARTRIDGES CONTAINED IN EQUIPMENT** or **FUEL CELL CARTRIDGES PACKED WITH EQUIPMENT,** containing liquefied flammable gas	2Y[(1)]		2.1		

[(1)] Not applicable to the carriage of dangerous goods under RID or ADR

UN No	Substance	EAC	APP	Hazards Class	Sub Risks	HIN
3479	**FUEL CELL CARTRIDGES** or **FUEL CELL CARTRIDGES CONTAINED IN EQUIPMENT** or **FUEL CELL CARTRIDGES PACKED WITH EQUIPMENT,** containing hydrogen in metal hydride	2W[(1)]		2.1		
3480	**LITHIUM ION BATTERIES** (including lithium ion polymer batteries)	4W[(1)]		9		
3481	**LITHIUM ION BATTERIES CONTAINED IN EQUIPMENT** or **LITHIUM ION BATTERIES PACKED WITH EQUIPMENT** (including lithium ion polymer batteries)	4W[(1)]		9		
3482	**ALKALI METAL DISPERSION, FLAMMABLE** or **ALKALINE EARTH METAL DISPERSION, FLAMMABLE**	4WE	A(fl)	4.3	3	X323
3483	**MOTOR FUEL ANTI-KNOCK MIXTURE, FLAMMABLE**	●3WE	A(fl)	6.1	3	663
3484	**HYDRAZINE AQUEOUS SOLUTION, FLAMMABLE** with more than 37% hydrazine, by mass	●2X	A(fl)	8	3, 6.1	886
3485	**CALCIUM HYPOCHLORITE, DRY, CORROSIVE** or **CALCIUM HYPOCHLORITE MIXTURE, DRY, CORROSIVE** with more than 39% available chlorine (8.8% available oxygen)	1W		5.1	8	58
3486	**CALCIUM HYPOCHLORITE MIXTURE, DRY, CORROSIVE** with more than 10% but not more than 39% available chlorine	1W		5.1	8	58
3487	**CALCIUM HYPOCHLORITE, HYDRATED, CORROSIVE** or **CALCIUM HYPOCHLORITE, HYDRATED MIXTURE, CORROSIVE** with not less than 5.5% but not more than 16% water	1W		5.1	8	58
3488	**TOXIC BY INHALATION LIQUID, FLAMMABLE, CORROSIVE, N.O.S.** with an LC_{50} lower than or equal to 200 ml/m³ and saturated vapour concentration greater than or equal to 500 LC_{50}	2WE	A(fl)	6.1	3, 8	663

(1) Not applicable to the carriage of dangerous goods under RID or ADR

UN No	Substance	EAC	APP	Hazards Class	Sub Risks	HIN
3489	**TOXIC BY INHALATION LIQUID, FLAMMABLE, CORROSIVE, N.O.S.** with an LC_{50} lower than or equal to 1000 ml/m³ and saturated vapour concentration greater than or equal to 10 LC_{50}	2WE	A(fl)	6.1	3, 8	663
3490	**TOXIC BY INHALATION LIQUID, WATER-REACTIVE, FLAMMABLE, N.O.S.** with an LC_{50} lower than or equal to 200 ml/m³ and saturated vapour concentration greater than or equal to 500 LC_{50}	4WE	A(fl)	6.1	3, 4.3	623
3491	**TOXIC BY INHALATION LIQUID, WATER-REACTIVE, FLAMMABLE, N.O.S.** with an LC_{50} lower than or equal to 1000 ml/m³ and saturated vapour concentration greater than or equal to 10 LC_{50}	4WE	A(fl)	6.1	3, 4.3	623
3492	**TOXIC BY INHALATION LIQUID, CORROSIVE, FLAMMABLE, N.O.S.** with an LC_{50} lower than or equal to 200 ml/m³ and saturated vapour concentration greater than or equal to 500 LC_{50}	2WE	A(fl)	6.1	8, 3	668
3493	**TOXIC BY INHALATION LIQUID, CORROSIVE, FLAMMABLE, N.O.S.** with an LC_{50} lower than or equal to 1000 ml/m³ and saturated vapour concentration greater than or equal to 10 LC_{50}	2WE	A(fl)	6.1	8, 3	668
3494	**PETROLEUM SOUR CRUDE OIL, FLAMMABLE, TOXIC,** packing groups I & II	●3WE	A(fl)	3	6.1	336
3494	**PETROLEUM SOUR CRUDE OIL, FLAMMABLE, TOXIC,** packing group III	●3W	A(fl)	3	6.1	36
3495	**IODINE**	2WE		8	6.1	86
3496	**BATTERIES, NICKEL-METAL HYDRIDE**	2Y[1]		9		
3497	**KRILL MEAL**	1Y		4.2		40
3498	**IODINE MONOCHLORIDE, LIQUID**	2X		8		80
3499	**CAPACITOR, ELECTRIC DOUBLE LAYER** (with an energy storage capacity greater than 0.3Wh)	1Z[1]		9		

[1] Not applicable to the carriage of dangerous goods under RID or ADR

UN No	Substance	EAC	APP	Hazards Class	Hazards Sub Risks	HIN
3500	CHEMICAL UNDER PRESSURE, N.O.S.	2ZE		2.2		20
3501	CHEMICAL UNDER PRESSURE, FLAMMABLE, N.O.S.	2YE		2.1		23
3502	CHEMICAL UNDER PRESSURE, TOXIC, N.O.S.	2XE	B	2.2	6.1	26
3503	CHEMICAL UNDER PRESSURE, CORROSIVE, N.O.S.	2XE	B	2.2	8	28
3504	CHEMICAL UNDER PRESSURE, FLAMMABLE, TOXIC, N.O.S.	2WE	A(fg)	2.1	6.1	263
3505	CHEMICAL UNDER PRESSURE, FLAMMABLE, CORROSIVE, N.O.S.	2WE	A(fg)	2.1	8	238
3506	MERCURY CONTAINED IN MANUFACTURED ARTICLES	2X[1]		8	6.1	
3507	URANIUM HEXAFLUORIDE, RADIOACTIVE MATERIAL, EXCEPTED PACKAGE, less than 0.1 kg per package, non-fissile or fissile-excepted	[2]		6.1	7, 8	
3508	CAPACITOR, ASYMMETRIC (with an energy storage capacity greater than 0.3Wh)	1Z[1]		9		
3509	PACKAGINGS, DISCARDED, EMPTY, UNCLEANED	2Z		9		90
3510	ADSORBED GAS, FLAMMABLE, N.O.S.	2SE[1]		2.1		
3511	ADSORBED GAS, N.O.S.	2TE[1]		2.2		
3512	ADSORBED GAS, TOXIC, N.O.S.	2RE[1]	B	2.3		
3513	ADSORBED GAS, OXIDIZING, N.O.S.	2S[1]		2.2	5.1	
3514	ADSORBED GAS, TOXIC, FLAMMABLE, N.O.S.	2PE[1]	A(fg)	2.3	2.1	
3515	ADSORBED GAS, TOXIC, OXIDIZING, N.O.S.	2PE[1]	B	2.3	5.1	
3516	ADSORBED GAS, TOXIC, CORROSIVE, N.O.S.	2RE[1]	B	2.3	8	
3517	ADSORBED GAS, TOXIC, FLAMMABLE, CORROSIVE, N.O.S.	2PE[1]	A(fg)	2.3	2.1, 8	
3518	ADSORBED GAS, TOXIC, OXIDIZING, CORROSIVE, N.O.S.	2PE[1]	B	2.3	5.1, 8	

(1) Not applicable to the carriage of dangerous goods under RID or ADR   (2) Radioactive material

UN No	Substance	EAC	APP	Hazards Class	Hazards Sub Risks	HIN
3519	BORON TRIFLUORIDE, ADSORBED	2RE[(1)]	B	2.3	8	
3520	CHLORINE, ADSORBED	2XE[(1)]	B	2.3	5.1, 8	
3521	SILICON TETRAFLUORIDE, ADSORBED	2PE[(1)]	B	2.3	8	
3522	ARSINE, ADSORBED	2PE[(1)]	A(fg)	2.3	2.1	
3523	GERMANE, ADSORBED	2PE[(1)]	A(fg)	2.3	2.1	
3524	PHOSPHORUS PENTAFLUORIDE, ADSORBED	2RE[(1)]	B	2.3	8	
3525	PHOSPHINE, ADSORBED	2PE[(1)]	A(fg)	2.3	2.1	
3526	HYDROGEN SELENIDE, ADSORBED	2WE[(1)]	A(fg)	2.3	2.1	
3527	POLYESTER RESIN KIT, solid base material	1W[(1)]		4.1		
3528	ENGINE, INTERNAL COMBUSTION, FLAMMABLE LIQUID POWERED or ENGINE, FUEL CELL, FLAMMABLE LIQUID POWERED or MACHINERY, INTERNAL COMBUSTION, FLAMMABLE LIQUID POWERED or MACHINERY, FUEL CELL, FLAMMABLE LIQUID POWERED	2YE[(1)]		3		
3529	ENGINE, INTERNAL COMBUSTION, FLAMMABLE GAS POWERED or ENGINE, FUEL CELL, FLAMMABLE GAS POWERED or MACHINERY, INTERNAL COMBUSTION, FLAMMABLE GAS POWERED or MACHINERY, FUEL CELL, FLAMMABLE GAS POWERED	2YE[(1)]		2.1		
3530	ENGINE, INTERNAL COMBUSTION or MACHINERY, INTERNAL COMBUSTION	2Y[(1)]		9		
3531	POLYMERIZING SUBSTANCE, SOLID, STABILIZED, N.O.S.	1W		4.1		40
3532	POLYMERIZING SUBSTANCE, LIQUID, STABILIZED, N.O.S.	2W		4.1		40
3533	POLYMERIZING SUBSTANCE, SOLID, TEMPERATURE CONTROLLED, N.O.S.	1W		4.1		40
3534	POLYMERIZING SUBSTANCE, LIQUID, TEMPERATURE CONTROLLED, N.O.S.	2W		4.1		40

(1) Not applicable to the carriage of dangerous goods under RID or ADR   (2) Radioactive material

Section 5

Alphabetical List of Dangerous Goods

Substance	UN No
Accumulators, electric, see	2794
	2795
	2800
	3028
	3292
ACETAL	1088
ACETALDEHYDE	1089
ACETALDEHYDE AMMONIA	1841
ACETALDEHYDE OXIME	2332
ACETIC ACID, GLACIAL	2789
ACETIC ACID SOLUTION, more than 80% acid, by mass	2789
ACETIC ACID SOLUTION, more than 10% but not more than 80% acid, by mass	2790
ACETIC ANHYDRIDE	1715
Acetoin, see	2621
ACETONE	1090
ACETONE CYANOHYDRIN, STABILIZED	1541
ACETONE OILS	1091
ACETONITRILE	1648
ACETYL BROMIDE	1716
ACETYL CHLORIDE	1717
ACETYLENE, DISSOLVED	1001
ACETYLENE, SOVLENT FREE	3374
Acetylene tetrabromide, see	2504
Acetylene tetrachloride, see	1702
ACETYL IODIDE	1898
ACETYL METHYL CARBINOL	2621
Acid butyl phosphate, see	1718
Acid mixtures, hydrofluoric and sulphuric, see	1786
Acid mixtures, nitrating acid, see	1796
Acid mixtures, spent, nitrating acid, see	1826
Acraldehyde, inhibited, see	1092

Substance	UN No
ACRIDINE	2713
ACROLEIN DIMER, STABILIZED	2607
ACROLEIN, STABILIZED	1092
ACRYLAMIDE, SOLID	2074
ACRYLAMIDE SOLUTION	3426
ACRYLIC ACID, STABILIZED	2218
ACRYLONITRILE, STABILIZED	1093
Actinolite, see	2212
Activated carbon, see	1362
Activated charcoal, see	1362
ADHESIVES, containing flammable liquid	1133
ADIPONITRILE	2205
ADSORBED GAS, FLAMMABLE, N.O.S.	3510
ADSORBED GAS, N.O.S.	3511
ADSORBED GAS, OXIDIZING, N.O.S.	3513
ADSORBED GAS, TOXIC, CORROSIVE, N.O.S.	3516
ADSORBED GAS, TOXIC, FLAMMABLE, CORROSIVE, N.O.S.	3517
ADSORBED GAS, TOXIC, FLAMMABLE, N.O.S.	3514
ADSORBED GAS, TOXIC, N.O.S.	3512
ADSORBED GAS, TOXIC, OXIDIZING, CORROSIVE, N.O.S.	3518
ADSORBED GAS, TOXIC, OXIDIZING, N.O.S.	3515
AEROSOLS	1950
AIR, COMPRESSED	1002
Air bag inflators, see	3268
Air bag modules, see	3268
Aircraft evacuation slides, see	2990

ALPHABETICAL LIST OF DANGEROUS GOODS

Substance	UN No
AIRCRAFT HYDRAULIC POWER UNIT FUEL TANK (containing a mixture of anhydrous hydrazine and methylhydrazine) (M86 fuel)	3165
Aircraft survival kits, see	2990
AIR, REFRIGERATED LIQUID	1003
ALCOHOLATES SOLUTIONS, N.O.S., in alcohol	3274
Alcohol, denatured, see	1986 1987
Alcohol, industrial, see	1986 1987
ALCOHOLS, N.O.S.	1987
ALCOHOLS, FLAMMABLE, TOXIC, N.O.S.	1986
ALCOHOLIC BEVERAGES	3065
Aldehyde, see	1989
ALDEHYDES, N.O.S.	1989
ALDEHYDES, FLAMMABLE, TOXIC, N.O.S.	1988
ALDOL	2839
ALKALI METAL ALCOHOLATES, SELF-HEATING, CORROSIVE, N.O.S.	3206
ALKALI METAL ALLOY, LIQUID, N.O.S.	1421
ALKALI METAL AMALGAM, LIQUID	1389
ALKALI METAL AMALGAM, SOLID	3401
ALKALI METAL AMIDES	1390
ALKALI METAL DISPERSION	1391
ALKALI METAL DISPERSION, FLAMMABLE	3482
Alkaline corrosive battery fluid, see	2797
ALKALINE EARTH METAL ALCOHOLATES, N.O.S.	3205
ALKALINE EARTH METAL ALLOY, N.O.S.	1393

Substance	UN No
ALKALINE EARTH METAL AMALGAM, LIQUID	1392
ALKALINE EARTH METAL AMALGAM, SOLID	3402
ALKALINE EARTH METAL DISPERSION	1391
ALKALINE EARTH METAL DISPERSION, FLAMMABLE	3482
ALKALOIDS, LIQUID, N.O.S.	3140
ALKALOIDS, SOLID, N.O.S.	1544
ALKALOID SALTS, LIQUID, N.O.S.	3140
ALKALOID SALTS, SOLID, N.O.S.	1544
Alkyl aluminium halides, see	3394
ALKYLPHENOLS, LIQUID, N.O.S. (including C2-C12 homologues)	3145
ALKYLPHENOLS, SOLID, N.O.S. (including C2-C12 homologues)	2430
ALKYL SULPHONIC ACIDS, LIQUID, with more than 5% free sulphuric acid	2584
ALKYL SULPHONIC ACIDS, LIQUID, with not more than 5% free sulphuric acid	2586
ALKYL SULPHONIC ACIDS, SOLID, with more than 5% free sulphuric acid	2583
ALKYL SULPHONIC ACIDS, SOLID, with not more than 5% sulphuric acid	2585
ALKYL SULPHURIC ACIDS	2571
Allene, see	2200
ALLYL ACETATE	2333
ALLYL ALCOHOL	1098
ALLYLAMINE	2334
ALLYL BROMIDE	1099
ALLYL CHLORIDE	1100
Allyl chlorocarbonate, see	1722
ALLYL CHLOROFORMATE	1722

Substance	UN No
ALLYL ETHYL ETHER	2335
ALLYL FORMATE	2336
ALLYL GLYCIDYL ETHER	2219
ALLYL IODIDE	1723
ALLYL ISOTHIOCYANATE, STABILIZED	1545
ALLYLTRICHLOROSILANE, STABILIZED	1724
Aluminium alkyl halides, liquid, see	3394
Aluminium alkyl halides, solid, see	3393
Aluminium alkyl hydrides, see	3394
Aluminium alkyls, see	3394
ALUMINIUM BOROHYDRIDE	2870
ALUMINIUM BOROHYDRIDE IN DEVICES	2870
ALUMINIUM BROMIDE, ANHYDROUS	1725
ALUMINIUM BROMIDE SOLUTION	2580
ALUMINIUM CARBIDE	1394
ALUMINIUM CHLORIDE, ANHYDROUS	1726
ALUMINIUM CHLORIDE SOLUTION	2581
Aluminium dross, see	3170
ALUMINIUM FERROSILICON POWDER	1395
ALUMINIUM HYDRIDE	2463
ALUMINIUM NITRATE	1438
ALUMINIUM PHOSPHIDE	1397
ALUMINIUM PHOSPHIDE PESTICIDE	3048
ALUMINIUM POWDER, COATED	1309
ALUMINIUM POWDER, UNCOATED	1396
ALUMINIUM REMELTING BY-PRODUCTS	3170

Substance	UN No
ALUMINIUM RESINATE	2715
ALUMINIUM SILICON POWDER, UNCOATED	1398
ALUMINIUM SMELTING BY-PRODUCTS	3170
AMINES, FLAMMABLE, CORROSIVE, N.O.S.	2733
AMINES, LIQUID, CORROSIVE, N.O.S.	2735
AMINES, LIQUID, CORROSIVE, FLAMMABLE, N.O.S.	2734
AMINES, SOLID, CORROSIVE, N.O.S.	3259
Aminobenzene, see	1547
2-Aminobenzotrifluoride, see	2942
3-Aminobenzotrifluoride, see	2948
Aminobutane, see	1125
2-AMINO-4-CHLOROPHENOL	2673
2-AMINO-5-DIETHYLAMINO-PENTANE	2946
2-AMINO-4,6-DINITROPHENOL, WETTED with not less than 20% water by mass	3317
2-(2-AMINOETHOXY) ETHANOL	3055
N-AMINOETHYLPIPERAZINE	2815
1-Amino-2-nitrobenzene, see	1661
1-Amino-3-nitrobenzene, see	1661
1-Amino-4-nitrobenzene, see	1661
AMINOPHENOLS (o-,m-,p-)	2512
AMINOPYRIDINES (o-,m-,p-)	2671
AMMONIA, ANHYDROUS	1005
AMMONIA SOLUTION, relative density (specific gravity) between 0.880 and 0.957 at 15°C in water, with more than 10% and not more than 35% ammonia	2672

Substance	UN No
AMMONIA SOLUTION, relative density (specific gravity) less than 0.880 at 15°C in water, with more than 35% and not more than 50% ammonia	2073
AMMONIA SOLUTION, relative density (specific gravity) less than 0.880 at 15°C in water, with more than 50% ammonia	3318
AMMONIUM ARSENATE	1546
Ammonium bichromate, see	1439
Ammonium bifluoride solid, see	1727
Ammonium bifluoride solution, see	2817
Ammonium bisulphate, see	2506
Ammonium bisulphite solution, see	2693
AMMONIUM DICHROMATE	1439
AMMONIUM DINITRO-o-CRESOLATE, SOLID	1843
AMMONIUM DINITRO-o-CRESOLATE, SOLUTION	3424
AMMONIUM FLUORIDE	2505
AMMONIUM FLUOROSILICATE	2854
Ammonium hexafluorosilicate, see	2854
AMMONIUMHYDROGEN DIFLUORIDE, SOLID	1727
AMMONIUMHYDROGEN DIFLUORIDE SOLUTION	2817
AMMONIUM HYDROGEN SULPHATE	2506
Ammonium hydrosulphide solution (treat as ammonium sulphide solution), see	2683
AMMONIUM METAVANDATE	2859
AMMONIUM NITRATE, with not more than 0.2% total combustible substances, including any organic substance calculated as carbon, to the exclusion of any other added substance	1942
AMMONIUM NITRATE BASED FERTILIZER	2067

Substance	UN No
AMMONIUM NITRATE EMULSION, intermediate for blasting explosives	3375
AMMONIUM NITRATE GEL, intermediate for blasting explosives	3375
AMMONIUM NITRATE LIQUID (hot concentrated solution)	2426
AMMONIUM NITRATE SUSPENSION, intermediate for blasting explosives	3375
AMMONIUM PERCHLORATE	1442
Ammonium permanganate, see	1482
AMMONIUM PERSULPHATE	1444
AMMONIUM PICRATE, WETTED, with not less than 10% water by mass	1310
AMMONIUM POLYSULPHIDE SOLUTION	2818
AMMONIUM POLYVANADATE	2861
Ammonium silicofluoride, see	2854
AMMONIUM SULPHIDE SOLUTION	2683
Ammunition, lachrymatory, see	2017
AMMUNITION, TEAR-PRODUCING, NON-EXPLOSIVE without burster or expelling charge, non-fused	2017
AMMUNITION, TOXIC, NON-EXPLOSIVE without burster or expelling charge, non-fused	2016
Amosite, see	2212
Amphibole asbestos, see	2212
AMYL ACETATES	1104
AMYL ACID PHOSPHATE	2819
Amyl aldehyde, see	2058
AMYLAMINE	1106
AMYL BUTYRATES	2620
AMYL CHLORIDE	1107
n-**AMYLENE,** see	1108

Substance	UN No
AMYL FORMATES	1109
AMYL MERCAPTAN	1111
n-AMYL METHYL KETONE	1110
AMYL NITRATE	1112
AMYL NITRITE	1113
AMYLTRICHLOROSILANE	1728
Anaesthetic ether, see	1155
ANILINE	1547
Aniline chloride, see	1548
ANILINE HYDROCHLORIDE	1548
Aniline oil, see	1547
Aniline salt, see	1548
ANISIDINES	2431
ANISOLE	2222
ANISOYL CHLORIDE	1729
Anthophyllite, see	2212
Antimonous chloride, see	1733
ANTIMONY COMPOUND, INORGANIC, LIQUID, N.O.S.	3141
ANTIMONY COMPOUND, INORGANIC, SOLID, N.O.S.	1549
Antimony hydride, see	2676
ANTIMONY LACTATE	1550
Antimony (III) lactate, see	1550
ANTIMONY PENTACHLORIDE, LIQUID	1730
ANTIMONY PENTACHLORIDE, SOLUTION	1731
ANTIMONY PENTAFLUORIDE	1732
Antimony perchloride, liquid, see	1730
ANTIMONY POTASSIUM TARTRATE	1551
ANTIMONY POWDER	2871
ANTIMONY TRICHLORIDE	1733
A.n.t.u., see	1651

Substance	UN No
ARGON, COMPRESSED	1006
ARGON, REFRIGERATED LIQUID	1951
Arsenates, liquid, n.o.s., see	1556
Arsenates, solid, n.o.s., see	1557
ARSENIC	1558
ARSENIC ACID, LIQUID	1553
ARSENIC ACID, SOLID	1554
ARSENICAL DUST	1562
Arsenical flue dust, see	1562
ARSENICAL PESTICIDE, LIQUID, FLAMMABLE, TOXIC, flash point less than 23°C	2760
ARSENICAL PESTICIDE, LIQUID, TOXIC, FLAMMABLE, flash point 23°C or above	2993
ARSENICAL PESTICIDE, LIQUID, TOXIC	2994
ARSENICAL PESTICIDE, SOLID, TOXIC	2759
ARSENIC BROMIDE	1555
Arsenic (III) bromide, see	1555
Arsenic chloride, see	1560
ARSENIC COMPOUND, LIQUID, N.O.S., inorganic, including: Arsenates, n.o.s.; Arsenites, n.o.s.; Arsenic sulphides, n.o.s.	1556
ARSENIC COMPOUND, SOLID, N.O.S., inorganic, including Arsenates, n.o.s.; Arsenites, n.o.s.; Arsenic sulphides, n.o.s.	1557
Arsenic (III) oxide, see	1561
Arsenic (V) oxide, see	1559
ARSENIC PENTOXIDE	1559
Arsenic sulphides, see	1556 1557
ARSENIC TRICHLORIDE	1560
ARSENIC TRIOXIDE	1561
Arsenious chloride, see	1560

Substance	UN No
Arsenites, n.o.s., liquid, see	1556
Arsenites, n.o.s., solid, see	1557
Arsenous chloride, see	1560
ARSINE	2188
ARSINE, ADSORBED	3522
ARTICLES PRESSURISED, HYDRAULIC (containing non-flammable gas)	3164
ARTICLES PRESSURISED, PNEUMATIC (containing non-flammable gas)	3164
ARYLSULPHONIC ACIDS, LIQUID, with more than 5% free sulphuric acid	2584
ARYLSULPHONIC ACIDS, LIQUID, with not more than 5% free sulphuric acid	2586
ARYLSULPHONIC ACIDS, SOLID, with more than 5% free sulphuric acid	2583
ARYLSULPHONIC ACIDS, SOLID, with not more than 5% free sulphuric acid	2585
ASBESTOS, AMPHIBOLE (amosite, tremolite, actinolite, anthophyllite, crocidolite)	2212
ASBESTOS, CHRYSOTILE	2590
Asphalt, see	1999 3256 3257
AVIATION REGULATED LIQUID, N.O.S.	3334
AVIATION REGULATED SOLID, N.O.S.	3335
AZODICARBONAMIDE	3242
BARIUM	1400
BARIUM ALLOYS, PYROPHORIC	1854
BARIUM AZIDE, WETTED, with not less than 50% water by mass	1571
Barium binoxide, see	1449
BARIUM BROMATE	2719

Substance	UN No
BARIUM CHLORATE, SOLID	1445
BARIUM CHLORATE SOLUTION	3405
BARIUM COMPOUND, N.O.S.	1564
BARIUM CYANIDE	1565
Barium dioxide, see	1449
BARIUM HYPOCHLORITE, with more than 22% available chlorine	2741
BARIUM NITRATE	1446
BARIUM OXIDE	1884
BARIUM PERCHLORATE, SOLID	1447
BARIUM PERCHLORATE SOLUTION	3406
BARIUM PERMANGANATE	1448
BARIUM PEROXIDE	1449
Barium selenate, see	2630
Barium selenite, see	2630
Barium superoxide, see	1449
BATTERIES, CONTAINING SODIUM	3292
BATTERIES, DRY, CONTAINING POTASSIUM HYDROXIDE SOLID, electric, storage	3028
BATTERIES, NICKEL-METAL HYDRIDE	3496
BATTERIES, WET, FILLED WITH ACID, electric, storage	2794
BATTERIES, WET, FILLED WITH ALKALI, electric, storage	2795
BATTERIES, WET, NON-SPILLABLE, electric, storage	2800
BATTERY FLUID, ACID	2796
BATTERY FLUID, ALKALI	2797
BATTERY POWERED EQUIPMENT	3171
BATTERY POWERED VEHICLE	3171
BENZALDEHYDE	1990
BENZENE	1114
BENZENESULPHONYL CHLORIDE	2225

Substance	UN No
Benzenethiol, see	2337
BENZIDINE	1885
Benzole, see	1114
Benzolene, see	1268
BENZONITRILE	2224
BENZOQUINONE	2587
Benzosulphochloride, see	2225
BENZOTRICHLORIDE	2226
BENZOTRIFLUORIDE	2338
BENZOYL CHLORIDE	1736
BENZYL BROMIDE	1737
BENZYL CHLORIDE	1738
Benzyl chlorocarbonate, see	1739
BENZYL CHLOROFORMATE	1739
Benzyl cyanide, see	2470
BENZYLDIMETHYLAMINE	2619
BENZYLIDENE CHLORIDE	1886
BENZYL IODIDE	2653
BERYLLIUM COMPOUND, N.O.S.	1566
BERYLLIUM NITRATE	2464
BERYLLIUM POWDER	1567
BHUSA	1327
BICYCLO[2.2.1]HEPTA-2,5-DIENE, STABILIZED	2251
Biflourides, n.o.s., see	1740
BIOLOGICAL SUBSTANCE, CATEGORY B	3373
(BIO) MEDICAL WASTE, N.O.S.	3291
BIPYRIDILIUM PESTICIDE, LIQUID, FLAMMABLE, TOXIC, flash point less than 23°C	2782
BIPYRIDILIUM PESTICIDE, LIQUID, TOXIC, FLAMMABLE, flash point 23°C or above	3015
BIPYRIDILIUM PESTICIDE, LIQUID, TOXIC	3016

Substance	UN No
BIPYRIDILIUM PESTICIDE, SOLID, TOXIC	2781
BISULPHATES, AQUEOUS SOLUTION	2837
BISULPHITES, AQUEOUS SOLUTION, N.O.S.	2693
Bitumen, see	1999 3256 3257
Bleaching powder, see	2208
BOMBS, SMOKE, NON-EXPLOSIVE, with corrosive liquid, without initiating device	2028
Borate and chlorate mixture, see	1458
BORNEOL	1312
BORON TRIBROMIDE	2692
BORON TRICHLORIDE	1741
BORON TRIFLUORIDE	1008
BORON TRIFLUORIDE ACETIC ACID COMPLEX, LIQUID	1742
BORON TRIFLUORIDE ACETIC ACID COMPLEX, SOLID	3419
BORON TRIFLUORIDE, ADSORBED	3519
BORON TRIFLUORIDE DIETHYL ETHERATE	2604
BORON TRIFLUORIDE DIMETHYL ETHERATE	2965
BORON TRIFLUORIDE DIHYDRATE	2851
BORON TRIFLUORIDE PROPIONIC ACID COMPLEX, LIQUID	1743
BORON TRIFLUORIDE PROPIONIC ACID COMPLEX, SOLID	3420
BROMATES, INORGANIC, N.O.S.	1450
BROMATES, INORGANIC, AQUEOUS SOLUTION, N.O.S.	3213
BROMINE	1744
BROMINE CHLORIDE	2901

Substance	UN No
BROMINE PENTAFLUORIDE	1745
BROMINE SOLUTION	1744
BROMINE TRIFLUORIDE	1746
BROMOACETIC ACID, SOLID	3425
BROMOACETIC ACID SOLUTION	1938
BROMOACETONE	1569
omega-Bromoacetophenone, see	2645
BROMOACETYL BROMIDE	2513
BROMOBENZENE	2514
BROMOBENZYL CYANIDES, LIQUID	1694
BROMOBENZYL CYANIDES, SOLID	3449
1-BROMOBUTANE	1126
2-BROMOBUTANE	2339
BROMOCHLOROMETHANE	1887
1-BROMO-3-CHLOROPROPANE	2688
1-Bromo-2,3-epoxypropane, see	2558
Bromoethane, see	1891
2-BROMOETHYL ETHYL ETHER	2340
BROMOFORM	2515
Bromomethane, see	1062
1-BROMO-3-METHYLBUTANE	2341
BROMOMETHYLPROPANES	2342
2-BROMO-2-NITROPROPANE-1,3-DIOL	3241
2-BROMOPENTANE	2343
BROMOPROPANES	2344
3-BROMOPROPYNE	2345
BROMOTRIFLUOROETHYLENE	2419
BROMOTRIFLUOROMETHANE	1009
BRUCINE	1570
BUTADIENES, STABILIZED	1010

Substance	UN No
BUTADIENES AND HYDROCARBON MIXTURE, STABILIZED	1010
BUTANE	1011
BUTANEDIONE	2346
Butane-1-thiol, see	2347
Butan-2-ol, see	1120
BUTANOLS	1120
1-Butanol, see	1120
Butanol, secondary, see	1120
Butanol, tertiary, see	1120
Butanone, see	1193
2-Butenal, see	1143
Butene, see	1012
But-1-ene-3-one, see	1251
1,2-Buteneoxide, see	3022
2-Buten-1-ol, see	2614
BUTYL ACETATES	1123
Butyl acetate, secondary, see	1123
BUTYL ACID PHOSPHATE	1718
BUTYL ACRYLATES, STABILIZED	2348
Butyl alcohols, see	1120
n-BUTYLAMINE	1125
N-BUTYLANILINE	2738
BUTYLBENZENES	2709
sec-Butyl benzene, see	2709
n-Butyl bromide, see	1126
n-Butyl chloride, see	1127
n-BUTYL CHLOROFORMATE	2743
tert-BUTYLCYCLOHEXYL CHLOROFORMATE	2747
1- BUTYLENE	1012
cis-2-BUTYLENE	1012
BUTYLENES	1012

Substance	UN No
1,2-BUTYLENE OXIDE, STABILIZED	3022
Butyl ethers, see	1149
Butyl ethyl ether, see	1179
n-BUTYL FORMATE	1128
tert-BUTYL HYPOCHLORITE	3255
N,n-BUTYLIMIDAZOLE	2690
N,n-Butyliminazole, see	2690
n-BUTYL ISOCYANATE	2485
tert-BUTYL ISOCYANATE	2484
Butyl lithium, see	3394
BUTYL MERCAPTAN	2347
n-BUTYL METHACRYLATE, STABILIZED	2227
BUTYL METHYL ETHER	2350
BUTYL NITRITES	2351
Butylphenols, liquid, see	3145
Butylphenols, solid, see	2430
BUTYL PROPIONATES	1914
p-tert-Butyltoluene, see	2667
BUTYLTOLUENES	2667
BUTYLTRICHLOROSILANE	1747
5-tert-BUTYL-2,4,6-TRINITRO-m-XYLENE	2956
BUTYL VINYL ETHER, STABILIZED	2352
But-1-yne, see	2452
1,4-BUTYNEDIOL	2716
2-Butyne-1, 4-diol, see	2716
BUTYRALDEHYDE	1129
BUTYRALDOXIME	2840
BUTYRIC ACID	2820
BUTYRIC ANHYDRIDE	2739
Butyrone, see	2710

Substance	UN No
BUTYRONITRILE	2411
Butyroyl chloride, see	2353
BUTYRYL CHLORIDE	2353
CACODYLIC ACID	1572
CADMIUM COMPOUND	2570
CAESIUM	1407
CAESIUM HYDROXIDE	2682
CAESIUM HYDROXIDE SOLUTION	2681
CAESIUM NITRATE	1451
Caffeine, see	1544
Cajeputene, see	2052
CALCIUM	1401
CALCIUM ALLOYS, PYROPHORIC	1855
CALCIUM ARSENATE	1573
CALCIUM ARSENATE AND CALCIUM ARSENITE, MIXTURE, SOLID	1574
Calcium bisulphite solutions, see	2693
CALCIUM CARBIDE	1402
CALCIUM CHLORATE	1452
CALCIUM CHLORATE, AQUEOUS SOLUTION	2429
CALCIUM CHLORITE	1453
CALCIUM CYANAMIDE, with more than 0.1% calcium carbide	1403
CALCIUM CYANIDE	1575
CALCIUM DITHIONITE	1923
CALCIUM HYDRIDE	1404
Calcium hydrosulphite, see	1923
CALCIUM HYPOCHLORITE, DRY or CALCIUM HYPOCHLORITE MIXTURE, DRY, with more than 39% available chlorine (8.8% available oxygen)	1748

Substance	UN No
CALCIUM HYPOCHLORITE, DRY, CORROSIVE or **CALCIUM HYPOCHLORITE MIXTURE, DRY, CORROSIVE**	3485
CALCIUM HYPOCHLORITE, HYDRATED or **CALCIUM HYPOCHLORITE, HYDRATED MIXTURE,** with not less than 5.5% but not more than 16% water	2880
CALCIUM HYPOCHLORITE, HYDRATED, CORROSIVE	3487
CALCIUM HYPOCHLORITE, HYDRATED MIXTURE, CORROSIVE	3487
CALCIUM HYPOCHLORITE MIXTURE, DRY, with more than 10% but not more than 39% available chlorine	2208
CALCIUM HYPOCHLORITE MIXTURE, DRY, CORROSIVE	3486
CALCIUM MANGANESE SILICON	2844
CALCIUM NITRATE	1454
CALCIUM OXIDE	1910
CALCIUM PERCHLORATE	1455
CALCIUM PERMANGANATE	1456
CALCIUM PEROXIDE	1457
CALCIUM PHOSPHIDE	1360
CALCIUM, PYROPHORIC	1855
CALCIUM RESINATE	1313
CALCIUM RESINATE, FUSED	1314
Calcium selenate, see	2630
CALCIUM SILICIDE	1405
Calcium silicon, see	1405
Calcium superoxide, see	1457
Camphanone, see	2717
CAMPHOR OIL	1130
CAMPHOR, synthetic	2717

Substance	UN No
CAPACITOR, ASYMMETRIC (with an energy storage capacity greater than 0.3Wh)	3508
CAPACITOR, ELECTRIC DOUBLE LAYER (with an energy storage capacity greater than 0.3Wh)	3499
CAPROIC ACID	2829
CARBAMATE PESTICIDE, LIQUID, FLAMMABLE, TOXIC, flash point less than 23°C	2758
CARBAMATE PESTICIDE, LIQUID, TOXIC, FLAMMABLE, flash point 23°C or above	2991
CARBAMATE PESTICIDE, LIQUID, TOXIC	2992
CARBAMATE PESTICIDE, SOLID, TOXIC	2757
Carbolic acid, see	1671 2312 2821
CARBON, ACTIVATED	1362
CARBON, animal or vegetable origin	1361
Carbon bisulphide, see	1131
Carbon, black, animal or vegetable origin, see	1361
CARBON DIOXIDE	1013
Carbon dioxide and ethylene oxide mixtures, see	1041 1952 3300
CARBON DIOXIDE, REFRIGERATED LIQUID	2187
CARBON DIOXIDE, SOLID	1845
CARBON DISULPHIDE	1131
Carbonic anhydride, see	1013 1845 2187
CARBON MONOXIDE, COMPRESSED	1016
Carbon oxysulphide, see	2204
CARBON TETRABROMIDE	2516

Substance	UN No
CARBON TETRACHLORIDE	1846
Carbonyl chloride, see	1076
CARBONYL FLUORIDE	2417
CARBONYL SULPHIDE	2204
Casingead gasolene, see	1203
CASTOR BEANS or **CASTOR MEAL** or **CASTOR POMACE** or **CASTOR FLAKE**	2969
CAUSTIC ALKALI LIQUID, N.O.S.	1719
Caustic potash, see	1814
Caustic soda, see	1824
Caustic soda liquor, see	1824
CELLS, CONTAINING SODIUM	3292
CELLULOID in blocks, rods, rolls, sheets, tubes, etc., except scrap	2000
CELLULOID, SCRAP	2002
Cement, see	1133
CERIUM, slabs, ingots, or rods	1333
CERIUM, turnings or gritty powder	3078
Cer mishmetall, see	1323
Charcoal, activated, see	1362
Charcoal, non-activated, see	1361
CHEMICAL KIT	3316
CHEMICAL SAMPLE, TOXIC	3315
CHEMICAL UNDER PRESSURE, N.O.S.	3500
CHEMICAL UNDER PRESSURE, FLAMMABLE, N.O.S.	3501
CHEMICAL UNDER PRESSURE, TOXIC, N.O.S.	3502
CHEMICAL UNDER PRESSURE, CORROSIVE, N.O.S.	3503
CHEMICAL UNDER PRESSURE, FLAMMABLE, TOXIC, N.O.S.	3504
CHEMICAL UNDER PRESSURE, FLAMMABLE, CORROSIVE, N.O.S.	3505
Chile saltpetre, see	1498

Substance	UN No
CHLORAL, ANHYDROUS, STABILIZED	2075
CHLORATE AND BORATE MIXTURE	1458
CHLORATE AND MAGNESIUM CHLORIDE MIXTURE, SOLID	1459
CHLORATE AND MAGNESIUM CHLORIDE MIXTURE SOLUTION	3407
CHLORATES, INORGANIC, N.O.S.	1461
CHLORATES, INORGANIC, AQUEOUS SOLUTION, N.O.S.	3210
CHLORIC ACID AQUEOUS SOLUTION, with not more than 10% chloric acid	2626
CHLORINE	1017
CHLORINE, ADSORBED	3520
CHLORINE PENTAFLUORIDE	2548
CHLORINE TRIFLUORIDE	1749
CHLORITES, INORGANIC, N.O.S.	1462
CHLORITE SOLUTION	1908
Chloroacetaldehyde, see	2232
CHLOROACETIC ACID, MOLTEN	3250
CHLOROACETIC ACID, SOLID	1751
CHLOROACETIC ACID SOLUTION	1750
CHLOROACETONE, STABILIZED	1695
CHLOROACETONITRILE	2668
CHLOROACETOPHENONE, LIQUID	3416
CHLOROACETOPHENONE, SOLID	1697
CHLOROACETYL CHLORIDE	1752
CHLOROANILINES, LIQUID	2019
CHLOROANILINES, SOLID	2018
CHLOROANISIDINES	2233
CHLOROBENZENE	1134
CHLOROBENZOTRIFLUORIDES	2234
CHLOROBENZYL CHLORIDES, LIQUID	2235

Substance	UN No
CHLOROBENZYL CHLORIDES, SOLID	3427
1-Chloro-3-bromopropane, see	2688
1-Chlorobutane, see	1127
2-Chlorobutane, see	1127
CHLOROBUTANES	1127
CHLOROCRESOLS, SOLID	3437
CHLOROCRESOLS, SOLUTION	2669
CHLORODIFLUORO-BROMOMETHANE	1974
1-CHLORO-1, 1-DIFLUOROETHANE	2517
CHLORODIFLUOROMETHANE	1018
CHLORODIFLUOROMETHANE AND CHLOROPENTAFLUORO-ETHANE MIXTURE, with fixed boiling point, with approximately 49% chlorodifluoromethane	1973
3-Chloro-1,2-dihydroxypropane, see	2689
Chlorodimethyl ether, see	1239
CHLORODINITROBENZENES, LIQUID	1577
CHLORODINITROBENZENES, SOLID	3441
2-CHLOROETHANAL	2232
Chloroethane, see	1037
Chloroethane nitrile, see	2668
2-Chloroethanol, see	1135
CHLOROFORM	1888
CHLOROFORMATES, TOXIC CORROSIVE, FLAMMABLE, N.O.S.	2742
CHLOROFORMATES, TOXIC, CORROSIVE, N.O.S.	3277
Chloromethane, see	1063
1-Chloro-3-methylbutane, see	1107
2-Chloro-2-methylbutane, see	1107

Substance	UN No
CHLOROMETHYL CHLOROFORMATE	2745
Chloromethyl cyanide, see	2668
CHLOROMETHYL ETHYL ETHER	2354
Chloromethyl methyl ether, see	1239
3-CHLORO-4-METHYLPHENYLISOCYANATE, LIQUID	2236
3-CHLORO-4-METHYLPHENYLISOCYANATE, SOLID	3428
3-Chloro-2-methylprop-1-ene, see	2554
CHLORONITROANILINES	2237
CHLORONITROBENZENES, LIQUID	3409
CHLORONITROBENZENES, SOLID	1578
CHLORONITROTOLUENES, LIQUID	2433
CHLORONITROTOLUENES, SOLID	3457
CHLOROPENTAFLUOROETHANE	1020
CHLOROPHENOLATES, LIQUID	2904
CHLOROPHENOLATES, SOLID	2905
CHLOROPHENOLS, LIQUID	2021
CHLOROPHENOLS, SOLID	2020
CHLOROPHENYLTRICHLOROSILANE	1753
CHLOROPICRIN	1580
CHLOROPICRIN AND METHYL BROMIDE MIXTURE, with more than 2% chloropicrin	1581
CHLOROPICRIN AND METHYL CHLORIDE MIXTURE	1582
CHLOROPICRIN MIXTURE, N.O.S.	1583
CHLOROPLATINIC ACID, SOLID	2507
CHLOROPRENE, STABILIZED	1991
1-CHLOROPROPANE	1278
2-CHLOROPROPANE	2356
3-Chloro-propanediol-1,2, see	2689

Substance	UN No
3-CHLOROPROPANOL-1	2849
2-CHLOROPROPENE	2456
3-Chloropropene, see	1100
3-Chloroprop-1-ene, see	1100
2-CHLOROPROPIONIC ACID	2511
2-CHLOROPYRIDINE	2822
CHLOROSILANES, CORROSIVE, N.O.S.	2987
CHLOROSILANES, CORROSIVE, FLAMMABLE, N.O.S.	2986
CHLOROSILANES, FLAMMABLE, CORROSIVE, N.O.S.	2985
CHLOROSILANES, TOXIC, CORROSIVE, N.O.S.	3361
CHLOROSILANES, TOXIC, CORROSIVE, FLAMMABLE, N.O.S.	3362
CHLOROSILANES, WATER-REACTIVE, FLAMMABLE, CORROSIVE, N.O.S.	2988
CHLOROSULPHONIC ACID, (with or without sulphur trioxide)	1754
1-CHLORO-1,2,2,2-TETRAFLUOROETHANE	1021
CHLOROTOLUENES	2238
4-CHLORO-o-TOLUIDINE HYDROCHLORIDE, SOLID	1579
4-CHLORO-o-TOLUIDINE HYDROCHLORIDE SOLUTION	3410
CHLOROTOLUIDINES, LIQUID	3429
CHLOROTOLUIDINES, SOLID	2239
1-CHLORO-2,2,2,-TRIFLUORO-ETHANE	1983
Chlorotrifluoroethylene, see	1082
CHLOROTRIFLUOROMETHANE	1022
CHLOROTRIFLUOROMETHANE AND TRIFLUOROMETHANE AZEOTROPIC MIXTURE, with approximately 60% chlorotrifluoromethane	2599

Substance	UN No
Chromic acid, solid, see	1463
CHROMIC ACID SOLUTION	1755
Chromic anhydride, solid, see	1463
CHROMIC FLUORIDE, SOLID	1756
CHROMIC FLUORIDE SOLUTION	1757
Chromic nitrate, see	2720
Chromium (VI) dichloride dioxide, see	1758
Chromium (III) fluoride, solid, see	1756
Chromium (III) nitrate, see	2750
CHROMIUM NITRATE	2720
CHROMIUM OXYCHLORIDE	1758
CHROMIUM TRIOXIDE, ANHYDROUS	1463
CHROMOSULPHURIC ACID	2240
Chrysotile, see	2590
Cinene, see	2052
Cinnamene, see	2055
Cinnamol, see	2055
CLINICAL WASTE, UNSPECIFIED, N.O.S. or MEDICAL WASTE, N.O.S. or REGULATED MEDICAL WASTE, N.O.S.	3291
CLINICAL WASTE, UNSPECIFIED, N.O.S. or MEDICAL WASTE, N.O.S. or REGULATED MEDICAL WASTE, N.O.S., in refrigerated liquid nitrogen	3291
COAL GAS, COMPRESSED	1023
COAL TAR DISTILLATES, FLAMMABLE	1136
Coal tar naphtha, see	1268
Coal tar oil, see	1136
COATING SOLUTION	1139
COBALT NAPHTHENATES, POWDER	2001
COBALT RESINATE, PRECIPITATED	1318

Substance	UN No
Cocculus, see	3172 3462
Collodion cottons, see	2059 2555 2556 2557
COMPRESSED GAS, FLAMMABLE, N.O.S.	1954
COMPRESSED GAS, N.O.S.	1956
COMPRESSED GAS, OXIDISING, N.O.S.	3156
COMPRESSED GAS, TOXIC, CORROSIVE, N.O.S.	3304
COMPRESSED GAS, TOXIC, FLAMMABLE, CORROSIVE, N.O.S.	3305
COMPRESSED GAS, TOXIC, FLAMMABLE, N.O.S.	1953
COMPRESSED GAS, TOXIC, N.O.S.	1955
COMPRESSED GAS, TOXIC, OXIDISING, CORROSIVE, N.O.S.	3306
COMPRESSED GAS, TOXIC, OXIDISING, N.O.S.	3303
COPPER ACETOARSENITE	1585
COPPER ARSENITE	1586
Copper (II) arsenite, see	1586
COPPER BASED PESTICIDE, LIQUID, FLAMMABLE, TOXIC, flash point less than 23°C	2776
COPPER BASED PESTICIDE, LIQUID, TOXIC	3010
COPPER BASED PESTICIDE, LIQUID, TOXIC, FLAMMABLE, flash point 23°C or above	3009
COPPER BASED PESTICIDE, SOLID, TOXIC	2775
COPPER CHLORATE	2721
Copper (II) chlorate, see	2721
COPPER CHLORIDE	2802
COPPER CYANIDE	1587

Substance	UN No
Copper selenate, see	2630
Copper selenite, see	2630
COPRA	1363
CORROSIVE LIQUID, ACIDIC, INORGANIC, N.O.S.	3264
CORROSIVE LIQUID, ACIDIC, ORGANIC, N.O.S.	3265
CORROSIVE LIQUID, BASIC, INORGANIC, N.O.S.	3266
CORROSIVE LIQUID, BASIC, ORGANIC, N.O.S.	3267
CORROSIVE LIQUID, FLAMMABLE, N.O.S.	2920
CORROSIVE LIQUID, N.O.S.	1760
CORROSIVE LIQUID, OXIDISING, N.O.S.	3093
CORROSIVE LIQUID, SELF-HEATING, N.O.S.	3301
CORROSIVE LIQUID, TOXIC, N.O.S.	2922
CORROSIVE LIQUID, WATER-REACTIVE, N.O.S.	3094
CORROSIVE SOLID, ACIDIC, INORGANIC, N.O.S.	3260
CORROSIVE SOLID, ACIDIC, ORGANIC, N.O.S.	3261
CORROSIVE SOLID, BASIC, INORGANIC, N.O.S.	3262
CORROSIVE SOLID, BASIC, ORGANIC, N.O.S.	3263
CORROSIVE SOLID, FLAMMABLE, N.O.S.	2921
CORROSIVE SOLID, N.O.S.	1759
CORROSIVE SOLID, OXIDISING, N.O.S.	3084
CORROSIVE SOLID, SELF-HEATING, N.O.S.	3095
CORROSIVE SOLID, TOXIC, N.O.S.	2923

Substance	UN No
CORROSIVE SOLID, WATER-REACTIVE, N.O.S.	3096
COTTON WASTE, OILY	1364
COTTON, WET	1365
COUMARIN DERIVATIVE PESTICIDE, LIQUID, FLAMMABLE, TOXIC, flash point less than 23°C	3024
COUMARIN DERIVATIVE PESTICIDE, LIQUID, TOXIC, FLAMMABLE, flash point 23°C or above	3025
COUMARIN DERIVATIVE PESTICIDE, LIQUID, TOXIC	3026
COUMARIN DERIVATIVE PESTICIDE, SOLID, TOXIC	3027
Creosote, see	2810
Creosote salts, see	1334
CRESOLS, LIQUID	2076
CRESOLS, SOLID	3455
CRESYLIC ACID	2022
Crocidolite, see	2212
CROTONALDEHYDE or **CROTONALDEHYDE, STABILIZED**	1143
CROTONIC ACID, LIQUID	3472
CROTONIC ACID, SOLID	2823
Crotonic aldehyde, stabilized, see	1143
CROTONYLENE	1144
Crude naphtha, see	1268
Cumene, see	1918
Cupric chlorate, see	2721
CUPRIETHYLENEDIAMINE SOLUTION	1761
Cut backs, see	1999 3256 3257
CYANIDE SOLUTION, N.O.S.	1935
CYANIDES, INORGANIC, SOLID, N.O.S.	1588

Substance	UN No
Cyanides, organic, flammable, toxic, n.o.s., see	3273
Cyanides, organic, toxic, n.o.s., see	3276 3439
Cyanides, organic, toxic, flammable, n.o.s., see	3275
Cyanoacetonitrile, see	2647
CYANOGEN	1026
CYANOGEN BROMIDE	1889
CYANOGEN CHLORIDE, STABILIZED	1589
CYANURIC CHLORIDE	2670
CYCLOBUTANE	2601
CYCLOBUTYL CHLOROFORMATE	2744
1,5,9-CYCLODODECATRIENE	2518
CYCLOHEPTANE	2241
CYCLOHEPTATRIENE	2603
1,3,5-Cyloheptatriene, see	2603
CYCLOHEPTENE	2242
1,4-Cyclohexadienedione, see	2587
CYCLOHEXANE	1145
Cyclohexanethiol, see	3054
CYCLOHEXANONE	1915
CYCLOHEXENE	2256
CYCLOHEXENYLTRICHLOROSILANE	1762
CYCLOHEXYL ACETATE	2243
CYCLOHEXYLAMINE	2357
CYCLOHEXYL ISOCYANATE	2488
CYCLOHEXYL MERCAPTAN	3054
CYCLOHEXYLTRICHLOROSILANE	1763
Cyclooctadiene phosphines, see	2940
CYCLOOCTADIENES	2520
CYCLOOCTATETRAENE	2358
CYCLOPENTANE	1146

Substance	UN No
CYCLOPENTANOL	2244
CYCLOPENTANONE	2245
CYCLOPENTENE	2246
CYCLOPROPANE	1027
CYMENES	2046
Cymol, see	2046
DANGEROUS GOODS IN APPARATUS	3363
DANGEROUS GOODS IN MACHINERY	3363
Deanol, see	2051
DECABORANE	1868
DECAHYDRONAPHTHALENE	1147
Decalin, see	1147
n-DECANE	2247
DESENSITIZED EXPLOSIVE, LIQUID, N.O.S.	3379
DESENSITIZED EXPLOSIVE, SOLID, N.O.S.	3380
DEUTERIUM, COMPRESSED	1957
DEVICES, SMALL, HYDROCARBON GAS POWERED, with release device	3150
DIACETONE ALCOHOL	1148
DIALLYLAMINE	2359
DIALLYL ETHER	2360
4,4'-DIAMINODIPHENYL-METHANE	2651
1,2-Diaminoethane, see	1604
Diaminopropylamine, see	2269
DI-n-AMYLAMINE	2841
Dibenzopyridine, see	2713
DIBENZYLDICHLOROSILANE	2434
DIBORANE	1911
1,2-DIBROMOBUTAN-3-ONE	2648
DIBROMOCHLOROPROPANES	2872

Substance	UN No
1,2-Dibromo-3-chloropropane, see	2872
DIBROMODIFLUOROMETHANE	1941
DIBROMOMETHANE	2664
DI-n-BUTYLAMINE	2248
DIBUTYLAMINOETHANOL	2873
2-Dibutylaminoethanol, see	2873
N,N-Di-n-butylaminoethanol, see	2873
DIBUTYL ETHERS	1149
DICHLOROACETIC ACID	1764
1,3-DICHLOROACETONE	2649
DICHLOROACETYL CHLORIDE	1765
DICHLOROANILINES, LIQUID	1590
DICHLOROANILINES, SOLID	3442
o-DICHLOROBENZENE	1591
2,2'-DICHLORODIETHYL ETHER	1916
DICHLORODIFLUOROMETHANE	1028
DICHLORODIFLUOROMETHANE AND DIFLUOROETHANE AZEOTROPIC MIXTURE, with approximately 74% dichlorodifluoromethane	2602
Dichlorodifluoromethane and ethylene oxide mixture, see	3070
DICHLORODIMETHYL ETHER, SYMMETRICAL	2249
1,1-DICHLOROETHANE	2362
1,2-Dichloroethane, see	1184
1,2-DICHLOROETHYLENE	1150
Di(2-chloroethyl) ether, see	1916
DICHLOROFLUOROMETHANE	1029
alpha-Dichlorohydrin, see	2750
DICHLOROISOCYANURIC ACID, DRY or DICHLOROISOCYANURIC ACID SALTS	2465
DICHLOROISOPROPYL ETHER	2490
DICHLOROMETHANE	1593

Substance	UN No
1,1-DICHLORO-1-NITROETHANE	2650
DICHLOROPENTANES	1152
Dichlorophenols, see	2020 2021
DICHLOROPHENYL ISOCYANATES	2250
DICHLOROPHENYLTRI-CHLOROSILANE	1766
1,2-DICHLOROPROPANE	1279
1,3-Dichloro-2-propanone, see	2649
1,3-DICHLOROPROPANOL-2	2750
DICHLOROPROPENES	2047
DICHLOROSILANE	2189
1,2-DICHLORO-1,1,2,2-TETRAFLUOROETHANE	1958
Dichloro-s-triazine-2,4,6-trione, see	2465
1,4-Dicyanobutane, see	2205
Dicycloheptadiene, see	2251
DICYCLOHEXYLAMINE	2565
Dicyclohexylamine nitrite, see	2687
DICYCLOHEXYLAMMONIUM NITRITE	2687
DICYCLOPENTADIENE	2048
1,2-DI-(DIMETHYLAMINO) ETHANE	2372
DIDYMIUM NITRATE	1465
DIESEL FUEL	1202
1,1-Diethoxyethane, see	1088
1,2-Diethoxyethane, see	1153
DIETHOXYMETHANE	2373
3,3-DIETHOXYPROPENE	2374
DIETHYLAMINE	1154
2-DIETHYLAMINOETHANOL	2686
3-DIETHYLAMINOPROPYLAMINE	2684
N,N-DIETHYLANILINE	2432

Substance	UN No
DIETHYLBENZENE	2049
Diethylcarbinol, see	1105
DIETHYL CARBONATE	2366
DIETHYLDICHLOROSILANE	1767
Diethylenediamine, see	2579
DIETHYLENETRIAMINE	2079
N,N-Diethylethanolamine, see	2686
DIETHYL ETHER	1155
N,N-DIETHYLETHYLENEDIAMINE	2685
Di-(2-ethylhexyl) phosphoric acid, see	1902
DIETHYL KETONE	1156
DIETHYL SULPHATE	1594
DIETHYL SULPHIDE	2375
DIETHYLTHIOPHOSPHORYL CHLORIDE	2751
Diethyl zinc, see	3394
2-4-Difluoroaniline, see	2941
Difluorochloroethane, see	2517
1,1-DIFLUOROETHANE	1030
1,1-DIFLUOROETHYLENE	1959
DIFLUOROMETHANE	3252
Difluoromethane, pentafluoroethane and 1,1,1,2-tetrafluoroethane azeotropic mixture, with approximately 23% difluoromethane and 25% pentafluoroethane, see	3340
Difluoromethane, pentafluoroethane, and 1,1,1,2-tetrafluoroethane azeotropic mixture, with approximately 20% difluoromethane and 40% pentafluoroethane, see	3338
Difluoromethane, pentafluoroethane, and 1,1,1,2-tetrafluoroethane azeotropic mixture, with approximately 10% difluoromethane and 70% pentafluoroethane, see	3339

Substance	UN No
DIFLUOROPHOSPHORIC ACID, ANHYDROUS	1768
2,3-DIHYDROPYRAN	2376
DIISOBUTYLAMINE	2361
DIISOBUTYLENE, ISOMERIC COMPOUNDS	2050
alpha-Diisobutylene, see	2050
beta-Diisobutylene, see	2050
DIISOBUTYL KETONE	1157
DIISOOCTYL ACID PHOSPHATE	1902
DIISOPROPYLAMINE	1158
DIISOPROPYL ETHER	1159
DIKETENE, STABILIZED	2521
1,1-DIMETHOXYETHANE	2377
1,2-DIMETHOXYETHANE	2252
Dimethoxystrychnine, see	1570
DIMETHYLAMINE ANHYDROUS	1032
DIMETHYLAMINE AQUEOUS SOLUTION	1160
2-DIMETHYLAMINO-ACETONITRILE	2378
2-DIMETHYLAMINOETHANOL	2051
2-DIMETHYLAMINOETHYL ACRYLATE	3302
2-DIMETHYLAMINOETHYL METHACRYLATE	2522
N,N-DIMETHYLANILINE	2253
Dimethylarsenic acid, see	1572
N,N-Dimethylbenzylamine, see	2619
2,3-DIMETHYLBUTANE	2457
1,3-DIMETHYLBUTYLAMINE	2379
DIMETHYLCARBAMOYL CHLORIDE	2262
DIMETHYL CARBONATE	1161
DIMETHYLCYCLOHEXANES	2263
N,N-DIMETHYLCYCLOHEXYLAMINE	2264

Substance	UN No
DIMETHYLDICHLOROSILANE	1162
DIMETHYLDIETHOXYSILANE	2380
DIMETHYLDIOXANES	2707
DIMETHYL DISULPHIDE	2381
Dimethylethanolamine, see	2051
DIMETHYL ETHER	1033
N,N-DIMETHYLFORMAMIDE	2265
DIMETHYLHYDRAZINE, SYMMETRICAL	2382
DIMETHYLHYDRAZINE, UNSYMMETRICAL	1163
1,1-Dimethylhydrazine, see	1163
N,N-Dimethyl-4-nitrosoaniline, see	1369
2,2-DIMETHYLPROPANE	2044
DIMETHYL-N-PROPYLAMINE	2266
DIMETHYL SULPHATE	1595
DIMETHYL SULPHIDE	1164
DIMETHYL THIOPHOSPHORYL CHLORIDE	2267
Dimethyl zinc, see	3394
DINITROANILINES	1596
DINITROBENZENES, LIQUID	1597
DINITROBENZENES, SOLID	3443
Dinitrochlorobenzene, see	1577
DINITROGEN TETROXIDE	1067
DINITRO-o-CRESOL	1598
DINITROPHENOL SOLUTION	1599
DINITROPHENOL, WETTED, with not less than 15% water by mass	1320
DINITROPHENOLATES, WETTED, with not less than 15% water by mass	1321
DINITRORESORCINOL, WETTED, with not less than 15% water by mass	1322
DINITROTOLUENES, LIQUID	2038

Substance	UN No
DINITROTOLUENES, MOLTEN	1600
DINITROTOLUENES, SOLID	3454
DIOXANE	1165
DIOXOLANE	1166
DIPENTENE	2052
DIPHENYLAMINE CHLOROARSINE	1698
DIPHENYLCHLOROARSINE, LIQUID	1699
DIPHENYLCHLOROARSINE, SOLID	3450
DIPHENYLDICHLOROSILANE	1769
DIPHENYLMETHYL BROMIDE	1770
DIPICRYL SULPHIDE, WETTED, with not less than 10% water by mass	2852
DIPROPYLAMINE	2383
Dipropylene triamine, see	2269
DI-n-PROPYL ETHER	2384
DIPROPYL KETONE	2710
DISINFECTANT, LIQUID, CORROSIVE, N.O.S.	1903
DISINFECTANT, LIQUID, TOXIC, N.O.S.	3142
DISINFECTANT, SOLID, TOXIC, N.O.S.	1601
DISODIUM TRIOXOSILICATE	3253
DIVINYL ETHER, STABILIZED	1167
DODECYLTRICHLOROSILANE	1771
Dry ice, see	1845
DYE or DYE INTERMEDIATE, LIQUID, CORROSIVE, N.O.S.	2801
DYE or DYE INTERMEDIATE, LIQUID, TOXIC, N.O.S.	1602
DYE or DYE INTERMEDIATE, SOLID, CORROSIVE, N.O.S.	3147
DYE or DYE INTERMEDIATE, SOLID, TOXIC, N.O.S.	3143

Substance	UN No
Electric storage, batteries, see	2794 2795 2800 3028
Electrolyte (acid or alkaline) for batteries, see	2796 2797
ELEVATED TEMPERATURE LIQUID, FLAMMABLE, N.O.S., with flash point above 60°C, at or above its flash point and at or above 100°C	3256
ELEVATED TEMPERATURE LIQUID, FLAMMABLE, N.O.S., with flash point above 60°C, at or above its flash point and below 100°C	3256
ELEVATED TEMPERATURE LIQUID, N.O.S., at or above 100°C and below its flash point (including molten metals, molten salts etc)	3257
ELEVATED TEMPERATURE SOLID, N.O.S., at or above 240°C	3258
Enamel, see	1263 3066 3469 3470
ENGINE, FUEL CELL, FLAMMABLE GAS POWERED	3166
ENGINE, FUEL CELL, FLAMMABLE GAS POWERED	3529
ENGINE, FUEL CELL, FLAMMABLE LIQUID POWERED	3166
ENGINE, FUEL CELL, FLAMMABLE LIQUID POWERED	3528
ENGINE, INTERNAL COMBUSTION	3166
ENGINE, INTERNAL COMBUSTION, FLAMMABLE GAS POWERED	3529
ENGINE, INTERNAL COMBUSTION, FLAMMABLE LIQUID POWERED	3528
ENVIRONMENTALLY HAZARDOUS SUBSTANCE, LIQUID, N.O.S.	3082

Substance	UN No
ENVIRONMENTALLY HAZARDOUS SUBSTANCE, SOLID, N.O.S.	3077
EPIBROMOHYDRIN	2558
EPICHLOROHYDRIN	2023
1,2-Epoxybutane, stabilized, see	3022
Epoxyethane, see	1040
1,2-EPOXY-3-ETHOXYPROPANE	2752
2,3-Epoxy-1-propanal, see	2622
2,3-Epoxypropyl ethyl ether, see	2752
ESTERS, N.O.S.	3272
ETHANE	1035
ETHANE, REFRIGERATED LIQUID	1961
Ethanethiol, see	2363
ETHANOL or ETHANOL SOLUTION	1170
ETHANOL AND GASOLINE MIXTURE or ETHANOL AND MOTOR SPIRIT or ETHANOL AND PETROL MIXTURE with more than 10% ethanol	3475
ETHANOLAMINE or ETHANOLAMINE SOLUTION	2491
Ether, see	1155
ETHERS, N.O.S.	3271
2-Ethoxyethanol, see	1171
2-Ethoxyethyl acetate, see	1172
Ethoxy propane-1, see	2615
ETHYL ACETATE	1173
ETHYLACETYLENE, STABILIZED	2452
ETHYL ACRYLATE, STABILIZED	1917
ETHYL ALCOHOL or ETHYL ALCOHOL SOLUTION, see	1170
ETHYLAMINE	1036
ETHYLAMINE, AQUEOUS SOLUTION, with not less than 50% but not more than 70% ethylamine	2270
ETHYL AMYL KETONE	2271

Substance	UN No
N-ETHYLANILINE	2272
2-ETHYLANILINE	2273
ETHYLBENZENE	1175
N-ETHYL-N-BENZYLANILINE	2274
N-ETHYLBENZYLTOLUIDINES, LIQUID	2753
N-ETHYLBENZYLTOLUIDINES, SOLID	3460
ETHYL BORATE	1176
ETHYL BROMIDE	1891
ETHYL BROMOACETATE	1603
2-ETHYLBUTANOL	2275
2-ETHYLBUTYL ACETATE	1177
ETHYL BUTYL ETHER	1179
2-ETHYLBUTYRALDEHYDE	1178
ETHYL BUTYRATE	1180
ETHYL CHLORIDE	1037
ETHYL CHLOROACETATE	1181
Ethyl chlorocarbonate, see	1182
ETHYL CHLOROFORMATE	1182
ETHYL-2-CHLOROPROPIONATE	2935
Ethyl-alpha-chloropropionate, see	2935
ETHYL CHLOROTHIOFORMATE	2826
ETHYL CROTONATE	1862
ETHYLDICHLOROARSINE	1892
ETHYLDICHLOROSILANE	1183
ETHYLENE, ACETYLENE AND PROPYLENE MIXTURE, REFRIGERATED LIQUID, containing at least 71.5% ethylene, with not more than 22.5% acetylene and not more than 6% propylene	3138
ETHYLENE CHLOROHYDRIN	1135
ETHYLENE	1962
ETHYLENEDIAMINE	1604

Substance	UN No
ETHYLENE DIBROMIDE	1605
Ethylene dibromide and methyl bromide, liquid mixture, see	1647
ETHYLENE DICHLORIDE	1184
ETHYLENE GLYCOL DIETHYL ETHER	1153
ETHYLENE GLYCOL MONOETHYL ETHER	1171
ETHYLENE GLYCOL MONOETHYL ETHER ACETATE	1172
ETHYLENE GLYCOL MONOMETHYL ETHER	1188
ETHYLENE GLYCOL MONOMETHYL ETHER ACETATE	1189
ETHYLENEIMINE, STABILIZED	1185
ETHYLENE OXIDE	1040
ETHYLENE OXIDE AND CARBON DIOXIDE MIXTURE, with more than 87% ethylene oxide	3300
ETHYLENE OXIDE AND CARBON DIOXIDE MIXTURE, with more than 9% but not more than 87% ethylene oxide	1041
ETHYLENE OXIDE AND CARBON DIOXIDE MIXTURE, with not more than 9% ethylene oxide	1952
ETHYLENE OXIDE AND CHLOROTETRAFLUOROETHANE MIXTURE, with not more than 8.8% ethylene oxide	3297
ETHYLENE OXIDE AND DICHLORODIFLUOROMETHANE MIXTURE, with not more than 12.5% ethylene oxide	3070
ETHYLENE OXIDE AND PENTAFLUOROETHANE MIXTURE, with not more than 7.9% ethylene oxide	3298
ETHYLENE OXIDE AND PROPYLENE OXIDE MIXTURE, with not more than 30% ethylene oxide	2983

Substance	UN No
ETHYLENE OXIDE AND TETRAFLUOROETHANE MIXTURE, with not more than 5.6% ethylene oxide	3299
ETHYLENE OXIDE WITH NITROGEN, up to a total pressure of 1MPa (10bar) at 50°C	1040
ETHYLENE, REFRIGERATED LIQUID	1038
Ethyl ether, see	1155
ETHYL FLUORIDE	2453
ETHYL FORMATE	1190
2-ETHYLHEXYLAMINE	2276
2-ETHYLHEXYL CHLOROFORMATE	2748
Ethylidene chloride, see	2362
ETHYL ISOBUTYRATE	2385
ETHYL ISOCYANATE	2481
ETHYL LACTATE	1192
ETHYL MERCAPTAN	2363
ETHYL METHACRYLATE, STABILIZED	2277
ETHYL METHYL ETHER	1039
ETHYL METHYL KETONE	1193
ETHYL NITRITE SOLUTION	1194
ETHYL ORTHOFORMATE	2524
ETHYL OXALATE	2525
ETHYLPHENYLDICHLOROSILANE	2435
1-ETHYLPIPERIDINE	2386
ETHYL PROPIONATE	1195
ETHYL PROPYL ETHER	2615
Ethyl silicate, see	1292
Ethyl sulphate, see	1594
N-ETHYLTOLUIDINES	2754
ETHYLTRICHLOROSILANE	1196
EXTRACTS, AROMATIC, LIQUID	1169

Substance	UN No
EXTRACTS, FLAVOURING, LIQUID	1197
FABRICS, ANIMAL, VEGETABLE or **SYNTHETIC, N.O.S.,** with oil	1373
FABRICS IMPREGNATED WITH WEAKLY NITRATED NITROCELLULOSE, N.O.S.	1353
FERRIC ARSENATE	1606
FERRIC ARSENITE	1607
FERRIC CHLORIDE, ANHYDROUS	1773
FERRIC CHLORIDE SOLUTION	2582
FERRIC NITRATE	1466
FERROCERIUM	1323
FERROSILICON, with 30% or more but less than 90% silicon	1408
FERROUS ARSENATE	1608
FERROUS METAL BORINGS, SHAVINGS, TURNINGS, or **CUTTINGS,** in a form liable to self-heating	2793
FERTILIZER AMMONIATING SOLUTION, with free ammonia	1043
Fertilizers with ammonium nitrate, n.o.s., see	2067
FIBRES, ANIMAL or **VEGETABLE,** burnt, wet or damp	1372
FIBRES, ANIMAL, VEGETABLE or **SYNTHETIC, N.O.S.** with oil	1373
FIBRES, IMPREGNATED WITH WEAKLY NITRATED NITROCELLULOSE, N.O.S.	1353
FIBRES, VEGETABLE, DRY	3360
Fillers, liquid, see	1263 3066 3469 3470
Films, nitrocellulose base, from which gelatine has been removed, film scrap, see	2002
FILMS, NITROCELLULOSE BASE, gelatin coated, except scrap	1324

Substance	UN No
FIRE EXTINGUISHER CHARGES, corrosive liquid	1774
FIRE EXTINGUISHERS, with compressed or liquefied gas	1044
FIRELIGHTERS, SOLID, with flammable liquid	2623
FIRST AID KIT	3316
FISH MEAL or **FISH SCRAP, STABILIZED**	2216
FISH MEAL or **FISH SCRAP, UNSTABILIZED**	1374
Flammable gas in lighters, see	1057
FLAMMABLE LIQUID, CORROSIVE, N.O.S.	2924
FLAMMABLE LIQUID, N.O.S.	1993
FLAMMABLE LIQUID, TOXIC, CORROSIVE, N.O.S.	3286
FLAMMABLE LIQUID, TOXIC, N.O.S.	1992
FLAMMABLE SOLID, INORGANIC, N.O.S.	3178
FLAMMABLE SOLID, CORROSIVE, INORGANIC, N.O.S.	3180
FLAMMABLE SOLID, TOXIC, INORGANIC, N.O.S.	3179
FLAMMABLE SOLID, ORGANIC, N.O.S.	1325
FLAMMABLE SOLID, CORROSIVE, ORGANIC, N.O.S.	2925
FLAMMABLE SOLID, ORGANIC, MOLTEN, N.O.S.	3176
FLAMMABLE SOLID, OXIDISING, N.O.S.	3097
FLAMMABLE SOLID, TOXIC, ORGANIC, N.O.S.	2926
Flue dusts, toxic, see	1562
Fluoric acid, see	1790
FLUORINE, COMPRESSED	1045
FLUOROACETIC ACID	2642

Substance	UN No
FLUOROANILINES	2941
2-Fluoroaniline, see	2941
4-Fluoroaniline, see	2941
o-Fluoroaniline, see	2941
p-Fluoroaniline, see	2941
FLUOROBENZENE	2387
FLUOROBORIC ACID	1775
Fluoroethane, see	2453
Fluoroform, see	1984
Fluoromethane, see	2454
FLUOROPHOSPHORIC ACID, ANHYDROUS	1776
FLUOROSILICATES, N.O.S.	2856
FLUOROSILICIC ACID	1778
FLUOROSULPHONIC ACID	1777
FLUOROTOLUENES	2388
FORMALDEHYDE SOLUTION, with not less than 25% formaldehyde	2209
FORMALDEHYDE SOLUTION, FLAMMABLE	1198
Formalin, see	1198 2209
Formamidine sulphinic acid, see	3341
FORMIC ACID, with more than 85% acid by mass	1779
FORMIC ACID, with more than 5% acid but not more than 85% acid	3412
Formic aldehyde, see	1198 2209
2-Formyl-3,4-dihydro-2H-pyran, see	2607
FUEL, AVIATION, TURBINE ENGINE	1863
FUEL CELL CARTRIDGES or **FUEL CELL CARTRIDGES CONTAINED IN EQUIPMENT** or **FUEL CELL CARTRIDGES PACKED WITH EQUIPMENT,** containing flammable liquids	3473

Substance	UN No
FUEL CELL CARTRIDGES or **FUEL CELL CARTRIDGES CONTAINED IN EQUIPMENT** or **FUEL CELL CARTRIDGES PACKED WITH EQUIPMENT,** containing water-reactive substances	3476
FUEL CELL CARTRIDGES or **FUEL CELL CARTRIDGES CONTAINED IN EQUIPMENT** or **FUEL CELL CARTRIDGES PACKED WITH EQUIPMENT,** containing corrosive substance	3477
FUEL CELL CARTRIDGES or **FUEL CELL CARTRIDGES CONTAINED IN EQUIPMENT** or **FUEL CELL CARTRIDGES PACKED WITH EQUIPMENT,** containing liquefied flammable gas	3478
FUEL CELL CARTRIDGES or **FUEL CELL CARTRIDGES CONTAINED IN EQUIPMENT** or **FUEL CELL CARTRIDGES PACKED WITH EQUIPMENT,** containing hydrogen in metal hydride	3479
Fumaroyl dichloride, see	1780
FUMARYL CHLORIDE	1780
FUMIGATED CARGO TRANSPORT UNIT	3359
FURALDEHYDES	1199
FURAN	2389
FURFURYL ALCOHOL	2874
FURFURYLAMINE	2526
Furyl carbinol, see	2874
FUSEL OIL	1201
GALLIUM	2803
GAS CARTRIDGES, without a release device, non-refillable, see	2037
Gas drips, hydrocarbon, see	3295
GAS OIL	1202
GASOLINE	1203
Gasoline and ethanol mixture, with more than 10% ethanol, see	3475

ALPHABETICAL LIST OF DANGEROUS GOODS

Substance	UN No
Gasoline, casinghead, see	1203
GAS, REFRIGERATED LIQUID, FLAMMABLE, N.O.S.	3312
GAS, REFRIGERATED LIQUID, N.O.S.	3158
GAS, REFRIGERATED LIQUID, OXIDISING, N.O.S.	3311
GAS SAMPLE, NON-PRESSURISED, FLAMMABLE, N.O.S., not refrigerated liquid	3167
GAS SAMPLE, NON-PRESSURISED, TOXIC, N.O.S., not refrigerated liquid	3169
GAS SAMPLE, NON-PRESSURISED, TOXIC, FLAMMABLE, N.O.S., not refrigerated liquid	3168
GENETICALLY MODIFIED MICRO-ORGANISMS or **GENETICALLY MODIFIED ORGANISMS**	3245
GENETICALLY MODIFIED MICRO-ORGANISMS or **GENETICALLY MODIFIED ORGANISMS**, in refrigerated liquid nitrogen	3245
GERMANE	2192
GERMANE, ADSORBED	3523
Germanium hydride, see	2192
Glycerol-1, 3-dichlorohydrin, see	2750
GYLCEROL alpha-MONO-CHLOROHYDRIN	2689
Glyceryl trinitrate, see	1204 3064
GLYCIDALDEHYDE	2622
GUANIDINE NITRATE	1467
Gutta percha solution, see	1287
HAFNIUM POWDER, DRY	2545
HAFNIUM POWDER, WETTED, with not less than 25% water	1326
HALOGENATED MONOMETHYLDIPHENYLMETHANES, LIQUID	3151

Substance	UN No
HALOGENATED MONOMETHYLDIPHENYLMETHANES, SOLID	3152
HAY	1327
HEATING OIL, LIGHT	1202
Heavy Hydrogen, see	1957
HELIUM, COMPRESSED	1046
HELIUM, REFRIGERATED LIQUID	1963
HEPTAFLUOROPROPANE	3296
n-HEPTALDEHYDE	3056
n-Heptanal, see	3056
HEPTANES	1206
4-Heptanone, see	2710
n-HEPTENE	2278
HEXACHLOROACETONE	2661
HEXACHLOROBENZENE	2729
HEXACHLOROBUTADIENE	2279
Hexachloro-1,3-butadiene, see	2279
HEXACHLOROCYCLO-PENTADIENE	2646
HEXACHLOROPHENE	2875
Hexachloro-2-propanone, see	2661
HEXADECYLTRICHLOROSILANE	1781
HEXADIENES	2458
HEXAETHYL TETRAPHOSPHATE	1611
HEXAETHYL TETRAPHOSPHATE AND COMPRESSED GAS MIXTURE	1612
HEXAFLUOROACETONE	2420
HEXAFLUOROACETONE HYDRATE, LIQUID	2552
HEXAFLUOROACETONE HYDRATE, SOLID	3436
HEXAFLUOROETHANE (REFRIGERANT GAS R116)	2193
HEXAFLUOROPHOSPHORIC ACID	1782

Substance	UN No
HEXAFLUOROPROPYLENE	1858
Hexahydrocresol, see	2617
Hexahydromethyl phenol, see	2617
HEXALDEHYDE	1207
HEXAMETHYLENEDIAMINE, SOLID	2280
HEXAMETHYLENEDIAMINE SOLUTION	1783
HEXAMETHYLENE DIISOCYANATE	2281
HEXAMETHYLENEIMINE	2493
HEXAMETHYLENETETRAMINE	1328
Hexamine, see	1328
HEXANES	1208
Hexanoic acid, see	2829
HEXANOLS	2282
1-HEXENE	2370
HEXYLTRICHLOROSILANE	1784
HYDRAZINE, ANHYDROUS	2029
HYDRAZINE, AQUEOUS SOLUTION, with not less than 37% hydrazine by mass	2030
HYDRAZINE, AQUEOUS SOLUTION, with not more than 37% hydrazine by mass	3293
HYDRAZINE AQUEOUS SOLUTION, FLAMMABLE with more than 37% hydrazine, by mass	3484
Hydrides, metal, water-reactive, n.o.s., see	1409
HYDRIODIC ACID	1787
Hydriodic acid, anhydrous, see	2197
HYDROBROMIC ACID	1788
HYDROCARBON GAS MIXTURE, COMPRESSED, N.O.S.	1964
HYDROCARBON GAS MIXTURE, LIQUEFIED, N.O.S.	1965

Substance	UN No
HYDROCARBON GAS REFILLS FOR SMALL DEVICES, with release device	3150
HYDROCARBONS, LIQUID N.O.S.	3295
HYDROCHLORIC ACID	1789
HYDROCYANIC ACID, AQUEOUS SOLUTIONS, with not more than 20% hydrogen cyanide	1613
Hydrofluoboric acid, see	1775
HYDROFLUORIC ACID	1790
HYDROFLUORIC ACID AND SULPHURIC ACID MIXTURE	1786
Hydrofluosilicic acid, see	1778
Hydrogen arsenide, see	2188
HYDROGEN BROMIDE, ANHYDROUS	1048
Hydrogen bromide solution, see	1788
HYDROGEN CHLORIDE, ANHYDROUS	1050
HYDROGEN CHLORIDE, REFRIGERATED LIQUID	2186
HYDROGEN, COMPRESSED	1049
HYDROGEN CYANIDE, AQUEOUS SOLUTION, with not more than 20% hyrdrogen cyanide	1613
HYDROGEN CYANIDE, SOLUTION IN ALCOHOL, with not more than 45% hydrogen cyanide	3294
HYDROGEN CYANIDE, STABILIZED, containing less than 3% water and absorbed in a porous inert material	1614
HYDROGEN CYANIDE, STABILIZED, containing less than 3% material	1051
HYDROGENDIFLUORIDES, SOLID, N.O.S.	1740
HYDROGENDIFLUORIDES, SOLUTION, N.O.S.	3471
HYDROGEN FLUORIDE, ANHYDROUS	1052

Substance	UN No
Hydrogen fluoride solution, see	1790
HYDROGEN IN METAL HYDRIDE STORAGE SYSTEM or **HYDROGEN IN A METAL HYDRIDE STORAGE SYSTEM CONTAINED IN EQUIPMENT** or **HYDROGEN IN A METAL HYDRIDE STORAGE SYSTEM PACKED WITH EQUIPMENT'**	3468
HYDROGEN IODIDE, ANHYDROUS	2197
Hydrogen iodide solution, see	1787
HYDROGEN AND METHANE MIXTURE, COMPRESSED	2034
HYDROGEN PEROXIDE AND PEROXYACETIC ACID MIXTURE, STABILIZED, with acid(s), water and not more than 5% peroxyacetic acid	3149
HYDROGEN PEROXIDE, AQUEOUS SOLUTION, with not less than 8% but less than 20% hydrogen peroxide (stabilized as necessary)	2984
HYDROGEN PEROXIDE, AQUEOUS SOLUTION, with not less than 20% but not more than 60% hydrogen peroxide (stabilized as necessary)	2014
HYDROGEN PEROXIDE, STABILIZED or **HYDROGEN PEROXIDE AQUEOUS SOLUTION, STABILIZED,** with more than 60% hydrogen peroxide	2015
HYDROGEN, REFRIGERATED LIQUID	1966
HYDROGEN SELENIDE, ABSORBED	3526
HYDROGEN SELENIDE, ANHYDROUS	2202
Hydrogen silicide, see	2203
HYDROGEN SULPHIDE	1053
Hydroselenic acid, see	2202
Hydrosilicofluoric acid, see	1778

Substance	UN No
1-HYDROXYBENZOTRIAZOLE MONOHYDRATE	3474
3-Hydroxybutan-2-one, see	2621
HYDROXYLAMINE SULPHATE	2865
1-Hydroxy-3-methyl-2-penten-4-yne, see	2705
3-Hydroxyphenol, see	2876
HYPOCHLORITE SOLUTION	1791
HYPOCHLORITES, INORGANIC, N.O.S.	3212
3,3'-IMINODIPROPYLAMINE	2269
India rubber, see	1287
INFECTIOUS SUBSTANCE, AFFECTING HUMANS	2814
INFECTIOUS SUBSTANCE, AFFECTING ANIMALS only	2900
Ink, printer's, flammable, see	1210
INSECTICIDE GAS, N.O.S.	1968
INSECTICIDE GAS, FLAMMABLE, N.O.S.	3354
INSECTICIDE GAS, TOXIC, N.O.S.	1967
INSECTICIDE GAS, TOXIC, FLAMMABLE, N.O.S.	3355
IODINE	3495
IODINE MONOCHLORIDE, LIQUID	3498
IODINE MONOCHLORIDE, SOLID	1792
IODINE PENTAFLUORIDE	2495
2-IODOBUTANE	2390
Iodomethane, see	2644
IODOMETHYLPROPANES	2391
IODOPROPANES	2392
alpha-Iodotoluene, see	2653
I.p.d.i, see	2290
Iron chloride anhydrous, see	1773
Iron chloride solution, see	2582

Substance	UN No
IRON OXIDE, SPENT	1376
IRON PENTACARBONYL	1994
Iron perchloride anhydrous, see	1773
Iron powder, pyrophoric, see	1383
Iron sesquichloride anhydrous, see	1773
IRON SPONGE, SPENT, obtained from coal gas purification	1376
Iron swarf, see	2793
ISOBUTANE	1969
ISOBUTANOL	1212
Isobutene, see	1055
ISOBUTYL ACETATE	1213
ISOBUTYL ACRYLATE, STABILIZED	2527
ISOBUTYL ALCOHOL	1212
ISOBUTYL ALDEHYDE	2045
ISOBUTYLAMINE	1214
ISOBUTYLENE	1055
ISOBUTYL FORMATE	2393
ISOBUTYL ISOBUTYRATE	2528
ISOBUTYL ISOCYANATE	2486
ISOBUTYL METHACRYLATE, STABILIZED	2283
ISOBUTYL PROPIONATE	2394
ISOBUTYRALDEHYDE	2045
ISOBUTYRIC ACID	2529
ISOBUTYRONITRILE	2284
ISOBUTYRYL CHLORIDE	2395
ISOCYANATES, FLAMMABLE, TOXIC, N.O.S., or **ISOCYANATE SOLUTION, FLAMMABLE, TOXIC, N.O.S.**	2478
ISOCYANATES, TOXIC, N.O.S., or **ISOCYANATE SOLUTION, TOXIC, N.O.S.**	2206

Substance	UN No
ISOCYANATES, TOXIC, FLAMMABLE, N.O.S., or **ISOCYANATE SOLUTION, TOXIC, FLAMMABLE, N.O.S.**	3080
ISOCYANATOBENZOTRIFLUORIDES	2285
3-Isocyanatomethyl-3,5,5-trimethylcyclohexyl isocyanate, see	2290
Isododecane, see	2286
ISOHEPTENE	2287
ISOHEXENE	2288
Isooctane, see	1262
ISOOCTENE	1216
Isopentane, see	1265
ISOPENTENES	2371
Isopentylamine, see	1106
Isopentyl nitrite, see	1113
ISOPHORONEDIAMINE	2289
ISOPHORONE DIISOCYANATE	2290
ISOPRENE, STABILIZED	1218
ISOPROPANOL	1219
ISOPROPENYL ACETATE	2403
ISOPROPENYLBENZENE	2303
ISOPROPYL ACETATE	1220
ISOPROPYL ACID PHOSPHATE	1793
ISOPROPYL ALCOHOL	1219
ISOPROPYLAMINE	1221
ISOPROPYLBENZENE	1918
ISOPROPYL BUTYRATE	2405
Isopropyl chloride, see	2356
ISOPROPYL CHLOROACETATE	2947
ISOPROPYL CHLOROFORMATE	2407
ISOPROPYL 2-CHLOROPROPIONATE	2934
Isopropyl-alpha-chloropropionate, see	2934

Substance	UN No
Isopropyl ether, see	1159
Isopropylethylene, see	2561
Isopropyl formate, see	1281
ISOPROPYL ISOBUTYRATE	2406
ISOPROPYL ISOCYANATE	2483
Isopropyl mercaptan, see	2402
ISOPROPYL NITRATE	1222
ISOPROPYL PROPIONATE	2409
Isopropyltoluene, see	2046
Isopropyltoluol, see	2046
ISOSORBIDE-5-MONONITRATE	3251
ISOSORBIDE DINITRATE MIXTURE, with not less than 60% lactose, mannose, starch, or calcium hydrogen phosphate	2907
Isovaleraldehyde, see	2058
KEROSENE	1223
KETONES, LIQUID, N.O.S.	1224
KRILL MEAL	3497
KRYPTON, COMPRESSED	1056
KRYPTON, REFRIGERATED LIQUID	1970
Lacquer, see	1263 3066 3469 3470
Lacquer base or lacquer chips, nitrocellulose, dry, see	2557
Lacquer base or lacquer chips, plastic, wet, with alcohol or solvent, see	1263 2059 2555 2556
Lacquer base, liquid, see	1263 3066 3469 3470
LEAD ACETATE	1616
Lead (II) acetate, see	1616
LEAD ARSENATES	1617

Substance	UN No
LEAD ARSENITES	1618
Lead chloride, solid, see	2291
LEAD COMPOUND, SOLUBLE, N.O.S.	2291
LEAD CYANIDE	1620
Lead (II) cyanide, see	1620
LEAD DIOXIDE	1872
LEAD NITRATE	1469
Lead (II) Nitrate, see	1469
LEAD PERCHLORATE, SOLID	1470
LEAD PERCHLORATE SOLUTION	3408
Lead (II) perchlorate	1470 3408
Lead peroxide, see	1872
LEAD PHOSPHITE, DIBASIC	2989
LEAD SULPHATE, with more than 3% free acid	1794
Lead tetraethyl, see	1649
Lead tetramethyl, see	1649
LIFE-SAVING APPLIANCES, NOT SELF-INFLATING, containing dangerous goods as equipment	3072
LIFE-SAVING APPLIANCES, SELF-INFLATING	2990
LIGHTERS or **LIGHTER REFILLS,** containing flammable gas	1057
Limonene, inactive, see	2052
LIQUEFIED GAS, N.O.S.	3163
LIQUEFIED GAS, FLAMMABLE, N.O.S.	3161
LIQUEFIED GAS, OXIDISING, N.O.S.	3157
LIQUEFIED GAS, TOXIC, N.O.S.	3162
LIQUEFIED GAS, TOXIC, CORROSIVE, N.O.S.	3308
LIQUEFIED GAS, TOXIC, FLAMMABLE, CORROSIVE, N.O.S.	3309

Substance	UN No
LIQUEFIED GAS, TOXIC, OXIDISING, CORROSIVE, N.O.S.	3310
LIQUEFIED GAS, TOXIC, OXIDISING, N.O.S.	3307
LIQUEFIED GAS, TOXIC, FLAMMABLE, N.O.S.	3160
LIQUEFIED GASES, non-flammable, charged with nitrogen, carbon dioxide or air	1058
Liquefied petroleum gas, see	1075
LITHIUM	1415
Lithium alkyls, liquid, see	3394
Lithium alkyls, solid, see	3393
LITHIUM ALUMINIUM HYDRIDE	1410
LITHIUM ALUMINIUM HYDRIDE, ETHEREAL	1411
LITHIUM BOROHYDRIDE	1413
LITHIUM FERROSILICON	2830
LITHIUM HYDRIDE	1414
LITHIUM HYDRIDE, FUSED SOLID	2805
LITHIUM HYDROXIDE	2680
LITHIUM HYDROXIDE SOLUTION	2679
LITHIUM HYPOCHLORITE, DRY or **LITHIUM HYPOCHLORITE MIXTURE**	1471
Lithium in cartouches, see	1415
LITHIUM ION BATTERIES (including lithium ion polymer batteries)	3480
LITHIUM ION BATTERIES CONTAINED IN EQUIPMENT or **LITHIUM ION BATTERIS PACKED WITH EQUIPMENT**	3481
LITHIUM METAL BATTERIES (including lithium alloy batteries)	3090
LITHIUM METAL BATTERIES CONTAINED IN EQUIPMENT or **LITHIUM METAL BATTERIES PACKED WITH EQUIPMENT**	3091
LITHIUM NITRATE	2722

Substance	UN No
LITHIUM NITRIDE	2806
LITHIUM PEROXIDE	1472
Lithium silicide, see	1417
LITHIUM SILICON	1417
L.n.g., see	1972
LONDON PURPLE	1621
L.p.g., see	1075
Lye, see	1823
Lythene, see	1268
MACHINERY, FUEL CELL, FLAMMABLE LIQUID POWERED	3528
MACHINERY, INTERNAL COMBUSTION, FLAMMABLE GAS POWERED or **MACHINERY, FUEL CELL, FLAMMABLE GAS POWERED**	3529
MACHINERY, INTERNAL COMBUSTION, FLAMMABLE LIQUID POWERED	3528
MAGNESIUM or **MAGNESIUM ALLOYS,** with more than 50% magnesium in pellets, turnings or ribbons	1869
Magnesium alkyls, see	3394
MAGNESIUM ALLOYS, POWDER	1418
MAGNESIUM ALUMINIUM PHOSPHIDE	1419
MAGNESIUM ARSENATE	1622
Magnesium bisulphite solution, see	2693
MAGNESIUM BROMATE	1473
MAGNESIUM CHLORATE	2723
Magnesium chloride and chlorate mixtures, see	1459 3407
MAGNESIUM DIAMIDE	2004
Magnesium diphenyl, see	3393
MAGNESIUM FLUOROSILICATE	2853
MAGNESIUM GRANULES, COATED, microns	2950

Substance	UN No
MAGNESIUM HYDRIDE	2010
MAGNESIUM NITRATE	1474
MAGNESIUM PERCHLORATE	1475
MAGNESIUM PEROXIDE	1476
MAGNESIUM PHOSPHIDE	2011
MAGNESIUM POWDER	1418
Magnesium scrap, see	1869
MAGNESIUM SILICIDE	2624
Magnesium silicofluoride, see	2853
MAGNETIZED MATERIAL	2807
MALEIC ANHYDRIDE or **MALEIC ANHYDRIDE, MOLTEN**	2215
Malonic dinitrile, see	2647
Malonodinitrile, see	2647
MALONONITRILE	2647
MANEB, STABILISED or **MANEB PREPARATIONS, STABILIZED** against self-heating	2968
MANEB or **MANEB PREPARATION** with not less than 60% maneb	2210
Manganese ethylene-di-dithiocarbamate, see	2210
Manganese ethylene-1,2-di-dithiocarbamate, see	2210
MANGANESE NITRATE	2724
Manganese (II) nitrate, see	2724
MANGANESE RESINATE	1330
Manganous nitrate, see	2724
MATCHES, FUSEE	2254
MATCHES, SAFETY, (book, card or strike on box	1944
MATCHES, "STRIKE ANYWHERE"	1331
MATCHES, WAX "VESTA"	1945
MEDICAL WASTE, N.O.S.	3291
MEDICINE, LIQUID, FLAMMABLE, TOXIC, N.O.S.	3248
MEDICINE, LIQUID, TOXIC, N.O.S.	1851
MEDICINE, SOLID, TOXIC, N.O.S.	3249
p-Mentha-1,8-diene, see	2052
MERCAPTANS, LIQUID, FLAMMABLE, TOXIC, N.O.S., or **MERCAPTAN MIXTURE, LIQUID, FLAMMABLE, TOXIC, N.O.S.**	1228
MERCAPTANS, LIQUID, FLAMMABLE, N.O.S. or **MERCAPTAN MIXTURE, LIQUID, FLAMMABLE, N.O.S.**	3336
MERCAPTANS, LIQUID, TOXIC, FLAMMABLE, N.O.S. or **MERCAPTAN MIXTURE, LIQUID, TOXIC, FLAMMABLE, N.O.S.**	3071
2-Mercaptoethanol, see	2966
2-Mercaptopropionic acid, see	2936
MERCURIC ARSENATE	1623
MERCURIC CHLORIDE	1624
MERCURIC NITRATE	1625
MERCURIC POTASSIUM CYANIDE	1626
Mercuric sulphate, see	1645
Mercurol, see	1639
Mercurous bisulphate, see	1645
MERCUROUS NITRATE	1627
Mercurous sulphate, see	1645
MERCURY	2809
MERCURY ACETATE	1629
MERCURY AMMONIUM CHLORIDE	1630
MERCURY BASED PESTICIDE, LIQUID, FLAMMABLE, TOXIC, flash point less than 23°C	2778
MERCURY BASED PESTICIDE, LIQUID, TOXIC, FLAMMABLE, flash point 23°C or above	3011
MERCURY BASED PESTICIDE, LIQUID, TOXIC	3012

Substance	UN No
MERCURY BASED PESTICIDE, SOLID, TOXIC	2777
MERCURY BENZOATE	1631
Mercury bichloride, see	1624
MERCURY BROMIDES	1634
MERCURY COMPOUND, LIQUID, N.O.S.	2024
MERCURY COMPOUND, SOLID, N.O.S.	2025
MERCURY CONTAINED IN MANUFACTURED ARTICLES	3506
MERCURY CYANIDE	1636
MERCURY GLUCONATE	1637
MERCURY IODIDE	1638
MERCURY NUCLEATE	1639
MERCURY OLEATE	1640
MERCURY OXIDE	1641
MERCURY OXYCYANIDE, DESENSITIZED	1642
MERCURY POTASSIUM IODIDE	1643
MERCURY SALICYLATE	1644
MERCURY SULPHATE	1645
MERCURY THIOCYANATE	1646
Mesitylene, see	2325
MESITYL OXIDE	1229
Metal alkyl halides, water-reactive, n.o.s or metal aryl halides, water-reactive, n.o.s., see	3394
Metal alkyl hydrides, water-reactive, n.o.s or metal aryl hydrides, water-reactive, n.o.s., see	3394
Metal alkyls, water-reactive, n.o.s or metal aryls, water-reactive, n.o.s., see	3393
METAL CARBONYLS, LIQUID, N.O.S.	3281
METAL CARBONYLS, SOLID, N.O.S.	3466

Substance	UN No
METAL CATALYST, DRY	2881
METAL CATALYST, WETTED with a visible excess of liquid	1378
METALDEHYDE	1332
METAL HYDRIDES, FLAMMABLE, N.O.S.	3182
METAL HYDRIDES, WATER-REACTIVE, N.O.S.	1409
METAL POWDER, FLAMMABLE, N.O.S.	3089
METAL POWDER, SELF-HEATING, N.O.S.	3189
METAL SALTS OF ORGANIC COMPOUNDS, FLAMMABLE, N.O.S.	3181
METALLIC SUBSTANCE, WATER-REACTIVE, N.O.S.	3208
METALLIC SUBSTANCE, WATER-REACTIVE, SELF-HEATING, N.O.S.	3209
METHACRYLALDEHYDE, STABILIZED	2396
METHACRYLIC ACID, STABILIZED	2531
METHACRYLONITRILE, STABILIZED	3079
METHALLYL ALCOHOL	2614
Methanal, see	1198 2209
Methane and hydrogen mixture, see	2034
METHANE, COMPRESSED	1971
METHANE, REFRIGERATED LIQUID	1972
METHANESULPHONYL CHLORIDE	3246
METHANOL	1230
2-Methoxyethyl acetate, see	1189
METHOXYMETHYL ISOCYANATE	2605
4-METHOXY-4-METHYLPENTAN-2-ONE	2293

Substance	UN No
1-Methoxy-2-nitrobenzene, see	2730 3458
1-Methoxy-3-nitrobenzene, see	2730 3458
1-Methoxy-4-nitrobenzene, see	2730
1-METHOXY-2-PROPANOL	3092
METHYL ACETATE	1231
METHYLACETYLENE AND PROPADIENE MIXTURE, STABILIZED	1060
beta-Methyl acrolein, see	1143
METHYL ACRYLATE, STABILIZED	1919
METHYLAL	1234
Methyl alcohol, see	1230
Methyl allyl alcohol, see	2614
METHYLALLYL CHLORIDE	2554
METHYLAMINE, ANHYDROUS	1061
METHYLAMINE, AQUEOUS SOLUTION	1235
METHYLAMYL ACETATE	1233
Methyl amyl alcohol, see	2053
Methyl amyl ketone, see	1110
N-METHYLANILINE	2294
Methylated spirit, see	1986 1987
alpha-METHYLBENZYL ALCOHOL, LIQUID	2937
alpha-METHYLBENZYL ALCOHOL, SOLID	3438
METHYL BROMIDE, with not more than 2% chloropicrin	1062
Methyl bromide and chloropicrin mixture, see	1581
METHYL BROMIDE AND ETHYLENE DIBROMIDE MIXTURE, LIQUID	1647
METHYL BROMOACETATE	2643
2-METHYLBUTANAL	3371

Substance	UN No
3-METHYLBUTAN-2-ONE	2397
2-METHYL-1-BUTENE	2459
2-METHYL-2-BUTENE	2460
3-METHYL-1-BUTENE	2561
N-METHYLBUTYLAMINE	2945
METHYL tert-BUTYL ETHER	2398
METHYL BUTYRATE	1237
METHYL CHLORIDE	1063
Methyl chloride and chloropicrin mixture, see	1582
METHYL CHLORIDE AND METHYLENE CHLORIDE MIXTURE	1912
METHYL CHLOROACETATE	2295
Methyl chlorocarbonate, see	1238
Methyl chloroform, see	2831
METHYL CHLOROFORMATE	1238
METHYL CHLOROMETHYL ETHER	1239
METHYL 2-CHLOROPROPIONATE	2933
Methyl alpha-chloropropionate, see	2933
METHYLCHLOROSILANE	2534
Methyl cyanide, see	1648
METHYLCYCLOHEXANE	2296
METHYLCYCLOHEXANOLS, flammable	2617
METHYCYCLOHEXANONE	2297
METHYLCYCLOPENTANE	2298
METHYL DICHLOROACETATE	2299
METHYLDICHLOROSILANE	1242
Methylene bromide, see	2664
Methylene chloride, see	1593
Methylene chloride and methyl chloride mixture, see	1912
Methylene cyanide, see	2647

Substance	UN No
p,p'-Methylene dianiline, see	2651
Methylene dibromide, see	2664
2,2'-Methylene-di-(3,4,6-trichlorophenol), see	2875
Methyl ethyl ether, see	1039
METHYL ETHYL KETONE	1193
2-METHYL-5-ETHYLPYRIDINE	2300
METHYL FLUORIDE	2454
METHYL FORMATE	1243
2-METHYLFURAN	2301
Methyl glycol, see	1188
Methyl glycol acetate, see	1189
2-METHYL-2-HEPTANETHIOL	3023
5-METHYLHEXAN-2-ONE	2302
METHYLHYDRAZINE	1244
METHYL IODIDE	2644
METHYL ISOBUTYL CARBINOL	2053
METHYL ISOBUTYL KETONE	1245
METHYL ISOCYANATE	2480
METHYL ISOPROPENYL KETONE, STABILIZED	1246
METHYL ISOTHIOCYANATE	2477
METHYL ISOVALERATE	2400
METHYL MAGNESIUM BROMIDE IN ETHYL ETHER	1928
METHYL MERCAPTAN	1064
Methyl mercaptopropionaldehyde, see	2785
METHYL METHACRYLATE MONOMER, STABILIZED	1247
4-METHYLMORPHOLINE (N-METHYLMORPHOLINE)	2535
METHYL NITRITE	2455
METHYL ORTHOSILICATE	2606
METHYLPENTADIENE	2461

Substance	UN No
Methylpentanes, see	1208
2-METHYLPENTAN-2-OL	2560
4-Methylpentan-2-ol, see	2053
3-Methyl-2-penten-4-yn-1-ol, see	2705
METHYLPHENYLDICHLOROSILANE	2437
2-Methyl-2-phenylpropane, see	2709
1-METHYLPIPERIDINE	2399
METHYL PROPIONATE	1248
Methylpropylbenzene, see	2046
METHYL PROPYL ETHER	2612
METHYL PROPYL KETONE	1249
Methyl pyridines, see	2313
Methylstyrene, see	2618
alpha-Methylstyrene, see	2303
Methyl sulphate, see	1595
Methyl sulphide, see	1164
METHYLTETRAHYDROFURAN	2536
METHYL TRICHLOROACETATE	2533
METHYLTRICHLOROSILANE	1250
alpha-METHYLVALERALDEHYDE	2367
Methyl vinyl benzene, see	2618
METHYL VINYL KETONE, STABILIZED	1251
M.i.b.c., see	2053
Mirbane oil, see	1662
Mixtures A, A01, A02, A0, A1, B1, B2, B or C, see	1965
Mixture F1, F2 or F3, see	1078
MIXTURES OF 1.3-BUTADIENE AND HYDROCARBONS, STABILIZED	1010
Mixture P1 or P2, see	1060
MOLYBDENUM PENTACHLORIDE	2508

Substance	UN No
Monochloroacetic acid, see	1750 1751
Monochlorobenzene, see	1134
Monochlorodifluoromethane, see	1018
Monochlorodifluoromethane and monochloropentafluoroethane mixture, see	1973
Monochlorodifluoromonobromomethane, see	1974
Monochloropentafluoroethane and monochlorodifluoromethane mixture, see	1973
Monoethylamine, see	1036
Monopropylamine, see	1277
MONONITROTOLUIDINES	2660
MORPHOLINE	2054
MOTOR FUEL ANTI-KNOCK MIXTURE	1649
MOTOR FUEL ANTI-KNOCK MIXTURE, FLAMMABLE	3483
MOTOR SPIRIT	1203
Motor spirit and ethanol mixture, with more than 10% ethanol, see	3475
Muriatic acid, see	1789
MUSK XYLENE	2956
Mysorite, see	2212
Naphta, see	1268
Naphta, petroleum, see	1268
Naphta, solvent, see	1268
NAPHTHALENE, CRUDE	1334
NAPHTHALENE, MOLTEN	2304
NAPHTHALENE, REFINED	1334
alpha-**NAPHTHYLAMINE**	2077
beta-**NAPHTHYLAMINE, SOLID**	1650
beta-**NAPHTHYLAMINE SOLUTION**	3411
NAPHTHYLTHIOUREA	1651

Substance	UN No
1-Naphthylthiourea, see	1651
NAPHTHYLUREA	1652
NATURAL GAS, COMPRESSED, with high methane content	1971
NATURAL GAS, REFRIGERATED LIQUID, with high methane content	1972
Natural gasoline, see	1203
Neohexane, see	1208
NEON, COMPRESSED	1065
NEON, REFRIGERATED LIQUID	1913
Neothyl, see	2612
NICKEL CARBONYL	1259
NICKEL CYANIDE	1653
Nickel (II) cyanide, see	1653
NICKEL NITRATE	2725
Nickel (II) nitrate	2725
NICKEL NITRITE	2726
Nickel (II) nitrite, see	2726
Nickelous nitrate, see	2725
Nickelous nitrite, see	2726
Nickel tetracarbonyl, see	1259
NICOTINE	1654
NICOTINE COMPOUND, LIQUID, N.O.S. or **NICOTINE PREPARATION, LIQUID, N.O.S.**	3144
NICOTINE COMPOUND, SOLID, or **SOLUTION, N.O.S.** or **NICOTINE PREPARATION, SOLID,** or **SOLUTION, N.O.S.**	1655
NICOTINE HYDROCHLORIDE, LIQUID or **SOLUTION**	1656
NICOTINE HYDROCHLORIDE, SOLID	3444
NICOTINE SALICYLATE	1657
NICOTINE SULPHATE, SOLID	3445
NICOTINE SULPHATE SOLUTION	1658

Substance	UN No
NICOTINE TARTRATE	1659
NITRATES, INORGANIC, N.O.S.	1477
NITRATES, INORGANIC, AQUEOUS SOLUTION, N.O.S.	3218
NITRATING ACID, MIXTURE	1796
NITRATING ACID, MIXTURE, SPENT	1826
NITRIC ACID, other than red fuming nitric acid	2031
NITRIC ACID, RED FUMING	2032
NITRIC OXIDE, COMPRESSED	1660
NITRIC OXIDE AND DINITROGEN TETROXIDE MIXTURE	1975
NITRIC OXIDE AND NITROGEN DIOXIDE, MIXTURE	1975
NITRILES, FLAMMABLE, TOXIC, N.O.S.	3273
NITRILES, TOXIC, FLAMMABLE, N.O.S.	3275
NITRILES, LIQUID, TOXIC, N.O.S.	3276
NITRILES, SOLID, TOXIC, N.O.S.	3439
NITRITES, INORGANIC, N.O.S.	2627
NITRITES, INORGANIC, AQUEOUS SOLUTION, N.O.S.	3219
NITROANILINES (o-,m-,p-)	1661
NITROANISOLES, LIQUID	2730
NITROANISOLES, SOLID	3458
NITROBENZENE	1662
Nitrobenzene bromide, see	2732
NITROBENZENESULPHONIC ACID	2305
Nitrobenzol, see	1662
NITROBENZOTRIFLUORIDES, LIQUID	2306
NITROBENZOTRIFLUORIDES, SOLID	3431
NITROBROMOBENZENES, LIQUID	2732

Substance	UN No
NITROBROMOBENZENES, SOLID	3459
NITROCELLULOSE SOLUTIONS, FLAMMABLE, with not more than 12.6% nitrogen by dry mass, and not more than 55% nitrocellulose	2059
NITROCELLULOSE MEMBRANE FILTERS, with not more than 12.6% nitrogen by dry mass	3270
NITROCELLULOSE, with not more than 12.6% nitrogen by dry mass, MIXTURE, WITHOUT PLASTICIZER, WITH OR WITHOUT PIGMENT	2557
NITROCELLULOSE with ALCOHOL, not less than 25% alcohol	2556
NITROCELLULOSE WITH WATER not less than 25% water by mass	2555
Nitrochlorobenzene, see	1578 3409
3-NITRO-4-CHLOROBENZO-TRIFLUORIDE	2307
NITROCRESOLS, LIQUID	3434
NITROCRESOLS, SOLID	2446
NITROETHANE	2842
NITROGEN, COMPRESSED	1066
Nitrogen dioxide, see	1067
NITROGEN, REFRIGERATED LIQUID	1977
NITROGEN TRIFLUORIDE	2451
NITROGEN TRIOXIDE	2421
NITROGLYERIN MIXTURE, DESENSITIZED, LIQUID, N.O.S., with not more than 30% nitroglycerin by mass	3357
NITROGLYCERIN MIXTURE, DESENSITIZED, SOLID, N.O.S., with more than 2% but not more than 10% nitroglycerin by mass	3319
NITROGLYCERIN MIXTURE, DESENSITIZED, LIQUID, FLAMMABLE, N.O.S., with not more than 30% nitroglycerin by mass	3343

Substance	UN No
NITROGLYCERIN SOLUTION IN ALCOHOL, with not more than 1% nitroglycerin	1204
NITROGLYCERIN, SOLUTION, IN ALCOHOL, with more than 1% but not more than 5% nitroglycerin	3064
NITROGUANIDINE, WETTED, with not less than 20% water by mass	1336
NITROHYDROCHLORIC ACID	1798
NITROMETHANE	1261
Nitromuriatic acid, see	1798
NITRONAPHTHALENE	2538
NITROPHENOLS (o-,m-,p-)	1663
4-NITROPHENYLHYDRAZINE, with not less than 30% water by mass	3376
NITROPROPANES	2608
p-NITROSODIMETHYLANILINE	1369
NITROSTARCH, WETTED, with not less than 20% water by mass	1337
NITROSYL CHLORIDE	1069
NITROSYLSULPHURIC ACID, LIQUID	2308
NITROSYLSULPHURIC ACID, SOLID	3456
NITROTOLUENES, LIQUID	1664
NITROTOLUENES, SOLID	3446
NITROTOLUIDINES	2660
NITROUS OXIDE	1070
NITROUS OXIDE, REFRIGERATED LIQUID	2201
NITROXYLENES, LIQUID	1665
NITROXYLENES, SOLID	3447
Non-activated carbon, see	1361
Non-activated charcoal, see	1361
NONANES	1920
NONYLTRICHLOROSILANE	1799
2,5-NORBORNADIENE, STABILIZED	2251

Substance	UN No
Normal propyl alcohol, see	1274
OCTADECYLTRICHLOROSILANE	1800
OCTADIENE	2309
OCTAFLUOROBUT-2-ENE	2422
OCTAFLUOROCYCLOBUTANE	1976
OCTAFLUOROPROPANE	2424
OCTANES	1262
OCTYL ALDEHYDES,	1191
tert-Octyl mercaptan, see	3023
OCTYLTRICHLOROSILANE	1801
Oenanthol, see	3056
OIL GAS, COMPRESSED	1071
Oleum, see	1831
ORGANIC PEROXIDE TYPE B, LIQUID	3101
ORGANIC PEROXIDE TYPE B, LIQUID, TEMPERATURE CONTROLLED	3111
ORGANIC PEROXIDE TYPE B, SOLID	3102
ORGANIC PEROXIDE TYPE B, SOLID, TEMPERATURE CONTROLLED	3112
ORGANIC PEROXIDE TYPE C, LIQUID	3103
ORGANIC PEROXIDE TYPE C, LIQUID, TEMPERATURE CONTROLLED	3113
ORGANIC PEROXIDE TYPE C, SOLID	3104
ORGANIC PEROXIDE TYPE C, SOLID, TEMPERATURE CONTROLLED	3114
ORGANIC PEROXIDE TYPE D, LIQUID	3105
ORGANIC PEROXIDE TYPE D, LIQUID, TEMPERATURE CONTROLLED	3115
ORGANIC PEROXIDE TYPE D, SOLID	3106

Substance	UN No
ORGANIC PEROXIDE TYPE D, SOLID, TEMPERATURE CONTROLLED	3116
ORGANIC PEROXIDE TYPE E, LIQUID	3107
ORGANIC PEROXIDE TYPE E, LIQUID, TEMPERATURE CONTROLLED	3117
ORGANIC PEROXIDE TYPE E, SOLID	3108
ORGANIC PEROXIDE TYPE E, SOLID, TEMPERATURE CONTROLLED	3118
ORGANIC PEROXIDE TYPE F, LIQUID	3109
ORGANIC PEROXIDE TYPE F, LIQUID, TEMPERATURE CONTROLLED	3119
ORGANIC PEROXIDE TYPE F, SOLID	3110
ORGANIC PEROXIDE TYPE F, SOLID, TEMPERATURE CONTROLLED	3120
ORGANIC PIGMENTS SELF-HEATING	3313
ORGANOARSENIC COMPOUND, LIQUID, N.O.S.	3280
ORGANOARSENIC COMPOUND, SOLID, N.O.S.	3465
ORGANOCHLORINE PESTICIDE, LIQUID, FLAMMABLE, TOXIC, flash point less than 23°C	2762
ORGANOCHLORINE PESTICIDE, LIQUID, TOXIC, FLAMMABLE, flash point 23°C or above	2995
ORGANOCHLORINE PESTICIDE, LIQUID, TOXIC	2996
ORGANOCHLORINE PESTICIDE, SOLID, TOXIC	2761
ORGANOMETALLIC COMPOUND, LIQUID, TOXIC, N.O.S.	3282

Substance	UN No
Organometallic compound, solid, water-reactive, flammable, n.o.s., see	3396
Organometallic compound or organometallic compound solution or organometallic compound dispersion, water-reactive, flammable, n.o.s., see	3399
ORGANOMETALLIC COMPOUND, SOLID, TOXIC, N.O.S.	3467
ORGANOMETALLIC SUBSTANCE, SOLID, PYROPHORIC	3391
ORGANOMETALLIC SUBSTANCE, LIQUID, PYROPHORIC	3392
ORGANOMETALLIC SUBSTANCE, SOLID, PYROPHORIC, WATER-REACTIVE	3393
ORGANOMETALLIC SUBSTANCE, LIQUID, PYROPHORIC, WATER-REACTIVE	3394
ORGANOMETALLIC SUBSTANCE, SOLID, WATER-REACTIVE	3395
ORGANOMETALLIC SUBSTANCE, SOLID, WATER-REACTIVE, FLAMMABLE	3396
ORGANOMETALLIC SUBSTANCE, SOLID, WATER-REACTIVE, SELF-HEATING	3397
ORGANOMETALLIC SUBSTANCE, LIQUID, WATER-REACTIVE	3398
ORGANOMETALLIC SUBSTANCE, LIQUID, WATER-REACTIVE, FLAMMABLE	3399
ORGANOMETALLIC SUBSTANCE, SOLID, SELF-HEATING	4000
ORGANOPHOSPHORUS COMPOUND, TOXIC, FLAMMABLE, N.O.S.	3279
ORGANOPHOSPHORUS COMPOUND, LIQUID, TOXIC, N.O.S.	3278
ORGANOPHOSPHORUS COMPOUND, SOLID, TOXIC, N.O.S.	3464

Substance	UN No
ORGANOPHOSPHOROUS PESTICIDE, LIQUID, FLAMMABLE, TOXIC, flash point less than 23°C	2784
ORGANOPHOSPHORUS PESTICIDE, LIQUID, TOXIC, FLAMMABLE, flash point 23°C or above	3017
ORGANOPHOSPHORUS PESTICIDE, LIQUID, TOXIC	3018
ORGANOPHOSPHORUS PESTICIDE, SOLID, TOXIC	2783
ORGANOTIN COMPOUND, LIQUID, N.O.S.	2788
ORGANOTIN COMPOUND, SOLID, N.O.S.	3146
ORGANOTIN PESTICIDE, LIQUID, FLAMMABLE, TOXIC, flash point less than 23°C	2787
ORGANOTIN PESTICIDE, LIQUID, TOXIC, FLAMMABLE, flash point 23°C or above	3019
ORGANOTIN PESTICIDE, LIQUID, TOXIC	3020
ORGANOTIN PESTICIDE, SOLID, TOXIC	2786
Orthophosphoric acid, see	1805
OSMIUM TETROXIDE	2471
OXIDISING LIQUID, CORROSIVE, N.O.S.	3098
OXIDISING LIQUID, N.O.S.	3139
OXIDISING LIQUID, TOXIC, N.O.S.	3099
OXIDISING SOLID, CORROSIVE, N.O.S.	3085
OXIDISING SOLID, FLAMMABLE, N.O.S.	3137
OXIDISING SOLID, N.O.S.	1479
OXIDISING SOLID, TOXIC, N.O.S.	3087
OXIDISING SOLID, SELF-HEATING, N.O.S.	3100

Substance	UN No
OXIDISING SOLID, WATER-REACTIVE, N.O.S.	3121
Oxirane, see	1040
OXYGEN, COMPRESSED	1072
OXYGEN DIFLUORIDE, COMPRESSED	2190
OXYGEN GENERATOR, CHEMICAL	3356
OXYGEN, REFRIGERATED LIQUID	1073
1-Oxy-4-nitrobenzene, see	1663
PACKAGINGS, DISCARDED, EMPTY, UNCLEANED	3509
PAINT (including paint, lacquer, enamel, stain, shellac, varnish, polish, liquid filler and liquid lacquer base)	3066 3469 3470
PAINT, CORROSIVE, FLAMMABLE, or PAINT RELATED MATERIAL, CORROSIVE, FLAMMABLE	3470
PAINT, FLAMMABLE, CORROSIVE, or PAINT RELATED MATERIAL, FLAMMABLE, CORROSIVE	3469
PAINT RELATED MATERIAL (including paint thinning or reducing compound)	1263 3066 3469 3470
Paint thinning and reducing compound, see	1263 3066 3469 3470
PAPER, UNSATURATED OIL TREATED, incompletely dried (includes carbon paper)	1379
Paraffin, see	1223
PARAFORMALDEHYDE	2213
PARALDEHYDE	1264
PCBs, LIQUID	2315
PCBs, SOLID	3432
PENTABORANE	1380
PENTACHLOROETHANE	1669
PENTACHLOROPHENOL	3155

Substance	UN No
PENTAERYTHRITE TETRANITRATE (PENTAERYTHRITOL TRETRANITRATE; PETN) MIXTURE, DESENSITIZED, SOLID, N.O.S., with more than 10% but not more than 20% PETN by mass	3344
PENTAFLUOROETHANE	3220
Pentafluoroethane, 1,1,1-trifluoroethane, and 1,1,1,2- tetrafluoroethane azeotropic mixture with approximately 44% pentafluoroethane and 52% 1,1,1- triflluoroethane, see	3337
PENTAMETHYLHEPTANE	2286
Pentanal, see	2058
PENTANE-2,4-DIONE	2310
PENTANES, liquid	1265
3-Pentanol, see	1105
n-Pentanol, see	1265
PENTANOLS	1105
1-PENTENE	1108
1-PENTOL	2705
Pentyl nitrite, see	1113
PERCHLORATES, INORGANIC, N.O.S.	1481
PERCHLORATES, INORGANIC, AQUEOUS SOLUTION, N.O.S.	3211
PERCHLORIC ACID, with more than 50% but not more than 72% acid by mass	1873
PERCHLORIC ACID, with not more than 50% acid by mass	1802
Perchlorobenzene, see	2729
Perchlorocyclopentadiene, see	2646
Perchloroethylene, see	1897
PERCHLOROMETHYL MERCAPTAN	1670
PERCHLORYL FLUORIDE	3083
Perfluoroacetylchloride, see	3057

Substance	UN No
PERFLUORO (ETHYL VINYL ETHER)	3154
PERFLUORO (METHYL VINYL ETHER)	3153
Perfluoropropane, see	2424
PERFUMERY PRODUCTS, with flammable solvents	1266
PERMANGANATES, INORGANIC, N.O.S.	1482
PERMANGANATES, INORGANIC, AQUEOUS SOLUTION, N.O.S.	3214
PEROXIDES, INORGANIC, N.O.S.	1483
PERSULPHATES, INORGANIC, N.O.S.	3215
PERSULPHATES, INORGANIC, AQUEOUS SOLUTION, N.O.S.	3216
PESTICIDE, LIQUID, FLAMMABLE, TOXIC, N.O.S., flash point less than 23°C	3021
PESTICIDE, LIQUID, TOXIC, FLAMMABLE, N.O.S., flash point 23°C or above	2903
PESTICIDE, LIQUID, TOXIC, N.O.S.	2902
PESTICIDE, SOLID, TOXIC, N.O.S.	2588
Pesticides, toxic, under compressed gas, n.o.s., see	1950
PETROL	1203
Petroleum and ethanol mixture, with more than 10% ethanol, see	3475
PETROLEUM CRUDE OIL	1267
PETROLEUM DISTILLATES, N.O.S.	1268
Petroleum ether, see	1268
PETROLEUM GASES, LIQUEFIED	1075
Petroleum naphtha, see	1268
Petroleum oil, see	1268
PETROLEUM PRODUCTS, N.O.S.	1268
Petroleum raffinate, see	1268

Substance	UN No
Petroleum spirit, see	1268
PETROLEUM SOUR CRUDE OIL, FLAMMABLE, TOXIC	3494
PHENACYL BROMIDE	2645
PHENETIDINES	2311
PHENOL, MOLTEN	2312
PHENOL, SOLID	1671
PHENOL SOLUTION	2821
PHENOLATES, LIQUID	2904
PHENOLATES, SOLID	2905
PHENOLSULPHONIC ACID, LIQUID	1803
PHENOXYACETIC ACID DERIVATIVE PESTICIDE, LIQUID, FLAMMABLE, TOXIC, flash point less than 23°C	3346
PHENOXYACETIC ACID DERIVATIVE PESTICIDE, LIQUID, TOXIC	3348
PHENOXYACETIC ACID DERIVATIVE PESTICIDE, LIQUID, TOXIC, FLAMMABLE, flash point not less than 23°C	3347
PHENOXYACETIC ACID DERIVATIVE PESTICIDE, SOLID, TOXIC	3345
PHENYLACETONITRILE LIQUID	2470
PHENYLACETYL CHLORIDE	2577
Phenylamine, see	1547
1-Phenylbutane, see	2709
2-Phenylbutane, see	2709
PHENYLCARBYLAMINE CHLORIDE	1672
PHENYL CHLOROFORMATE	2746
Phenyl cyanide, see	2224
PHENYLENEDIAMINES(o-,m-,p)	1673
Phenylethylene, see	2055
PHENYLHYDRAZINE	2572

Substance	UN No
PHENYL ISOCYANATE	2487
Phenylisocyanodichloride, see	1672
PHENYL MERCAPTAN	2337
PHENYLMERCURIC ACETATE	1674
PHENYLMERCURIC COMPOUND, N.O.S.	2026
PHENYLMERCURIC HYDROXIDE	1894
PHENYLMERCURIC NITRATE	1895
PHENYLPHOSPHORUS DICHLORIDE	2798
PHENYLPHOSPHORUS THIODICHLORIDE	2799
2-Phenylpropene, see	2303
PHENYLTRICHLOROSILANE	1804
PHOSGENE	1076
9-PHOSPHABICYCLONONANES	2940
PHOSPHINE	2199
PHOSPHINE, ABSORBED	3525
Phosphoretted hydrogen, see	2199
PHOSPHORIC ACID, SOLUTION	1805
PHOSPHORIC ACID, SOLID	3453
Phosphoric acid, anhydrous, see	1807
PHOSPHOROUS ACID	2834
PHOSPHORUS, AMORPHOUS	1338
Phosphorus bromide, see	1808
Phosphorus chloride, see	1809
PHOSPHORUS HEPTASULPHIDE, free from yellow and white phosphorus	1339
PHOSPHORUS OXYBROMIDE	1939
PHOSPHORUS OXYBROMIDE, MOLTEN	2576
PHOSPHORUS OXYCHLORIDE	1810
PHOSPHORUS PENTABROMIDE	2691
PHOSPHORUS PENTACHLORIDE	1806

Substance	UN No
PHOSPHORUS PENTAFLUORIDE	2198
PHOSPHORUS PENTAFLUORIDE, ADSORBED	3524
PHOSPHORUS PENTASULPHIDE, free from yellow and white phosphorus	1340
PHOSPHORUS PENTOXIDE	1807
PHOSPHORUS SESQUISULPHIDE, free from yellow and white phosphorus	1341
Phosphorus (V) sulphide, free from yellow and white phosphorus, see	1340
Phosphorus sulphochloride, see	1837
PHOSPHORUS TRIBROMIDE	1808
PHOSPHORUS TRICHLORIDE	1809
PHOSPHORUS TRIOXIDE	2578
PHOSPHORUS TRISULPHIDE, free from yellow and white phosphorus	1343
PHOSPHORUS, WHITE, MOLTEN	2447
PHOSPHORUS, WHITE or **YELLOW, DRY** or **UNDER WATER** or **IN SOLUTION**	1381
Phosphoryl chloride, see	1810
PHTHALIC ANHYDRIDE, with more than 0.05% maleic anhydride	2214
PICOLINE	2313
Picric Acid, Wetted, see	1344 3364
Picrite, Wetted, see	1336
Picrotoxin, see	3172 3462
Picryl Chloride, Wetted, see	3365
alpha-PINENE	2368
PINE OIL	1272
PIPERAZINE	2579
PIPERIDINE	2401
Privaloyl chloride, see	2438

Substance	UN No
PLASTICS MOULDING COMPOUND in dough, sheet or extruded rope form, evolving flammable vapour	3314
PLASTICS, NITROCELLULOSE-BASED, SELF-HEATING, N.O.S.	2006
Polish, see	1263 3066 3469 3470
POLYAMINES, FLAMMABLE, CORROSIVE, N.O.S.	2733
POLYAMINES, LIQUID, CORROSIVE, N.O.S.	2735
POLYAMINES, LIQUID, CORROSIVE, FLAMMABLE, N.O.S.	2734
POLYAMINES, SOLID, CORROSIVE, N.O.S.	3259
POLYCHLORINATED BIPHENYLS, LIQUID	2315
POLYCHLORINATED BIPHENYLS, SOLID	3432
POLYESTER RESIN KIT, liquid base material	3269
POLYESTER RESIN KIT, solid base material	3527
POLYHALOGENATED BIPHENYLS, LIQUID	3151
POLYHALOGENATED BIPHENYLS, SOLID	3152
POLYHALOGENATED TERPHENYLS, LIQUID	3151
POLYHALOGENATED TERPHENYLS, SOLID	3152
POLYMERIC BEADS, EXPANDABLE, evolving flammable vapour	2211
POLYMERIZING SUBSTANCE, LIQUID, STABILIZED, N.O.S.	3531
POLYMERIZING SUBSTANCE, LIQUID, TEMPERATURE CONTROLLED, N.O.S.	3533

Substance	UN No
POLYMERIZING SUBSTANCE, LIQUID, TEMPERATURE CONTROLLED, N.O.S.	3534
POLYMERIZING SUBSTANCE, SOLID, TEMPERATURE CONTROLLED, N.O.S.	3532
Polystyrene beads, evolving flammable vapour, see	2211
POTASSIUM	2257
POTASSIUM ARSENATE	1677
POTASSIUM ARSENITE	1678
Potassium bifluoride, see	1811
Potassium bisulphate, see	2509
Potassium bisulphite solution, see	2693
POTASSIUM BOROHYDRIDE	1870
POTASSIUM BROMATE	1484
POTASSIUM CHLORATE	1485
POTASSIUM CHLORATE, AQUEOUS SOLUTION	2427
POTASSIUM CUPROCYANIDE	1679
POTASSIUM CYANIDE, SOLID	1680
POTASSIUM CYANIDE SOLUTION	3413
Potassium dicyanocuprate (I), see	1679
POTASSIUM DITHIONITE	1929
POTASSIUM FLUORIDE, SOLID	1812
POTASSIUM FLUORIDE SOLUTION	3422
POTASSIUM FLUOROACETATE	2628
POTASSIUM FLUOROSILICATE	2655
Potassium hexafluorosilicate, see	2655
Potassium hydrate, see	1814
POTASSIUM HYDROGENDIFLUORIDE, SOLID	1811
POTASSIUM HYDROGENDIFLUORIDE SOLUTION	3421
POTASSIUM HYDROGEN SULPHATE	2509

Substance	UN No
POTASSIUM HYDROSULPHITE	1929
Potassium hydroxide, liquid, see	1814
POTASSIUM HYDROXIDE, SOLID	1813
POTASSIUM HYDROXIDE SOLUTION	1814
POTASSIUM METAL ALLOYS, LIQUID	1420
POTASSIUM METAL ALLOYS, SOLID	3403
POTASSIUM METAVANADATE	2864
POTASSIUM MONOXIDE	2033
POTASSIUM NITRATE	1486
Potassium nitrate and sodium nitrate mixture, see	1499
POTASSIUM NITRATE and SODIUM NITRITE MIXTURE	1487
POTASSIUM NITRITE	1488
POTASSIUM PERCHLORATE	1489
POTASSIUM PERMANGANATE	1490
POTASSIUM PEROXIDE	1491
POTASSIUM PERSULPHATE	1492
POTASSIUM PHOSPHIDE	2012
Potassium selenate, see	2630
Potassium selenite, see	2630
Potassium silicofluoride, see	2655
POTASSIUM SODIUM ALLOYS, LIQUID	1422
POTASSIUM SODIUM ALLOYS, SOLID	3404
POTASSIUM SULPHIDE, ANHYDROUS or POTASSIUM SULPHIDE, with less than 30% water of crystallization	1382
POTASSIUM SULPHIDE, HYDRATED, with not less than 30% water of crystallization	1847
POTASSIUM SUPEROXIDE	2466
Potassium tetracyanomercurate (II), see	1626

Substance	UN No
PRINTING INK, FLAMMABLE or **PRINTING INK RELATED MATERIAL** (including printing ink thinning or reducing compound), flammable	1210
PROPADIENE, STABILIZED	2200
Propadiene and methyl acetylene mixture, stabilized, see	1060
PROPANE	1978
PROPANETHIOLS	2402
n-PROPANOL	1274
Propene, see	1077
PROPIONALDEHYDE	1275
PROPIONIC ACID, with not less than 10% and less than 90% acid by mass	1848
PROPIONIC ACID, with not less than 90% acid by mass	3463
PROPIONIC ANHYDRIDE	2496
PROPIONITRILE	2404
PROPIONYL CHLORIDE	1815
n-PROPYL ACETATE	1276
Propyl alcohol, normal, see	1274
PROPYLAMINE	1277
n-PROPYLBENZENE	2364
Propyl chloride, see	1278
n-PROPYL CHLOROFORMATE	2740
PROPYLENE	1077
PROPYLENE CHLOROHYDRIN	2611
1,2-PROPYLENEDIAMINE	2258
Propylene dichloride, see	1279
PROPYLENEIMINE, STABILIZED	1921
PROPYLENE OXIDE	1280
PROPYLENE TETRAMER	2850
Propylene trimer, see	2057
PROPYL FORMATES	1281
n-PROPYL ISOCYANATE	2482

Substance	UN No
Propyl mercaptan, see	2402
n-PROPYL NITRATE	1865
PROPYLTRICHLOROSILANE	1816
Pyrazine hexahydride, see	2579
PYRETHROID PESTICIDE, LIQUID, FLAMMABLE, TOXIC, flash point less than 23°C	3350
PYRETHROID PESTICIDE, LIQUID, TOXIC	3352
PYRETHROID PESTICIDE, LIQUID, TOXIC, FLAMMABLE, flash point not less than 23°C	3351
PYRETHROID PESTICIDE, SOLID, TOXIC	3349
PYRIDINE	1282
PYROPHORIC ALLOY, N.O.S.	1383
Pyrophoric organometallic compound, water-reactive, n.o.s., liquid, see	3394
Pyrophoric organometallic compound, water-reactive, n.o.s., solid, see	3393
PYROPHORIC LIQUID, INORGANIC, N.O.S.	3194
PYROPHORIC LIQUID, ORGANIC, N.O.S.	2845
PYROPHORIC METAL, N.O.S.	1383
PYROPHORIC SOLID, INORGANIC, N.O.S.	3200
PYROPHORIC SOLID, ORGANIC, N.O.S.	2846
PYROSULPHURYL CHLORIDE	1817
Pyroxylin solution, see	2059
PYRROLIDINE	1922
QUINOLINE	2656
Quinone, see	2587

Substance	UN No
RADIOACTIVE MATERIAL, EXCEPTED PACKAGE – ARTICLES MANUFACTURED FROM NATURAL DEPLETED URANIUM or DEPLETED URANIUM or NATURAL THORIUM	2909
RADIOACTIVE MATERIAL, EXCEPTED PACKAGE – EMPTY PACKAGING	2908
RADIOACTIVE MATERIAL, EXCEPTED PACKAGE – INSTRUMENTS or ARTICLES	2911
RADIOACTIVE MATERIAL, EXCEPTED PACKAGE – LIMITED QUANTITY OF MATERIAL	2910
RADIOACTIVE MATERIAL, LOW SPECIFIC ACTIVITY (LSA-I), non-fissile or fissile excepted	2912
RADIOACTIVE MATERIAL, LOW SPECIFIC ACTIVITY (LSA – II), FISSILE	3324
RADIOACTIVE MATERIAL, LOW SPECIFIC ACTIVITY (LSA -II), non-fissile or fissile excepted	3321
RADIOACTIVE MATERIAL, LOW SPECIFIC ACTIVITY (LSA – III), FISSILE	3325
RADIOACTIVE MATERIAL, LOW SPECIFIC ACTIVITY (LSA – III), non-fissile or fissile excepted	3322
RADIOACTIVE MATERIAL, SURFACE CONTAMINATED OBJECTS (SCO – I or SCO – II), FISSILE	3326
RADIOACTIVE MATERIAL, SURFACE CONTAMINATED OBJECTS (SCO – I or SCO – II), non-fissile or fissile excepted	2913
RADIOACTIVE MATERIAL, TRANSPORTED UNDER SPECIAL ARRANGEMENT, FISSILE	3331
RADIOACTIVE MATERIAL, TRANSPORTED UNDER SPECIAL ARRANGEMENT, non-fissile or fissile excepted	2919

Substance	UN No
RADIOACTIVE MATERIAL, TYPE A PACKAGE, FISSILE, non-special form	3327
RADIOACTIVE MATERIAL, TYPE A PACKAGE, non-special for, non-fissile or fissile excepted	2915
RADIOACTIVE MATERIAL, TYPE A PACKAGE, SPECIAL FORM, FISSILE	3333
RADIOACTIVE MATERIAL, TYPE A PACKAGE, SPECIAL FORM, non-fissile or fissile excepted	3332
RADIOACTIVE MATERIAL, TYPE B(M) PACKAGE, FISSILE	3329
RADIOACTIVE MATERIAL, TYPE B(M) PACKAGE, non-fissile or fissile excepted	2917
RADIOACTIVE MATERIAL, TYPE B(U) PACKAGE, FISSILE	3328
RADIOACTIVE MATERIAL, TYPE B(U) PACKAGE, non-fissile or fissile excepted	2916
RADIOACTIVE MATERIAL, TYPE C PACKAGE, FISSILE	3330
RADIOACTIVE MATERIAL, TYPE C PACKAGE, non-fissile or fissile excepted	3323
RADIOACTIVE MATERIAL, URANIUM HEXFLUORIDE, FISSILE	2977
RADIOACTIVE MATERIAL, URANIUM HEXAFLUORIDE, non-fissile or fissile excepted	2978
RAGS, OILY	1856
RECEPTACLES, SMALL, CONTAINING GAS, without release device, not refillable	2037
Red phosphorus, see	1338
REFRIGERANT GAS, N.O.S.	1078
Refrigerant Gas R 12, see	1028
Refrigerant Gas R 12b1, see	1974
Refrigerant Gas R 13, see	1022

Substance	UN No
Refrigerant Gas R 13b1, see	1009
Refrigerant Gas R 14, see	1982
Refrigerant Gas R 21, see	1029
Refrigerant Gas R22, see	1018
Refrigerant Gas R 23, see	1984
Refrigerant Gas R 32, see	3252
Refrigerant Gas R 40, see	1063
Refrigerant Gas R 41, see	2454
Refrigerant Gas R 114, see	1958
Refrigerant Gas R 115, see	1020
Refrigerant Gas R 116, see	2193
Refrigerant Gas R 124, see	1021
Refrigerant Gas R 125, see	3220
Refrigerant Gas R 133a, see	1983
Refrigerant Gas R 134a, see	3159
Refrigerant Gas R 142b, see	2517
Refrigerant Gas R 143a, see	2035
Refrigerant Gas R 152a, see	1030
Refrigerant Gas R 161, see	2453
Refrigerant Gas R 218, see	2424
Refrigerant Gas R 227, see	3296
Refrigerant Gas R 404a, see	3337
Refrigerant Gas R 407a, see	3338
Refrigerant Gas R 407b, see	3339
Refrigerant Gas R 407c, see	3340
Refrigerant Gas R 500, see	2602
Refrigerant Gas R 502, see	1973
Refrigerant Gas R 503, see	2599
Refrigerant Gas R 1113, see	1082
Refrigerant Gas R 1132a, see	1959
Refrigerant Gas R 1216, see	1858
Refrigerant Gas R 1318, see	2422
Refrigerant Gas Rc 318, see	1976

Substance	UN No
REFRIGERATING MACHINES, containing flammable, non-toxic, liquefied gas	3358
REFRIGERATING MACHINES, containing non-flammable, non-toxic, gases or ammonia solutions (UN 2672)	2857
REGULATED MEDICAL WASTE, N.O.S.	3291
RESIN SOLUTION, flammable	1866
Resorcin, see	2876
RESORCINOL	2876
ROSIN OIL	1286
RUBBER SCRAP or **RUBBER SHODDY,** powdered or granulated	1345
RUBBER SOLUTION	1287
RUBIDIUM	1423
RUBIDIUM HYDROXIDE	2678
RUBIDIUM HYDROXIDE SOLUTION	2677
Rubidium nitrate, see	1477
Saltpetre, see	1486
Sand acid, see	1778
SAFETY DEVICES, electrically initiated	3268
Seat-belt pretensioners, see	3268
SEED CAKE with more than 1.5% oil and not more than 11% moisture	1386
SEED CAKE with not more than 1.5% oil and not more than 11% moisture	2217
Seed expellers, see	1386 2217
SELENATES	2630
SELENIC ACID	1905
SELENITES	2630
SELENIUM COMPOUND, LIQUID, N.O.S.	3440

Substance	UN No
SELENIUM COMPOUND, SOLID, N.O.S.	3283
SELENIUM DISULPHIDE	2657
SELENIUM HEXAFLUORIDE	2194
SELENIUM OXYCHLORIDE	2879
SELF-HEATING LIQUID, CORROSIVE, INORGANIC, N.O.S.	3188
SELF-HEATING LIQUID, CORROSIVE, ORGANIC, N.O.S.	3185
SELF-HEATING LIQUID, INORGANIC, N.O.S.	3186
SELF-HEATING LIQUID, ORGANIC, N.O.S.	3183
SELF-HEATING LIQUID, TOXIC, INORGANIC, N.O.S.	3187
SELF-HEATING LIQUID, TOXIC, ORGANIC, N.O.S.	3184
SELF-HEATING SOLID, CORROSIVE, ORGANIC, N.O.S.	3126
SELF-HEATING SOLID, INORGANIC, N.O.S.	3190
SELF-HEATING SOLID, CORROSIVE, INORGANIC, N.O.S.	3192
SELF-HEATING SOLID, TOXIC, INORGANIC, N.O.S.	3191
SELF-HEATING SOLID, ORGANIC, N.O.S.	3088
SELF-HEATING SOLID, OXIDISING, N.O.S.	3127
SELF-HEATING SOLID, TOXIC, ORGANIC, N.O.S.	3128
SELF-REACTIVE LIQUID TYPE B	3221
SELF-REACTIVE LIQUID TYPE B, TEMPERATURE CONTROLLED	3231
SELF-REACTIVE LIQUID TYPE C	3223
SELF-REACTIVE LIQUID TYPE C, TEMPERATURE CONTROLLED	3233
SELF-REACTIVE LIQUID TYPE D	3225
SELF-REACTIVE LIQUID TYPE D, TEMPERATURE CONTROLLED	3235

Substance	UN No
SELF-REACTIVE LIQUID TYPE E,	3227
SELF-REACTIVE LIQUID TYPE E, TEMPERATURE CONTROLLED	3237
SELF-REACTIVE LIQUID TYPE F	3229
SELF-REACTIVE LIQUID TYPE F, TEMPERATURE CONTROLLED	3239
SELF-REACTIVE SOLID TYPE B	3222
SELF-REACTIVE SOLID TYPE B, TEMPERATURE CONTROLLED	3232
SELF-REACTIVE SOLID TYPE C	3224
SELF-REACTIVE SOLID TYPE C, TEMPERATURE CONTROLLED	3234
SELF-REACTIVE SOLID TYPE D	3226
SELF-REACTIVE SOLID TYPE D, TEMPERATURE CONTROLLED	3236
SELF-REACTIVE SOLID TYPE E	3228
SELF-REACTIVE SOLID TYPE E, TEMPERATURE CONTROLLED	3238
SELF-REACTIVE SOLID TYPE F	3230
SELF-REACTIVE SOLID TYPE F, TEMPERATURE CONTROLLED	3240
SHALE OIL	1288
Shellac, see	1263 3066 3469 3470
SILANE	2203
Silicofluoric acid, see	1778
Silicofluorides, n.o.s., see	2856
Silicon chloride, see	1818
SILICON POWDER, AMORPHOUS	1346
SILICON TETRACHLORIDE	1818
SILICON TETRAFLUORIDE	1859
SILICON TETRAFLUORIDE, ADSORBED	3521
SILVER ARSENITE	1683
SILVER CYANIDE	1684

Substance	UN No
SILVER NITRATE	1493
SILVER PICRATE, WETTED, with not less than 30% water by mass	1347
SLUDGE ACID	1906
SODA LIME, with more than 4% sodium hydroxide	1907
SODIUM	1428
SODIUM ALUMINATE, SOLID	2812
SODIUM ALUMINATE SOLUTION	1819
SODIUM ALUMINIUM HYDRIDE	2835
SODIUM AMMONIUM VANADATE	2863
SODIUM ARSANILATE	2473
SODIUM ARSENATE	1685
SODIUM ARSENITE, AQUEOUS SOLUTIONS	1686
SODIUM ARSENITE, SOLID	2027
SODIUM AZIDE	1687
Sodium bifluoride, see	2439
Sodium binoxide, see	1504
Sodium bisulphite solution, see	2693
SODIUM BOROHYDRIDE	1426
SODIUM BOROHYDRIDE AND SODIUM HYDROXIDE SOLUTION, with not more than 12% sodium borohydride and not more than 40% sodium hydroxide by mass	3320
SODIUM BROMATE	1494
SODIUM CACODYLATE	1688
SODIUM CARBONATE PEROXYHYDRATE	3378
SODIUM CHLORATE	1495
SODIUM CHLORATE, AQUEOUS SOLUTION	2428
SODIUM CHLORITE	1496
SODIUM CHLOROACETATE	2659

Substance	UN No
SODIUM CUPROCYANIDE, SOLID	2316
SODIUM CUPROCYANIDE SOLUTION	2317
SODIUM CYANIDE, SOLID	1689
SODIUM CYANIDE SOLUTION	3414
Sodium dicyanocuprate (I), solid, see	2316
Sodium dicyanocuprate (I), solution, see	2317
Sodium dimethylarsenate, see	1688
SODIUM DINITRO-o-CRESOLATE, WETTED, with not less than 10% water by mass	3369
SODIUM DINITRO-o-CRESOLATE, WETTED, with not less than 15% water by mass	1348
Sodium dioxide, see	1504
SODIUM DITHIONITE	1384
SODIUM FLUORIDE, SOLID	1690
SODIUM FLUORIDE SOLUTION	3415
SODIUM FLUOROACETATE	2629
SODIUM FLUOROSILICATE	2674
Sodium hexafluorosilicate, see	2674
Sodium hydrate, see	1824
SODIUM HYDRIDE	1427
Sodium hydrogen 4-aminophenylarsenate, see	2473
SODIUM HYDROGENDIFLUORIDE	2439
SODIUM HYDROSULPHIDE, with less than 25% water of crystallization	2318
SODIUM HYDROSULPHIDE, HYDRATED, with not less than 25% water of crystallization	2949
SODIUM HYDROSULPHITE	1384
SODIUM HYDROXIDE, SOLID	1823
SODIUM HYDROXIDE SOLUTION	1824

Substance	UN No
Sodium metasilicate pentahydrate, see	3253
SODIUM METHYLATE	1431
SODIUM METHYLATE SOLUTION, in alcohol	1289
SODIUM MONOXIDE	1825
SODIUM NITRATE	1498
SODIUM NITRATE AND POTASSIUM NITRATE MIXTURE	1499
SODIUM NITRITE	1500
Sodium nitrite and potassium nitrate mixture, see	1487
SODIUM PENTACHLOROPHENATE	2567
SODIUM PERBORATE MONOHYDRATE	3377
SODIUM PERCHLORATE	1502
SODIUM PERMANGANATE	1503
SODIUM PEROXIDE	1504
SODIUM PEROXOBORATE, ANHYDROUS	3247
SODIUM PERSULPHATE	1505
SODIUM PHOSPHIDE	1432
SODIUM PICRAMATE, WETTED, with not less than 20% water by mass	1349
Sodium potassium alloys, see	1422
Sodium selenate, see	2630
Sodium selenite, see	2630
Sodium silicofluoride, see	2674
SODIUM SULPHIDE, ANHYDROUS or **SODIUM SULPHIDE,** with less than 30% water of crystallization	1385
SODIUM SULPHIDE, HYDRATED, with not less than 30% water	1849
SODIUM SUPEROXIDE	2547
SOLIDS CONTAINING CORROSIVE LIQUID, N.O.S.	3244

Substance	UN No
SOLIDS CONTAINING FLAMMABLE LIQUID, N.O.S.	3175
SOLIDS CONTAINING TOXIC LIQUID, N.O.S.	3243
Solvents, flammable, n.o.s., see	1993
Solvents, flammable, toxic, n.o.s., see	1992
Stain, see	1263 3066 3469 3470
STANNIC CHLORIDE, ANHYDROUS	1827
STANNIC CHLORIDE PENTAHYDRATE	2440
STANNIC PHOSPHIDES	1433
Steel swarf, see	2793
STIBINE	2676
STRAW	1327
Strontium alloys, pyrophoric, see	1383
STRONTIUM ARSENITE	1691
STRONTIUM CHLORATE	1506
Strontium dioxide, see	1509
STRONTIUM NITRATE	1507
STRONTIUM PERCHLORATE	1508
STRONTIUM PEROXIDE	1509
STRONTIUM PHOSPHIDE	2013
STRYCHNINE or **STRYCHNINE SALTS**	1692
STYRENE MONOMER, STABILIZED	2055
Substances liable to spontaneous combustion, n.o.s., see	2845 2846 3194 3200
SUBSTITUTED NITROPHENOL PESTICIDE, LIQUID, FLAMMABLE, TOXIC, flash point less than 23°C	2780

Substance	UN No
SUBSTITUTED NITROPHENOL PESTICIDE, LIQUID, TOXIC, FLAMMABLE, flash point not less than 23°C	3013
SUBSTITUTED NITROPHENOL PESTICIDE, LIQUID, TOXIC	3014
SUBSTITUTED NITROPHENOL PESTICIDE, SOLID, TOXIC	2779
SULPHAMIC ACID	2967
SULPHUR	1350
SULPHUR CHLORIDES	1828
Sulphur dichloride, see	1828
SULPHUR DIOXIDE	1079
SULPHUR HEXAFLUORIDE	1080
SULPHUR, MOLTEN	2448
Sulphur monochloride, see	1828
Sulphuretted hydrogen, see	1053
SULPHURIC ACID, with more than 51% acid	1830
SULPHURIC ACID, with not more than 51% acid	2796
SULPHURIC ACID, FUMING	1831
SULPHURIC ACID, SPENT	1832
Sulphuric and hydrofluoric acid mixture, see	1786
SULPHUROUS ACID	1833
SULPHUR TETRAFLUORIDE	2418
SULPHUR TRIOXIDE, STABILIZED	1829
SULPHURYL CHLORIDE	1834
SULPHURYL FLUORIDE	2191
Talcum with tremolite and/or actinolite, see	2212
Tars, liquid, at or above 100°C and below its flashpoint, see	3257
TARS, LIQUID, including road oils and cutbacks bitumens, with a flashpoint not greater than 60°C	1999
Tars, liquid, with a flashpoint above 60°C at or above its flashpoint, see	3256
Tartar, emetic, see	1551
TEAR GAS CANDLES	1700
TEAR GAS SUBSTANCE, LIQUID, N.O.S.	1693
TEAR GAS SUBSTANCE, SOLID, N.O.S.	3448
TELLURIUM COMPOUND, N.O.S.	3284
TELLURIUM HEXAFLUORIDE	2195
TERPENE HYDROCARBONS, N.O.S.	2319
TERPINOLENE	2541
TETRABROMOETHANE	2504
1,1,2,2-TETRACHLOROETHANE	1702
TETRACHLOROETHYLENE	1897
TETRAETHYLDITHIOPYROPHOSPHATE	1704
TETRAETHYLENEPENTAMINE	2320
Tetraethyl lead, see	1649
TETRAETHYL SILICATE	1292
Tetraethyoxysilane, see	1292
Tetrafluorodichloroethane, see	1958
1,1,1,2-TETRAFLUOROETHANE	3159
TETRAFLUOROETHYLENE, STABILIZED	1081
TETRAFLUOROMETHANE, (REFRIGERANT GAS R14)	1982
1,2,3,6-TETRAHYDROBENZALDEHYDE	2498
TETRAHYDROFURAN	2056
TETRAHYDROFURFURYLAMINE	2943
Tetrahydro-1, 4-oxazine, see	2054
TETRAHYDROPHTHALIC ANHYDRIDES, with more than 0.05% maleic anhydride	2698
1,2,3,6-TERTRAHYDROPYRIDINE	2410

Substance	UN No
TETRAHYDROTHIOPHENE	2412
Tetramethoxysilane, see	2606
TETRAMETHYLAMMONIUM HYDROXIDE, SOLID	3423
TETRAMETHYLAMMONIUM HYDROXIDE SOLUTION	1835
Tetramethylene, see	2601
TETRAMETHYLENE CYANIDE	2205
Tetramethyl lead, see	1649
TETRAMETHYLSILANE	2749
TETRANITROMETHANE	1510
TETRAPROPYL ORTHOTITANATE	2413
TEXTILE WASTE, WET	1857
THALLIUM CHLORATE	2573
Thallium (I) chlorate, see	2573
THALLIUM COMPOUND, N.O.S.	1707
Thallium (I) nitrate, see	2727
THALLIUM NITRATE	2727
Thallous chlorate, see	2573
4-THIAPENTANAL	2785
Thia-4-pentanal, see	2785
THIOACETIC ACID	2436
THIOCARBAMATE PESTICIDE, LIQUID, FLAMMABLE, TOXIC, flash point less than 23°C	2772
THIOCARBAMATE PESTICIDE, LIQUID, TOXIC, FLAMMABLE, flash point 23°C or above	3005
THIOCARBAMATE PESTICIDE, LIQUID, TOXIC	3006
THIOCARBAMATE PESTICIDE, SOLID, TOXIC	2771
THIOGLYCOL	2966
THIOGLYCOLIC ACID	1940
THIOLACTIC ACID	2936
THIONYL CHLORIDE	1836

Substance	UN No
THIOPHENE	2414
Thiophenol, see	2337
THIOPHOSGENE	2474
THIOPHOSPHORYL CHLORIDE	1837
THIOUREA DIOXIDE	3341
Tin (IV) chloride, anhydrous, see	1827
Tin (IV) chloride pentahydrate, see	2440
TINCTURES, MEDICINAL	1293
Tin tetrachloride, see	1827
TITANIUM DISULPHIDE	3174
TITANIUM HYDRIDE	1871
TITANIUM POWDER, DRY	2546
TITANIUM POWDER, WETTED, with not less than 25% water	1352
TITANIUM SPONGE GRANULES or TITANIUM SPONGE POWDERS	2878
TITANIUM TETRACHLORIDE	1838
TITANIUM TRICHLORIDE MIXTURE	2869
TITANIUM TRICHLORIDE, PYROPHORIC	2441
TITANIUM TRICHLORIDE MIXTURE, PYROPHORIC	2441
TNT, WETTED, with not less than 10% water by mass, see	3366
TNT, WETTED, with not less than 30% water by mass, see	1356
Toe puffs, nitrocellulose base, see	1353
TOLUENE	1294
TOLUENE DI-ISOCYANATE	2078
TOLUIDINES, LIQUID	1708
TOLUIDINES, SOLID	3451
Toluol, see	1294
Toluylene diisocyanate, see	2078
2,4-TOLUYLENEDIAMINE, SOLID	1709

Substance	UN No
2,4-TOLUYLENEDIAMINE SOLUTION	3418
Tolylene diisocyanate, see	2078
Tolylethylene, inhibited, see	2618
TOXIC BY INHALATION LIQUID, N.O.S., with an LC_{50} lower than or equal to 200 ml/m³ and saturated vapour concentration greater than or equal to 500 LC_{50}	3381
TOXIC BY INHALATION LIQUID, N.O.S., with an LC_{50} lower than or equal to 1000 ml/m³ and saturated vapour concentration greater than or equal to 10 LC_{50}	3382
TOXIC BY INHALATION LIQUID, CORROSIVE, N.O.S., with an LC_{50} lower than or equal to 200 ml/m³ and saturated vapour concentration greater than or equal to 500 LC_{50}	3389
TOXIC BY INHALATION LIQUID, CORROSIVE, N.O.S., with an LC_{50} lower than or equal to 1000 ml/m³ and saturated vapour concentration greater than or equal to 10 LC_{50}	3390
TOXIC BY INHALATION LIQUID, CORROSIVE, FLAMMABLE, N.O.S. with an LC_{50} lower than or equal to 200 ml/m³ and saturated vapour concentration greater than or equal to 500 LC_{50}	3492
TOXIC BY INHALATION LIQUID, CORROSIVE, FLAMMABLE, N.O.S. with an LC_{50} lower than or equal to 1000 ml/m³ and saturated vapour concentration greater than or equal to 10 LC_{50}	3493
TOXIC BY INHALATION LIQUID, FLAMMABLE, N.O.S., with an LC_{50} lower than or equal to 200 ml/m³ and saturated vapour concentration greater than or equal to 500 LC_{50}	3383
TOXIC BY INHALATION LIQUID, FLAMMABLE, N.O.S., with an LC_{50} lower than or equal to 1000 ml/m³ and saturated vapour concentration greater than or equal to 10 LC_{50}	3384

Substance	UN No
TOXIC BY INHALATION LIQUID, FLAMMABLE, CORROSIVE, N.O.S. with an LC_{50} lower than or equal to 200 ml/m³ and saturated vapour concentration greater than or equal to 500 LC_{50}	3488
TOXIC BY INHALATION LIQUID, FLAMMABLE, CORROSIVE, N.O.S. with an LC_{50} lower than or equal to 1000 ml/m³ and saturated vapour concentration greater than or equal to 10 LC_{50}	3489
TOXIC BY INHALATION LIQUID, OXIDISING, N.O.S., with an LC_{50} lower than or equal to 200 ml/m³ and saturated vapour concentration greater than or equal to 500 LC_{50}	3387
TOXIC BY INHALATION LIQUID, OXIDISING, N.O.S., with an LC_{50} lower than or equal to 1000 ml/m³ and saturated vapour concentration greater than or equal to 10 LC_{50}	3388
TOXIC BY INHALATION LIQUID, WATER-REACTIVE, N.O.S., with an LC_{50} lower than or equal to 200 ml/m³ and saturated vapour concentration greater than or equal to 500 LC_{50}	3385
TOXIC BY INHALATION LIQUID, WATER-REACTIVE, N.O.S., with an LC_{50} lower than or equal to 1000 ml/m³ and saturated vapour concentration greater than or equal to 10 LC_{50}	3386
TOXIC BY INHALATION LIQUID, WATER-REACTIVE, FLAMMABLE, N.O.S. with an LC_{50} lower than or equal to 200 ml/m³ and saturated vapour concentration greater than or equal to 500 LC_{50}	3490
TOXIC BY INHALATION LIQUID, WATER-REACTIVE, FLAMMABLE, N.O.S. with an LC_{50} lower than or equal to 1000 ml/m³ and saturated vapour concentration greater than or equal to 10 LC_{50}	3491
TOXIC LIQUID, CORROSIVE, INORGANIC, N.O.S.	3289

Substance	UN No
TOXIC LIQUID, CORROSIVE, ORGANIC, N.O.S.	2927
TOXIC LIQUID, FLAMMABLE, ORGANIC, N.O.S.	2929
TOXIC LIQUID, INORGANIC, N.O.S.	3287
TOXIC LIQUID, ORGANIC, N.O.S.	2810
TOXIC LIQUID, OXIDISING, N.O.S.	3122
TOXIC LIQUID, WATER-REACTIVE, N.O.S.	3123
TOXIC SOLID, CORROSIVE, INORGANIC, N.O.S.	3290
TOXIC SOLID, CORROSIVE, ORGANIC, N.O.S.	2928
TOXIC SOLID, FLAMMABLE, ORGANIC, N.O.S.	2930
TOXIC SOLID, INORGANIC, N.O.S.	3288
TOXIC SOLID, SELF-HEATING, N.O.S.	3124
TOXIC SOLID, ORGANIC, N.O.S.	2811
TOXIC SOLID, OXIDISING, N.O.S.	3086
TOXIC SOLID, WATER-REACTIVE, N.O.S.	3125
TOXINS, EXTRACTED FROM LIVING SOURCES, LIQUID, N.O.S.	3172
TOXINS, EXTRACTED FROM LIVING SOURCES, SOLID, N.O.S.	3462
Tremolite, see	2212
TRIALLYLAMINE	2610
TRIALLYL BORATE	2609
TRIAZINE PESTICIDE, LIQUID FLAMMABLE, TOXIC, flash point less than 23°C	2764
TRIAZINE PESTICIDE, LIQUID TOXIC, FLAMMABLE, flash point 23°C or above	2997
TRIAZINE PESTICIDE, LIQUID, TOXIC	2998
TRIAZINE PESTICIDE, SOLID, TOXIC	2763
Tribromoborane, see	2692
TRIBUTYLAMINE	2542
TRIBUTYLPHOSPHANE	3254
Trichloroacetaldehyde, see	2075
TRICHLOROACETIC ACID	1839
TRICHLOROACETIC ACID SOLUTION	2564
Trichloroaceticaldehyde, see	2075
TRICHLOROACETYL CHLORIDE	2442
TRICHLOROBENZENES, LIQUID	2321
TRICHLOROBUTENE	2322
1,1,1-TRICHLOROETHANE	2831
TRICHLOROETHYLENE	1710
TRICHLOROISOCYANURIC ACID, DRY	2468
Trichloronitromethane, see	1580
TRICHLOROSILANE	1295
1,3,5-Trichloro-s-triazine-2,4,6-trione, see	2468
2,4,6-Trichloro-1,3,5-triazine, see	2670
TRICRESYL PHOSPHATE, with more than 3% ortho isomer	2574
TRIETHYLAMINE	1296
Triethyl borate, see	1176
TRIETHYLENETETRAMINE	2259
Triethyl orthoformate, see	2524
TRIETHYL PHOSPHITE	2323
TRIFLUOROACETIC ACID	2699
TRIFLUOROACETYL CHLORIDE	3057
Trifluorobromoemethane, see	1009
Trifluorochloroethane, see	1983
TRIFLUOROCHLOROETHYLENE, STABILIZED (REFRIGERANT GAS R 1113)	1082

Substance	UN No
Trifluorochloromethane, see	1022
1,1,1-TRIFLUOROETHANE	2035
TRIFLUOROMETHANE	1984
TRIFLUOROMETHANE, REFRIGERATED LIQUID	3136
2-TRIFLUOROMETHYLANILINE	2942
3-TRIFLUOROMETHYLANILINE	2948
TRIISOBUTYLENE	2324
TRIISOPROPYL BORATE	2616
TRIMETHYLACETYL CHLORIDE	2438
TRIMETHYLAMINE, ANHYDROUS	1083
TRIMETHYLAMINE, AQUEOUS SOLUTION, with not more than 50% trimethylamine, by mass	1297
1,3,5-TRIMETHYLBENZENE	2325
TRIMETHYL BORATE	2416
TRIMETHYLCHLOROSILANE	1298
TRIMETHYLCYCLOHEXYLAMINE	2326
Trimethylene chlorobromide, see	2688
TRIMETHYLHEXA-METHYLENEDIAMINES	2327
TRIMETHYLHEXAMETHYLENE DIISOCYANATE	2328
2,4,4-Trimethylpentene-1, see	2050
2,4,4-Trimethylpentene-2, see	2050
TRIMETHYL PHOSPHITE	2329
TRINITROBENZENE, WETTED, with not less than 10% water by mass	3367
TRINITROBENZENE, WETTED, with not less than 30% water by mass	1354
TRINITROBENZOIC ACID, WETTED, with not less than 10% water by mass	3368

Substance	UN No
TRINITROBENZOIC ACID, WETTED, with not less than 30% water by mass	1355
TRINITROCHLOROBENZENE, WETTED, with not less than 10% water by mass	3365
TRINITROPHENOL, WETTED, with not less than 10% water by mass	3364
TRINITROPHENOL, (PICRIC ACID) WETTED, with not less than 30% water by mass	1344
TRINITROTOLUENE, WETTED with not less than 10% water by mass	3366
TRINITROTOLUENE (TNT), WETTED, with not less than 30% water by mass	1356
TRIPROPYLAMINE	2260
TRIPROPYLENE	2057
Tropilidene, see	2603
TRIS-(1-AZIRIDINYL) PHOSPHINE OXIDE SOLUTION	2501
TUNGSTEN HEXAFLUORIDE	2196
TURPENTINE	1299
TURPENTINE SUBSTITUTE	1300
UNDECANE	2330
URANIUM HEXAFLUORIDE, RADIOACTIVE MATERIAL, EXCEPTED PACKAGE, less than 0.1 kg per package, non-fissile or fissile-excepted	3507
UREA HYDROGEN PEROXIDE	1511
UREA NITRATE, WETTED, with not less than 10% water by mass	3370
UREA NITRATE, WETTED, with not less than 20% water by mass	1357
Valeral, see	2058
VALERALDEHYDE	2058
n-Valeraldehyde, see	2058
Valeric aldehyde, see	2058
VALERYL CHLORIDE	2502

Substance	UN No
VANADIUM COMPOUNDS, N.O.S.	3285
Vanadium (IV) oxide suphate, see	2931
Vanadium oxysulphate, see	2931
VANADIUM OXYTRICHLORIDE	2443
VANADIUM PENTOXIDE, non-fused form	2862
VANADIUM TETRACHLORIDE	2444
VANADIUM TRICHLORIDE	2475
VANADYL SULPHATE	2931
Varnish, see	1263 3066 3469 3470
VEHICLE, FUEL CELL, FLAMMABLE GAS POWERED	3166
VEHICLE, FUEL CELL, FLAMMABLE LIQUID POWERED	3166
VEHICLE, FLAMMABLE GAS POWERED	3166
VEHICLE, FLAMMABLE LIQUID POWERED	3166
Viliaumite, see	1690
VINYL ACETATE, STABILIZED	1301
Vinylbenzene, see	2055
VINYL BROMIDE, STABILIZED	1085
VINYL BUTYRATE, STABILIZED	2838
VINYL CHLORIDE, STABILIZED	1086
VINYL CHLOROACETATE	2589
VINYL ETHYL ETHER, STABILIZED	1302
VINYL FLUORIDE, STABILIZED	1860
VINYLIDENE CHLORIDE, STABILIZED	1303
VINYL ISOBUTYL ETHER, STABILIZED	1304
VINYL METHYL ETHER, STABILIZED	1087
VINYLPYRIDINES, STABILIZED	3073
VINYLTOLUENES, STABILIZED	2618
VINYLTRICHLOROSILANE	1305
WATER-REACTIVE LIQUID, CORROSIVE, N.O.S.	3129
WATER-REACTIVE LIQUID, N.O.S.	3148
WATER-REACTIVE LIQUID, TOXIC, N.O.S.	3130
WATER-REACTIVE SOLID, CORROSIVE, N.O.S.	3131
WATER-REACTIVE SOLID, FLAMMABLE, N.O.S.	3132
WATER-REACTIVE SOLID, N.O.S.	2813
WATER-REACTIVE SOLID, OXIDISING, N.O.S.	3133
WATER-REACTIVE SOLID, TOXIC, N.O.S.	3134
WATER-REACTIVE SOLID, SELF-HEATING, N.O.S.	3135
White arsenic, see	1561
White spirit, see	1300
WOOD PRESERVATIVES, LIQUID	1306
WOOL WASTE, WET	1387
XANTHATES	3342
XENON	2036
XENON, REFRIGERATED LIQUID	2591
XYLENES	1307
XYLENOLS, LIQUID	3430
XYLENOLS, SOLID	2261
XYLIDINES, LIQUID	1711
XYLIDINES, SOLID	3452
Xylols, see	1307
XYLYL BROMIDE, LIQUID	1701
XYLYL BROMIDE, SOLID	3417
ZINC AMMONIUM NITRATE	1512
ZINC ARSENATE	1712
ZINC ARSENITE	1712

Substance	UN No
ZINC ARSENATE AND ZINC ARSENITE MIXTURE	1712
ZINC ASHES	1435
Zinc bisulphite solution, see	2693
ZINC BROMATE	2469
ZINC CHLORATE	1513
ZINC CHLORIDE, ANHYDROUS	2331
ZINC CHLORIDE SOLUTION	1840
ZINC CYANIDE	1713
ZINC DITHIONITE	1931
ZINC DUST	1436
ZINC FLUOROSILICATE	2855
Zinc hexafluorosilicate, see	2855
ZINC HYDROSULPHITE	1931
ZINC NITRATE	1514
ZINC PERMANGANATE	1515
ZINC PEROXIDE	1516
ZINC PHOSPHIDE	1714
ZINC POWDER	1436
ZINC RESINATE	2714
Zinc selenate, see	2630
Zinc selenite, see	2630
Zinc silicofluoride, see	2855
ZIRCONIUM HYDRIDE	1437
ZIRCONIUM, DRY, coiled wire, finished metal sheets, strip (thinner than 254 microns but not thinner than 18 microns)	2858
ZIRCONIUM, DRY, finished sheets, strip or coiled wire	2009
ZIRCONIUM NITRATE	2728
ZIRCONIUM PICRAMATE, WETTED, with not less than 20% water by mass	1517
ZIRCONIUM POWDER, DRY	2008

Substance	UN No
ZIRCONIUM POWDER, WETTED, with not less than 25% water	1358
ZIRCONIUM SCRAP	1932
ZIRCONIUM SUSPENDED IN A FLAMMABLE LIQUID	1308
ZIRCONIUM TETRACHLORIDE	2503

Acknowledgements

NCEC is indebted to all who have helped with the provision of information, expertise and validation to assist with the production of this edition and previous editions of this publication, in particular:

The Chief Fire and Rescue Adviser (part of Home Office)
Dennis Ricketts (formerly of CLG)
British Chemical Distributors Trade Association
British Compressed Gas Association
British Safety Industry Federation
Bureau Veritas
Chemical Industries Association
Chief Fire Officers Association
Department for Transport
Environment Agency
Fire Brigades Union
Fire Service College
Freight Transport Association
Greater Manchester Fire and Rescue Service
HazmatLINK Ltd
Health & Safety Executive
Her Majesty's Fire Service Inspectorate for Scotland
Independent Consultant (Bob Cumberland)
Lancashire Fire and Rescue Service
Local Government Association
London Fire & Emergency Planning Authority
Liquefied Petroleum Gas Association

Ministry of Defence
National Police Chief's Council (NPCC)
Network Rail
Retained Firefighters' Union
Road Haulage Association
United Kingdom Petroleum Industry Association
United Utilities plc